THE RAILWAYS OF NORTHUMBERLAND AND NEWCASTLE UPON TYNE 1828-1998

J A WELLS

First published in 1998 by
Powdene Publicity Ltd.,
Unit 17, St. Peter's Wharf,
Newcastle upon Tyne, NE6 1TZ.

Printed by
Chatsworth Studios

British Library Cataloguing in Publication Data

Wells, James Alan
The Railways of Northumberland and
Newcastle upon Tyne 1828-1998

1) North East England.
Railway Services, history.

ISBN 0 9520226 2 1

CONTENTS

Page

ILLUSTRATIONS

LIST OF MAPS, POSTERS, DIAGRAMS, TIMETABLES, etc.

Page

ACKNOWLEDGEMENTS

Very sincere thanks are expressed to:

Northumberland County Council Amenities Division:
D E Bonser, M Dimelow, Administration & Library staff
Northumberland County Records Office: Mrs S Bird
Beamish Museum Archives: J Lawson
Darlington Railway Centre & Museum: Mrs A Wilson
National Railway Museum Library, York
Newcastle City Library (Local Studies)
Nexus, Newcastle upon Tyne
North Eastern Railway Association
North Shields Library, North Tyneside (Local Studies)
Public Records Office, Kew
Staff of Powdene Publicity Ltd.
Stait & Son, Photographers, Morpeth;

George Mitcheson for all the time he spent preparing maps and diagrams, and for the use of his model railway for the picture of Whittingham (courtesy of the Railway Modeller);

and to the following for their own particular help in numerous ways:-

Stewart Bonney	Derek Patten
Ian S Carr	Frank Scott
George Charlton	Chris Shaw
Malcolm Charlton	Mr. & Mrs. P Short
John M Fleming	Mrs. June Wells
Keith Goodaire	David A Wells
Ken Morton	Mrs. Judith Black

To Simon and Philip Holgate,
also to members of our families
who gave over 200 years of
service to the railways.

LOCATIONS

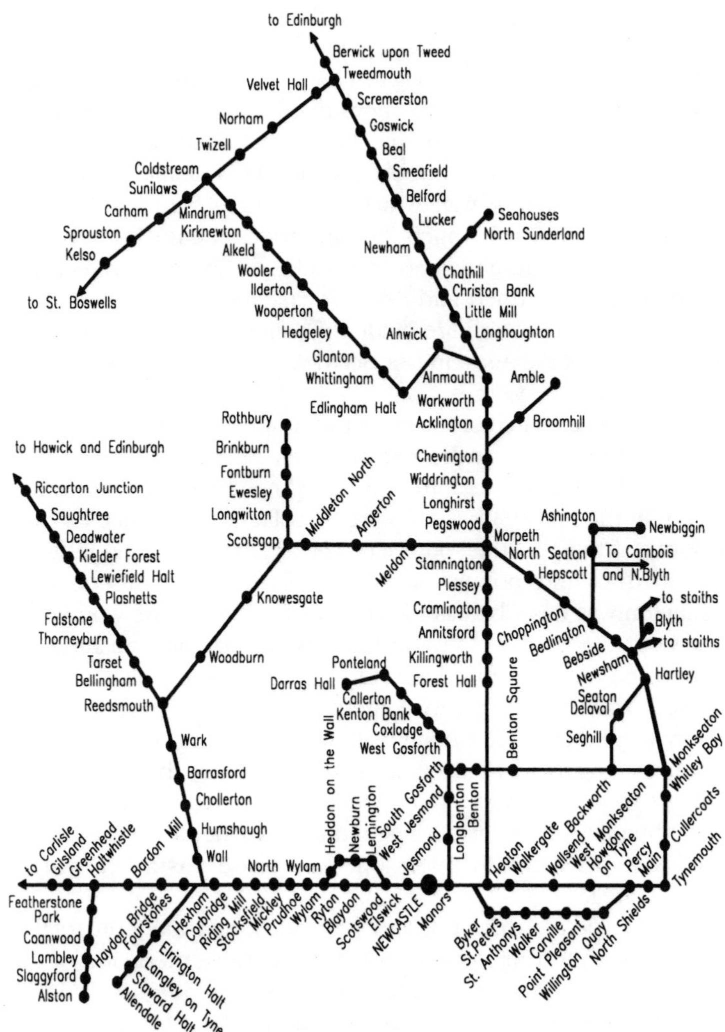

Railways of Northumberland

PREFACE

Northumberland is England's most northerly county whose immediate neighbours are now Tyne & Wear, Durham and Cumbria. Part of its boundaries are the river Tyne in the south and the river Tweed in the north, the latter marking in places the border between England and Scotland. All along its eastern side is the North Sea giving a spectacular coastline for more than 60 miles. Other principal rivers running into the sea are the Aln, Blyth, Coquet and Wansbeck.

Historically, the northernmost part of the Roman Empire was marked by Hadrian's Wall which stretched defiantly across the country and of which much remains today. Centuries later the Kingdom of Northumbria was the cradle of Christianity, recalling names such as Cuthbert and Bede. Formidable castles throughout the county are a powerful reminder of numerous conflicts with the Scots in the Middle Ages: in fact Berwick has been claimed by both countries over the years.

The principal source of wealth in the county was coal. Shafts were sunk and the coal was extracted, well over 8½ million tons in 1895 for example. As seams became exhausted new workings were introduced. In the mid-1930s there were 81 collieries in production, the majority of them in the south east corner. As the mining industry expanded so did populations in colliery districts. At one time Ashington was described as the largest pit village in the world. The Coal Company used the latest techniques for extracting, washing and grading the coal, and introduced various innovations which they had evolved. They had an extensive internal railway system for collecting empty wagons and distributing them to the different collieries in the group, loading them, then making up train loads for the railway companies to move. They also ran passenger trains for the miners.

Shipbuilding and engineering on the river Tyne were other major employers. In the early 1900s only the Clyde was a larger shipbuilding area.

From Morpeth northwards and westwards the main industry was farming but a further contrast was the extensive moorland of the higher parts of the county, some of which were subsequently developed into areas of forestry, particularly at Kielder.

The County Council was constituted in 1889 but for the purposes of administration the city of Newcastle upon Tyne was excluded from Northumberland's control having been given County Borough status the previous year. Gradually more of the city suburbs were taken from the county, and Tynemouth became a County

Borough in 1904. Local Government reorganisation in 1974 meant that a substantial section of the most populated area of the county passed into the control of the new Tyne & Wear authority, or into an extended city. If certain amendments had not been agreed Northumberland would have lost 45% of its population; even so it became one of the smallest counties for population but covering one of the largest and remotest areas. For the purpose of this book it is the original County of Northumberland which is considered together with Newcastle.

The evolution of the steam locomotive, which led to the rapid spread of railways throughout the world, came predominantly from Northumberland. Certain routes have been the subject of books and the district is mentioned in several publications relating to the north east as a whole, but this is the first attempt to unravel the complicated history of all the railways in the county and present them together in one volume. It has not been possible to include all the various colliery railways and, for reasons of space, the narrow gauge lines from quarries and works or as used, say, in the construction of Fontburn reservoir have been omitted. Nevertheless it was from the urgent necessity of transporting coal from collieries that railways developed.

Once it had been decided to build a railway full details of the proposed system had to be presented to Parliament for approval. If the Act was passed many problems lay ahead before the scheme was running satisfactorily. Some railways grew from strength to strength whereas others fought financial or other difficulties before being taken over in a very short time by a rival, or merged with a more powerful company.

Part I of this book considers individually the development of all the private railways in Northumberland and at Newcastle upon Tyne mainly from when the Act was passed (not when traffic started to run) and up to their demise. It concludes with the nationalised British Railways. The second part shows how the main lines and branches progressed after becoming part of larger organisations such as the North Eastern Railway, the North British Railway and the LNER. Comparisons are made between different periods particularly pre-1920, the 1930s and, where appropriate, the early 1950s. Part III reviews the legacies of the past which remain but which are used now in a different capacity. Finally the complex process of Privatisation looks encouragingly towards a revitalised railway system.

J. A. WELLS

NOTES

THE
RAILWAYS OF NORTHUMBERLAND
AND NEWCASTLE UPON TYNE

Part I

THE HISTORY OF THE RAILWAYS OF NORTHUMBERLAND

Early waggonways to British Rail

NORTHUMBERLAND'S RAILWAY PEDIGREE

Northumberland's railway pedigree is second to none dating back to 1609 when waggonways from collieries at Bedlington led to a short quay alongside the river Blyth. John Birkinshaw of Bedlington Iron Works patented an improved method of rolling sixteen-feet lengths of wrought iron rails in 1820. It is not widely known that the patent included the welding of rail ends though its use would be limited. These rails were used in various parts of the country.

Several notable railway pioneers were born in Northumberland. William Hedley (1779-1843) was born at Newburn but attended the village school at nearby Wylam. In his capacity of colliery manager there, he was aware of two steam locomotives working at Coxlodge a few miles away. Both had a cogged driving wheel which engaged semi-circular lugs on a rack-rail on one side of the track. He, however, was convinced that smooth wheels would work on smooth track to give adequate adhesion and proved that the actual weight of a locomotive had to be in proportion to the load it was expected to pull.

George Stephenson (1781-1848) was often described as the father of railways and his achievements are legendary. He was born at Wylam: incredibly so were two others. Timothy Hackworth (1786-1850) whose father was foreman of the colliery blacksmiths, assisted in the building of *Puffing Billy* (page 7) and became a very successful builder of locomotives. He was appointed engineer to the world's first public railway, the Stockton & Darlington. Nicholas Wood (1795-1865) was several years younger than George Stephenson but he too became a prominent engineer and the two worked together on developing railway engines at Killingworth colliery, north of Newcastle, where Nicholas was the viewer and George the enginewright.

Two other 'railway sons' of Northumberland must also be mentioned. John Urpeth Rastrick (1780-1856) was a native of Morpeth. He became the managing partner in the firm of Foster Rastrick & Co. which supplied a locomotive called *Stourbridge Lion* to the Delaware & Hudson Canal Company for its railroad which was opened in October 1829, one of the first in the USA. Prior to that he had designed and built the *Argenoria,* now resident in the National Railway Museum. Rastrick's greatest achievement was the

London & Brighton Railway built 1837-40 and claimed to be one of the most magnificently engineered railways in the world. He was one of the judges at the Rainhill Trials, as was Nicholas Wood. The other gentleman was Daniel Gooch who was born at Bedlington. In 1837, when he was just 21, he was appointed locomotive superintendent of the Great Western Railway. He founded the famous Swindon Works in 1841 and was later made a baronet, the first engineer to receive such an honour. His father was manager of the Iron Works.

Bedlington Iron Works began producing high quality locomotives from 1837. The first passenger train out of Kings Cross and the first trains in Holland and Italy were hauled by engines built at Bedlington.

George Stephenson opened locomotive works at Newcastle in 1823 in the name of his son, Robert. They were situated in Forth Street, alongside which the Central station was subsequently built. Those works gave a long and distinguished service to the growing railway industry. Their achievements included:

the first two steam engines, *La Flèche* and *Stephenson,* for a Belgian railway in 1835, the first in mainland Europe:

the first locomotive – named Dorchester – to work on the first Canadian railway, opened in July 1836:

and the first locomotives for use in Germany (1835), Russia (1836) and New South Wales, Australia (1854).

Northumberland can claim several other railway distinctions. The Newcastle & Carlisle Railway, opened throughout in 1838, was the first cross country line from east to west. In April 1840 passengers travelled from Carlisle to an Exhibition in Newcastle at special fares, making those trains the first railway excursions. The N & CR was also the first to experiment with a sanding apparatus to help prevent wheelslip. Of the numerous distinctive bridges and viaducts in the county, the earliest and largest 'elastic arch' railway bridge in the British Isles was opened at West Wylam in 1876. It was the forerunner of the Tyne bridge and a similar structure in Australia. The first electric trains in the country were introduced in 1904 by the North Eastern Railway around north Tyneside. In 1961 Blyth handled more rail-borne coal than any other port in Europe. The Metro system, the initial part of which was opened in 1980, was the first rapid light transit system in the United Kingdom.

WAGGONWAYS

Huntington Beaumont of Bilborough near Nottingham laid a primitive form of 'waggon way', made from roughly squared timber, near his home town in 1603, the first one known. Described in William Gray's Chorographia of 1649 as "a Gentleman of great ingenuity and rare parts" he leased pits at Bedlington from the Bishop of Durham in 1605. A wooden waggonway connected those pits to the river Blyth near to the present railway viaduct, and 21,571 tons of coal were shipped from there in 1609.

Where collieries were near a navigable river it was a comparatively simple task to take the coal to be loaded into ships. If the water was too shallow the coal was first loaded on to keels and transferred to sailing ships in deeper water. As the coal supply became exhausted or too costly to mine, pits were sunk further inland where miners could extract this valuable commodity from the rich seams which ran through south east Northumberland. It was then transported to a river for removal to other parts of the country or to be sent overseas. Agreement had to be reached with land owners for the use of waggonways across their property and fees paid accordingly. These were known as wayleaves.

W W Tomlinson recorded that the type of waggonway most in use was the *double way* which was built from six-feet lengths of fir fastened to hardwood *sleepers* and edged with *false rails* made of beech. With experience, rails were made first from cast iron and later wrought iron to give much longer wear.

To keep wheels on the track the system of fixing flat metal plates on the *inside* of the rails was found to be effective but subsequently flanges were put on to wheels rather than on the track. About 1800 most collieries were using a form of short, fish-bellied rails but in 1820 John Birkinshaw, principal agent at Michael Longridge's Bedlington Iron Works, patented his idea of rolling sixteen-feet lengths of malleable iron rail which proved to be very successful. George Stephenson used them on the three-mile waggonway between Glebe Colliery, Barrington, and the works. This type of track was used extensively on the Stockton & Darlington Railway and visitors came from many other

From time to time pieces of early trackwork are unearthed. These are examples from the Netherton waggonway, dug up during ploughing. The one in the foreground is approximately six inches long. (J A Wells)

embryonic railways to inspect it, including the Liverpool & Manchester, opened in 1829.

Before waggonways were laid to the river Tyne coal was taken through the harbours of Blyth and Seaton Sluice. In order to take coal to the shipping point at what originally was Old Hartley (the name was changed to Seaton Sluice in 1690) it was necessary to build a wooden bridge across Holywell Dene, the detailed cost of which was given to Lord Delaval in a letter dated 7 March 1784. There was a waggonway from Plessey to the river Blyth about six miles in length which, according to John Wallace in The History of Blyth, carried 21,786 chaldrons of coal during 1723. A horse and its driver would be expected to make three return trips each working day. Chaldron (pronounced sholdron) waggons became the standard transport for coal and carried 2 tons 13 hundredweights.

There was an enormous demand for coal but the tremendous costs for manpower in a labour-intensive industry together with fodder for horses meant that a question was being asked by colliery owners which, put simply, was: "How can more coal be moved over longer distances at less cost?" The answer would lie with the steam locomotive.

Two steam engines employed on the Kenton & Coxlodge waggonway used John Blenkinsopp's rack system. They were introduced between 1813 and 1815 and could haul 100 tons at walking pace thereby replacing up to 50 horses and 200 men. Rack rails, however, were expensive and the system was not widely adopted. William Hedley, in his capacity of colliery viewer (ie manager) for Christopher Blackett of Wylam colliery, carried out various experiments during 1812-13 relating to adhesion as a result of which *Puffing Billy, Wylam Dilly* and *Lady Mary* were built to work on the Wylam waggonway. 'Billy', as it was known locally, worked there for 48 years pulling loads of 50 tons. It is preserved in the Science Museum, London, the oldest locomotive in existence.

It was George Stephenson who really took the railway age from a rolling snowball to an avalanche of progress. His first locomotive, the *Blucher,* built at Killingworth colliery in 1814, could haul eight loaded waggons at 4 mph but he quickly produced machines which could move twenty full waggons without any trouble even in wet weather. These were used to demonstrate to visitors the power of steam engines. One of five he built for Hetton colliery, County Durham between 1819 and 1822 survived until 1908 after being rebuilt twice, but it was his *Locomotion no. 1* for the Stockton & Darlington Railway (1825) and the success of *Rocket,* which ran at 30 mph in the Rainhill Trials at Liverpool and proved the supremacy of steam over other forms of traction, with which most people are familiar. *Rocket* was a joint father and son venture as Robert had become a very prominent engineer in his own right. Nevertheless George was involved with numerous, complex railway projects, various experiments and ingenious ideas, apart from his locomotives, which earned him his name as the world's greatest railway engineer.

THE FAMILY TREE OF RAILWAYS IN NORTHUMBERLAND

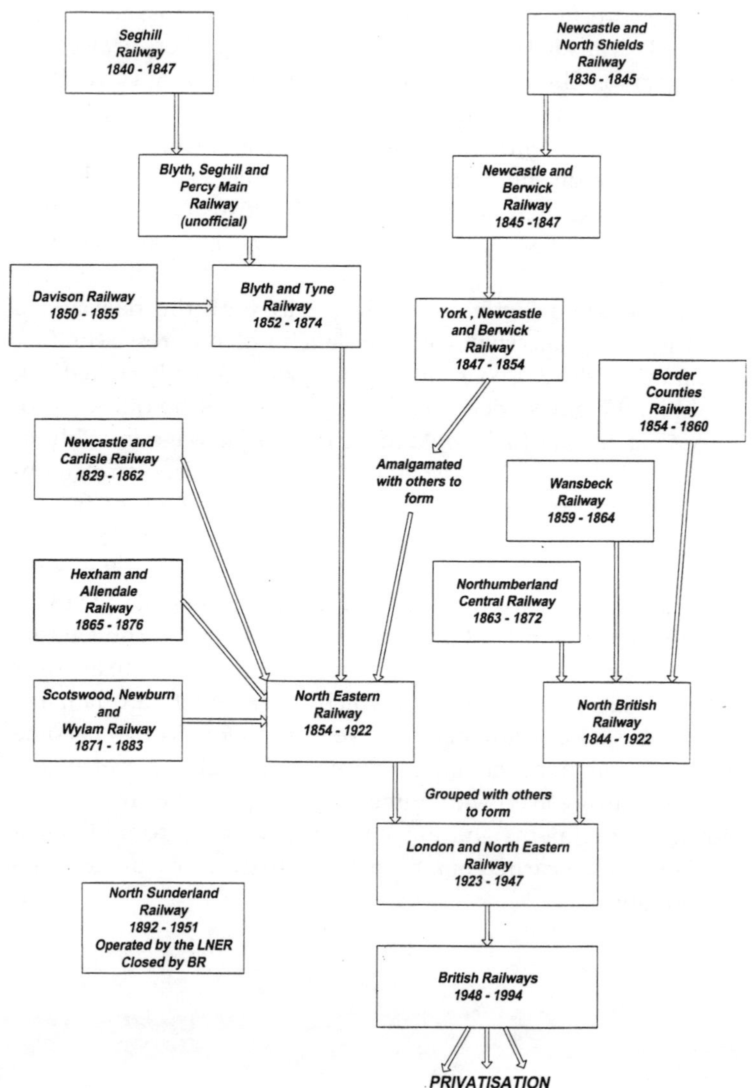

THE HARTLEYBURN & BRAMPTON JUNCTION RAILWAY

(Unofficial title)

OPENED 1828

Also known as The Midgeholme Railway, The Brampton & Midgeholme Railway, Hartleyburn Railway, Hartleyburn & Brampton Railway.

Lord Carlisle of Naworth, near Brampton, Cumberland (now Cumbria) owned a number of very productive collieries on his estate and leased others beyond its borders. A waggonway was in use in 1799 carrying coal to a staith to the east of Brampton. The waggonway was lengthened and by 1808 they were using cast iron and malleable iron rails on part of the route. These rails were the focus of much attention and aroused great interest over a wide area.

From 1819 the collieries agent for Lord Carlisle was James Thompson who in that same year was in correspondence with Bedlington Iron Works on the subject of rails. In consultation with George Stephenson – with whom he became a good friend – Mr Thompson, seeking to extract coal from other collieries, extended the line eastwards through Midgeholme (1828) to reach Halton Lea Gate in 1836 and Lambley colliery in 1849, both of which are in Northumberland. This track was laid to the standard Stephenson gauge of 4 feet 8½ inches and when the rest of the waggonway was converted it became Cumberland's first railway to main line standards capable of carrying steam locomotives. At its west end this railway formed a junction with the Newcastle & Carlisle Railway at Milton. This name was changed to Brampton Junction in September 1870. Brian Webb in *Lord Carlisle's Railways* describes James Thompson as "a man who has never been given the recognition he merits as a highly important railway pioneer of considerable vision ... who had helped to standardise the rail gauge of British and overseas railways ..." He was a member of the advisory team to the directors of the Newcastle & Carlisle Railway.

After its success at the Rainhill Trials, the Stephensons' *Rocket* worked on the Liverpool & Manchester Railway from 1829 but soon reached its limitations as loads became heavier. It was bought by Lord Carlisle in 1836 and commenced work on the Midgeholme section the following year in a modified form. This was the first locomotive actually bought rather than hired and it performed for some three years before being withdrawn. This famous engine, therefore, actually worked on a railway in Northumberland apart from its trials.

By 1835 three four-wheeled passenger coaches, horse-drawn, were in use on the Midgeholme railway. These were named Black Diamond, Experiment and Mountaineer. The fare from Midgeholme to Brampton was one shilling. People used the railway in order to reach Brampton market.

January 1852 brought the opening of a short branch just over a mile long from Lambley station to serve pits around Lambley Fell. It joined end on with what had become known as the Hartleyburn & Brampton Junction Railway, providing an outlet for coal on to the main line at Milton (ie Brampton) before the Alston branch was opened the following November.

THE NEWCASTLE & CARLISLE RAILWAY (1829-1862)

Two hundred years ago thoughts of linking Newcastle with Carlisle naturally focused on the building of a canal. Several schemes were discussed and surveyed in a bid to link the seas on the east and west of the country. A ship canal between the Solway Firth and Carlisle had been opened in March 1823 and hopes were expressed that this could be connected one day to the river Tyne. Had this been put into effect it would have needed no less than 117 locks. It had not gone unnoticed, however, that more and more schemes for railways were being actively pursued – the beginning of Railway Mania – and at a meeting held in Newcastle upon Tyne in March 1825 it was finally agreed that the advantages of a railway would far outweigh the proposals for a waterway.

It was envisaged that the railway would be a common highway to be used by carriers of all kinds for the payment of a toll. Horses would be used rather than locomotives. It was 1828 before the route was agreed but only after intense opposition by certain landowners who did not want a railway on any part of their land. Their intransigence continued during arguments in Parliament but after twenty days the Bill received the Royal assent on 22 May 1829. It approved the construction of a 63-

mile railway from The Close at Newcastle to Canal Basin at Carlisle, which at that time was the longest line that had been sanctioned. In that same year the old military road between the two cities was often choked with carts both day and night most of which took three days for the whole journey. There were two stage coaches a day, the *True Briton* and the *Royal Mail* which would normally take 8½ hours.

Work commenced at the west end of the line in 1830 between Blenkinsopp and Carlisle: at the eastern side it was decided to make a temporary terminus at Blaydon in County Durham until a bridge could be built over the Tyne. The first section of the railway to be ready for use was that between Blaydon and Hexham where, towards the end of 1834 goods were being conveyed in horse drawn trucks. By then of course it was realised that steam locomotives would be much more effective and more economical, so, in anticipation that approval would be given by Parliament for the Act to be amended to permit steam traction, the Newcastle & Carlisle Railway ordered three engines. One was from Robert Stephenson & Co., one from R & W Hawthorn and their third from Edward Bury, named *Rapid, Comet* and *Meteor* respectively. All three were 0-4-0 tender engines with wheels four feet in diameter, but different in design.

There was an Official Opening for passenger traffic on this section on 9 March 1835 featuring a ceremonial trip from Blaydon to Hexham and back using *Rapid* and *Comet.* The carriages attached to *Rapid* were named *Expedition, Sociable* and *Prospect;* those in the second train were *Despatch, Industry* and *Transit.* Tickets were issued to about 600 people. The trains also conveyed on flat trucks the road carriages of several gentlemen, plus a total of 23 open trucks fitted with bench seats. It was a lively, festive occasion with hundreds of eager, curious spectators coming from near and far. There were flags, bunting and banners wishing success to the railway. A brass band accompanied each train, with the musicians sitting on benches on the top of a carriage. As the trains pulled into Hexham they passed under a triumphal arch watched by "an immense assemblage of people". They were there to witness the beginning of an era which would bring prosperity to their region and open up the chance of broadening their horizons in travel. Life would never be the same again.

The amendment to the first Newcastle & Carlisle Railway Act was not agreed until 17 June 1835, owing to persistent objections by Charles Bacon Grey, Esq. of Twyford who had earlier taken out an injunction against the company to prevent the use of steam engines. This caused the line to be closed to passengers for some five weeks. He faced a storm of protest until civic and public opinion forced him to retract.

Three more sections of the N & CR were opened during 1836 namely:-

11 June from Blaydon to the eastern bank of the river Derwent ($1^1/_4$ miles);

28 June from Hexham to Haydon Bridge ($7^1/_2$ miles). Two trains were used for this event, hauled by the locos named *Samson* and *Hercules.* Both had been fitted with a steam whistle, the sounds from which were heard for the first time in the Tyne valley;

19 July from Carlisle to Blenkinsopp colliery (Greenhead), a distance of 20 miles.

This left the section between Haydon Bridge to just west of Haltwhistle to be completed and for which 1,400 men were employed. The gap was filled by transferring passengers and goods to road then back again to rail. There was also the pressing need to push the east end of the line nearer to Newcastle but before this was completed a line was laid from Blaydon to Redheugh, near Gateshead. From a busy quay there passengers and merchandise were conveyed across the Tyne by steamer or lighter to a wharf on the north side of the river near the old Tyne bridge.

By June 1838 the first uninterrupted railway line across Great Britain, from Gateshead to Carlisle, a distance of $60^3/_4$ miles, was completed. The directors travelled the length of the line on 15 June prior to the Grand Opening on 18 June – which was also Waterloo Day, marking the anniversary of Napoleon's defeat in 1815. The Newcastle & Carlisle Railway Company certainly believed in flamboyant publicity when they opened sections of the route, but this was to be something spectacular to mark a very auspicious occasion, unequalled, perhaps, in the history of railways!

A public holiday had been declared at Carlisle. At 6 am five special trains carrying civic dignitaries, invited guests and members of the public who had paid a fare of ten shillings (50p) left the border city for Redheugh where they arrived between 9.30 and 10 am. There the invited guests were conveyed across the river in the mayor's barge or a Trinity House vessel, while other passengers crossed in steam packets. Unfortunately, when a gangway collapsed a dozen or so people including a physician, two surgeons and two ladies in dainty, silk dresses fell into the river which was between three and four feet deep at that spot.

The civic bodies of Newcastle marched in procession with their colleagues from the west, taking them along Grey Street to point out some of the magnificent new buildings of which the City was very proud. They made their way to the Assembly Rooms for breakfast with the directors. Meanwhile, the Tyne was covered with boats of every description and the banks at Redheugh were "studded with myriads of human beings" as thirteen special trains, decorated for the occasion, were prepared for the journey to Carlisle. Some of the locomotives deserve special mention from those days of proud patriotism. *Wellington* was decorated with shields on either side bearing the portrait of the hero of Waterloo; *Nelson* carried a shield showing the victor of Trafalgar; *Meteor's* banner proclaimed ENGLAND EXPECTS EVERY MAN TO DO HIS DUTY; *Tyne* had been fitted with a steam organ, and *Goliah* was given the task of hauling nineteen vehicles, eventually to carry "about 600" passengers of the estimated 3,500 who made this historic trip through the Tyne valley.

The Gateshead Corporation had taken their seats early but the carriages reserved for those from Newcastle and Carlisle were invaded by the crowd. When the officials returned from the reception to Redheugh, at least an hour late, they had to hunt for seats. It was said that the chief magistrates of both cities had to travel in a sheep truck and the High Sheriff of Cumberland was squeezed into an open carriage attached to the first train! Even the new police on the trains – the Peelers, introduced on to the streets of Newcastle in May 1836 – could do little to help as the cavalcade prepared to move off. It was headed by *Rapid,* carrying the national flag, running on its own with an engineer on board to keep a check on the line ahead. All around was an imposing air of grandeur in spite of a moderate fog which quickly gave way to incessant rain. The last train did not reach Carlisle until after 6 pm, an hour after it should have left to return to Gateshead. What should have been an orderly search for refreshments soon became more like a stampede as people rushed back to the station, determined to find seats in covered carriages. When the doors were found to be locked "several ladies and portly town councillors with a temporary loss of dignity" scrambled in through the windows. Although they were well known to staff of the Newcastle Journal for similar selfish behaviour, they were not named.

As the engineer had to supervise personally the preparation of the trains prior to departure and travel ahead of the convoy in case anyone had changed switches (ie points), it was 10 pm before the first train departed, in a violent thunderstorm. At Milton the train headed by *Carlisle* ran into the back of the train ahead injuring two passengers. This meant that following trains were held up until 1 am when the tender and some carriages had been rerailed. Being in the dark among those lonely fells in open trucks and soaked to the skin, would be an experience few would want to repeat. The last train did not arrive at Redheugh until 6 o'clock on the 19th June, much to the relief of anxious relatives.

In spite of unforeseen difficulties in a very ambitious programme the Newcastle Journal referred to the railway as "a stupendous work, a new source of wealth ..." It was "a tract of country rarely visited and but little known ... which has been made to constitute a vast emporium of commerce." It was a splendid monument of the skill, ingenuity and perseverance of man.

Between 1837 and 1839 the route was extended from Blaydon towards Newcastle, crossing the Tyne at Scotswood by an unusual timber bridge standing 35 feet above the low water mark. It was designed by the company's engineer, John Blackmore. On 21 May a temporary terminus was opened near the Shot Tower though regular passenger services were not introduced until 21 October 1839. The penultimate link was to Forth Banks where the line was carried on an attractive viaduct of 44 arches: this was opened in November 1846. Finally, Newcastle and Carlisle trains began using the west end of the new Central station on 1st January 1851, four months after the east end was commissioned by the York, Newcastle & Berwick Railway.

Most of the Newcastle & Carlisle Railway was in Northumberland though from Scotswood Bridge almost to Wylam it was in County Durham, and after Rose Hill (later Gilsland) it passed into Cumberland. Up to 1844 parts of the route were still single track, for example that between Stocksfield and Hexham, but all was doubled in anticipation of extra traffic coming from the Newcastle & Darlington Junction Railway.

AN EPITAPH

My engine now is cold and still,
No water does my boiler fill;
My coke affords its flame no more,
My days of usefulness are o'er;
My wheels deny their wonted speed,
No more my guiding hand they heed,
My whistle, too, has lost its tone,
Its shrill and thrilling sounds are gone.
My valves are now thrown open wide,
My flanges all refuse to guide,
My clacks, also, though once so strong,
Refuse their aid in the busy throng;
No more I feel each urging breath,
My steam is all condensed in death,
Life's railways o'er, each station past,
In death I'm stopped, and rest at last.
Farewell, dear friends, and cease to weep,
In Christ I'm safe, in him I sleep.

Oswald Gardner was killed when a connecting rod on his engine broke near Stocksfield on Saturday 15 August 1840.

Although the major structures of this line were in Cumberland they deserve a mention for some amazing engineering triumphs. Wetheral bridge, designed by Francis Giles and built by W S Denton, was 564 feet in length, and carried on five arches across the river Eden at a height of 95 feet. It took 4½ years to build. Another of architectural merit was the seven arch Corby viaduct, constructed between 1831 and 1834, which was 480 feet long and some 70 feet high. There was also a skew bridge across the river Gelt which was one of the largest of its kind in the country. The mile long cutting through the Cowran Hills was 110 feet at its deepest part, 26 feet wide at rail level, and 305 feet between the highest points – all of which required the excavation of nearly a million cubic yards of earth. It was at that time the most extensive cutting ever completed in any country. Near Wylam a river wall 26 feet in height above the low water level was needed for ¾ mile. There were two short tunnels, one near Haltwhistle and the other at Corbridge. A trip over the line about 1840 would reveal 25 bridges over the railway, 36 under the tracks, 61 level crossings and 95 field crossings.

It is so easy to record a series of events in the evolution of a railway system, or to over-simplify that, for example, a certain viaduct "was built". None of these things could have happened without *people.* Yes, they needed the architects, financiers, inventors, lawyers, organisers, planners, surveyors ... and behind them the committees – but it was the armies of tough men who built the actual railways with picks, shovels, wheel barrows and with help from horses. The 'navigators' who had dug the canals became the 'navvies' who shaped the iron roads, often in appalling conditions, up and down the country. Apart from their great strength, they had developed a good knowledge of drainage, building embankments, boring tunnels and excavating cuttings which, coupled to their familiarity with rocks and clay, made them ideal for this type of work. Many were very shrewd but were known for their loyalty to their comrades. They often worked together in a 'butty-gang' of ten or twelve under contract to cut out and remove so much 'dirt'. Their dress was usually corduroy breeches held up by a broad leather belt and tied or buttoned at the knee; ribbed stockings and strong, high-laced boots. Those navvies were known for their huge appetites, particularly for meat, and for their ability to drink enormous amounts of liquor. This was good for local trade where they were working but often scared the life out of the natives! Nevertheless, they were visited regularly by clergymen for whom they had a great respect. Very often the railway builders were known only by their nicknames. There was Old Blackbird, Gorger, Hedgehog, Cat's Meat, the Duke of Wellington (because of his large nose), and Mary Ann who had an effeminate voice.

The Newcastle & Carlisle Railway owned about 50 locomotives with a maximum of 37 at any one time. These were supplied by R & W Hawthorn, Robert Stephenson & Co., and Thompson Bros. of Wylam, apart from the one from Edward Bury, number 3 *Meteor*. Originally all were tender engines, seven of them being four-wheelers. The rest were six-wheeled having either four or all six wheels coupled. Later some of the fleet were rebuilt as tank engines. In general they were painted red with black lining and the usual polished brass. All carried a number but the name was more prominent. It was this company that fitted the first sanding apparatus to locomotives to assist adhesion.

John Blackmore is also credited with the design of the company's carriages which were of three types – first class, second class and mixed. First class, of which there were twelve in 1839, had sprung seats and were lined and stuffed throughout. It is said the glass window sashes did not rattle like those of other companies. These coaches were painted yellow picked out in black and could seat eighteen passengers in three compartments. Mixed, or composite, carriages had one first class compartment and two for second class, seating in all 22. Second class, which were white picked out with green, held 24 passengers. These vehicles were open at the sides above the waist which, as one journalist put it, gave travellers "an extensive view of the countryside". According to Wishaw's analysis there were in 1839 six mixed and twelve second class vehicles. Mail coaches painted green were $13\frac{1}{2}$ feet long and four feet above the underframe except for the guard's compartment, which was six feet high. In 1839 the number of passengers carried on the railway was 236,288. The following year there were five through trains in each direction, two of which conveyed mail, taking 3-$3\frac{1}{4}$ hours. On the 'quick' trains fares were just over tuppence a mile for first class and 1.67 old pence for second class. With the possible exception of a train carrying passengers at a reduced fare to an event a short distance away in August 1839, in Yorkshire, it was the Newcastle & Carlisle Railway that introduced the excursion system in April 1840 by allowing visitors to travel from Carlisle to the Polytechnic Exhibition in Newcastle at special rates. This was followed by a Sunday trip to Carlisle for workers from Messrs R & W Hawthorn and their friends on 14 June. A similar outing on a Sunday in August 1840 was denounced by a vicar on placards and handbills stating:-

A REWARD

FOR

SABBATH BREAKING.

People taken safely and swiftly to

HELL!

NEXT LORD'S DAY,

BY THE

CARLISLE RAILWAY,

FOR 7s. 6d.

IT IS A PLEASURE TRIP!

Mad Sinners, will you put a Knife into your own Bowels?

Ye that have Shares in this Iniquity, your Profits will be a Share in JEHOVAH'S WRATH.

For goods and mineral traffic in its early days, the N & CR used 220 goods trucks and 570 chaldron waggons, plus cattle trucks and horse boxes. Trucks were often sheeted over and carried such commodities as coal, lime, iron ore, timber, bricks, slates, manure (fertilisers), grain, hay, wool, hides, sugar, glass and manufactured goods. In 1837 fish traffic included sole and turbot which had rarely been seen at Newcastle before then. Irish bacon was carried in 1839 and many cargoes including flax and timber from Baltic ports were taken from Newcastle to Carlisle then shipped to Liverpool. Livestock from Newcastle cattle market became another good source of revenue. Advertisements in local newspapers at Newcastle advised customers that goods could be collected and delivered.

From Newcastle the railway passed through Scotswood, Blaydon, Ryton, Wylam, Prudhoe, Stocksfield, Riding Mill, Corbridge, Hexham, Fourstones, Haydon Bridge, Bardon Mill, Haltwhistle, Greenhead and Rose Hill; then, in Cumberland, Low Row, Milton, How Mill, Wetheral and Scotby before reach-

Wylam is one of the world's oldest stations still in use for passengers. The station house (now used for business purposes) and the small booking office were completed shortly after the line was opened but the waiting area was added some years later. (J A Wells)

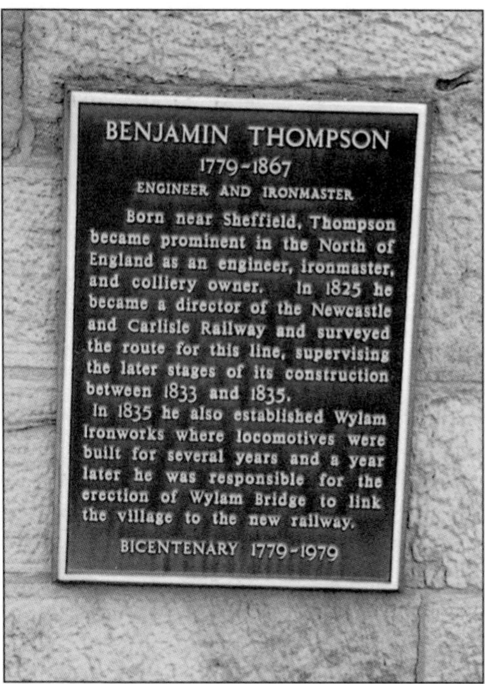

Plaque on the west wall of the station house.

ing the Carlisle station on London Road. The whole line seemed to be a long series of curves through beautiful scenery. Platforms were not provided, only a paved area, though at Hexham and Haltwhistle this was fenced in "to prevent fraud which is frequently committed by unprincipled persons on this railway". Some of the smaller station houses were of neat, rustic designs usually set back from the tracks. When a platform was eventually erected at those adjacent to the line, it was level with the window sills. At Wylam the station house stood at the end of the ramp of the Down (ie Carlisle) platform alongside the level crossing. The station buildings at Stocksfield and Haydon Bridge, both of which were temporary termini, were decorated with Gothic porticos. The company provided covered waiting areas for passengers at its stations but only rarely office buildings.

After 1836 white or coloured paper tickets were in general use on most passenger carrying lines in northern England, but as these had to be completed by hand it was usually a very slow process. At Milton station Thomas Edmondson introduced an ingenious idea which enabled an accurate check to be kept on tickets sold and cash received therefrom. His method was to issue from special racks cardboard tickets he had previously printed himself and numbered consecutively by hand. He invented and brought into use in August 1837 a ticket dating press, the principle of which was still used in booking offices through to the 1950s. The company extended this system to all its stations.

Attempts were made by both the Caledonian Railway and the York, Newcastle & Berwick Railway, to lease the Newcastle-Carlisle line. An agreement was signed with the latter and from 1st August 1848 control of the railway passed into their hands, though subsequently the Newcastle & Carlisle Railway resumed possession of its rolling stock and took management back into its own hands in 1859, following a legal dispute.

On 17 July 1862 the company became part of the North Eastern Railway. A concession of the deal allowed the North British Railway running powers between Hexham and Newcastle in exchange for a reciprocal agreement for the NER between Berwick and Edinburgh. When the North Eastern took over the Newcastle to Carlisle route, one of the first tasks facing them was to change the direction of running from right to left.

(For details of the branch to Alston see page 140)

A VANE IN A TEMPEST

An Irish navvy, named Ernest Vane, 'late of Kielder', happened, in larking with a mate, to break a pane of glass in the office window of Hexham station on Thursday night and because he was not suffered to depart without paying for the damage, he became quite uproarious and commenced a general assault on the said window, firing boots, bundles and anything he could lay hold of, at the offending glass, till he had knocked out eight additional squares, making nine in all.

He was brought before Simon Mewburn, Esq. yesterday and committed to one month's hard labour.

Newcastle Daily Chronicle 17 Aug. 1861.

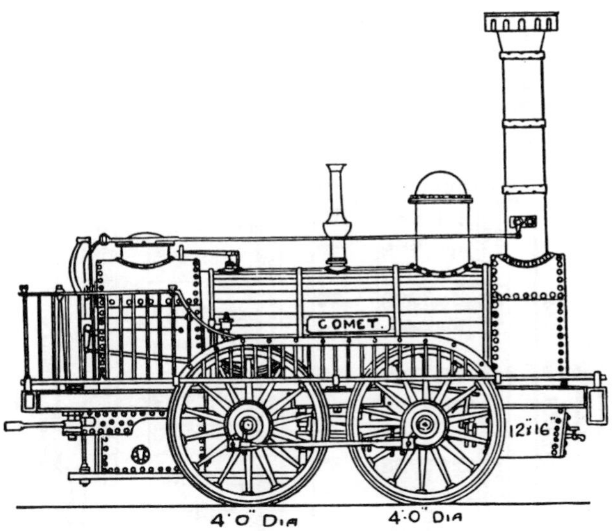

0-4-0 Locomotive 'Comet'. Built in 1835 for the Newcastle & Carlisle Railway by R & W Hawthorn, Newcastle upon Tyne.

It was the custom of some railways to provide local newspapers with weekly Returns showing income from passengers and goods. These would be of interest to shareholders but would also be a form of indirect advertising and may even have reminded their staff that the success or otherwise of the company depended on their efforts. Below are three such weeks relating to the Newcastle & Carlisle Railway in 1847 and comparing them with the same period the previous year.

NEWCASTLE AND CARLISLE RAILWAY			
Week Ending	6th February 1847	8th May 1847	7th August 1847
PASSENGERS MERCHANDISE TOTAL	£ 538-15-7 £1,245-13-2 £1,784- 8-9	£ 664-14-5 £1,526-12-0 £2,191- 6-5	£1,246-18-6 £1,507- 1-7 £2,754- 0-1
CORRESPONDING WEEK 1846	£1,612-16-10 INCREASE £171-11-11	£1,786-16-6 INCREASE £404-9-11	£2,134-3-8 INCREASE £619-16-5

NEWCASTLE-UPON-TYNE AND CARLISLE RAILWAY.

TIMES OF DEPARTURE OF THE TRAINS ON AND AFTER OCTOBER 1st, 1845.

GOING WEST THROUGH THE WEEK.

TRAINS	Leave Newcastle H. M.	Leave Gateshead H. M.	Leave Blaydon H. M.	Leave Stocksfield H. M.	Leave Hexham H. M.	Leave Haydon Bridge H. M.	Leave Haltwhistle H. M.	Leave Rose Hill H. M.	Leave Milton H. M.	Arrive at Carlisle H. M.
1. Morning	7 0	....	7 15	7 45	8 13	8 38	9 5	9 20	9 45	10 15
2. Morning (Mail)	10 0	9 50	10 15	10 45	11 13	11 38	12 5	12 20	12 45	1 15
3. Noon (Short)	12 0	....	12 15	12 46	1 18	............Arrives at Haydon Bridge at 2 o'clock.				
4. Afternoon	2 0	1 50	2 15	2 45	3 13	3 38	4 5	4 20	4 45	5 15
5. Afternoon	4 0	3 50	4 15	4 46	5 18	5 43	6 15	6 30	7 0	7 30
6. Evening	6 45	6 35	7 0	7 30	7 58	8 23	8 50	9 5	9 30	10 0

GOING WEST ON SUNDAYS.

TRAINS	Leave Newcastle H. M.	Leave Gateshead H. M.	Leave Blaydon H. M.	Leave Stocksfield H. M.	Leave Hexham H. M.	Leave Haydon Bridge H. M.	Leave Haltwhistle H. M.	Leave Rose Hill H. M.	Leave Milton H. M.	Arrive at Carlisle H. M.
1. Morning (Mail)	9 45	....	10 0	10 30	10 58	11 23	11 50	12 5	12 30	1 0
2. Afternoon	5 0	....	5 15	5 45	6 13	6 38	7 5	7 20	7 45	8 15

GOING EAST THROUGH THE WEEK.

TRAINS	Leave Carlisle H. M.	Leave Milton H. M.	Leave Rose Hill H. M.	Leave Haltwhistle H. M.	Leave Haydon Bridge H. M.	Leave Hexham H. M.	Leave Stocksfield H. M.	Leave Blaydon H. M.	Arrive at Gateshead H. M.	Arrive at Newcastle H. M.
1. Morning	5 45	6 20	6 40	6 55	7 20	7 45	8 10	8 45	9 5	9 0
2. Morning (Short)	............From Hexham only............					9 30	10 0	10 33	....	10 50
3. Morning	9 0	9 35	9 55	10 10	10 35	11 0	11 25	12 0	12 20	12 15
*4. Afternoon (Mail)	12 5	12 30	12 45	1 0	1 25	1 45	2 10	2 40	3 0	2 55
5. Afternoon	4 15	4 50	5 10	5 25	5 50	6 15	6 40	7 15	7 35	7 30
6. Evening	7 0	7 30	7 47	8 3	8 30	8 53	9 15	9 45	10 5	10 0

GOING EAST ON SUNDAYS.

TRAINS	Leave Carlisle H. M.	Leave Milton H. M.	Leave Rose Hill H. M.	Leave Haltwhistle H. M.	Leave Haydon Bridge H. M.	Leave Hexham H. M.	Leave Stocksfield H. M.	Leave Blaydon H. M.	Arrive at Gateshead H. M.	Arrive at Newcastle H. M.
1. Morning (Mail)	9 0	9 35	9 55	10 10	10 35	11 0	11 25	12 0	....	12 15
2. Afternoon	5 0	5 35	5 55	6 10	6 35	7 0	7 25	8 0	....	8 15

Newcastle: Printed at the Journal Office, by John Hernaman.

* N.B.—This Train will not call at Scotby, How Mill, or Low Row.

A Train will leave Newcastle Station for Blaydon every Evening, (Sundays excepted,) at a quarter before five o'clock, and return from Blaydon for Newcastle at a quarter-past five. And for the convenience of people attending Carlisle Market, a Train will leave Milton Station every Saturday Morning at half-past eight o'clock.

FARES—(For the whole Distance between Newcastle and Carlisle) 1st Class, 11s.; 2nd Class, 8s. 6d.——Children, under Two Years of Age, Free; above Two, and under Ten, Half Price.

Parties riding *inside* their own Carriages, to pay First Class Fares; parties riding *outside* their own Carriages, to pay Second Class Fares. Goods and Parcels conveyed with Safety and Dispatch, and at moderate Rates.

Railway Office, Forth, Newcastle-upon-Tyne, Oct. 1st, 1845. **JOHN ADAMSON, Secretary.**

1845 Timetable. The locomotive and rolling stock on such documents are typical of the time but do not necessarily reflect a particular line. They were from blocks held by the printer but used indiscriminately.

THE NEWCASTLE & NORTH SHIELDS RAILWAY (1836-1845)

Many people welcomed the coming of railways. Some could foresee the tremendous advantages they would bring – faster, cheaper and more comfortable travel, the wider movement of goods, food, materials and livestock; and transporting coal to factories, for export or for domestic use in areas where there were no stocks available. Others predicted dire consequences and tried to spread their fears in attempts to keep railways away. Cows would give less milk, hens would not lay eggs, homes would be burnt to the ground or crushed by collapsing embankments, the health of thousands would be ruined for the benefit of a few ... worst of all the human body would disintegrate if it travelled at over 30 miles per hour, wouldn't it? By petitions, newspaper campaigns, ill-informed criticisms and prejudice did the prophets of doom oppose the iron horse on the iron road.

The earliest scheme for a railway between Newcastle and the port of North Shields with branches to various shipping points was proposed in 1830 but opponents quickly pointed out that it would throw men out of work on the river Tyne and because trains would carry merchandise to the river mouth ships would not have to go so far up the river – thus Newcastle would lose some of its importance. Owners of gigs, coaches or steam packets would be affected. Tradesmen in North Shields objected that more people would shop in Newcastle. Lodging house keepers at Tynemouth were sure that business men would take the train to the coast, have a bathe in the sea and be back in Newcastle for breakfast. Various schemes were considered but opposing views brought the project to a halt in 1831 for two years.

One wit, with tongue in cheek, suggested that disused mine workings should be linked together to form an underground railway lit by gas where people could travel the length of the line in ten and a half minutes for two pence first class. There would be no delays caused by bad weather nor would passengers have to wait in the rain. There would be a constant temperature all the year round "similar to Tivoli in Italy" - and he even suggested this 'tuppenny tube' should be called the Newcastle, North Shields & Tynemouth Tivolian Railway!

In spite of everything a proposal to link Newcastle with North Shields was laid before Parliament in 1836 and was passed on 21 June of that year. There was no opposition to the Bill as it passed through the House of Lords.

The Newcastle & North Shields Railway appointed Robert Nicholson as engineer as he had surveyed the route in 1835. Two viaducts on the line reflected a level of skill that caused great interest to members of the British Association. Both were designed by John and Benjamin Green of Newcastle. Foundation stones were laid in January 1837. One viaduct, 918 feet in length, was carried across the Ouseburn valley on nine arches 108 feet above the stream. The other on seven arches over Willington dene was 1,048 feet long and 82 feet high. Although the abutments and piers were of stone, five of the Ouseburn arches and all seven of the one at Willington were of timber but it was the laminated method of construction that was so unusual, probably used for the first time in this country. Part of the design involved fourteen layers of three inch planks pinned together by tree nails and iron bolts.

Within a quarter of a mile of the Newcastle terminus there was a short tunnel just over 100 yards long. Gates were fitted at each end to make it serve as a carriage shed at night. Other earthworks on this seven mile line were an embankment 80 feet high and a cutting at Heaton three quarters of a mile long. Near Percy Main the line intersected nine waggonways leading to staiths on the river.

Trackwork for the permanent way was different from all others in northern England in that it was laid with flat-bottomed rails weighing 52lb to the yard, screwed down to longitudinal sleepers twelve inches broad by six inches thick and from 20 to 50 feet in length. There were crossbars of oak dovetailed into them every eight feet. It is said this method of track laying gave a very smooth ride. At first the route was single track but it had all been doubled by April 1840. This style of track was of great interest to other companies. The steepest gradients were between Wallsend and Howdon where in a stretch about two miles long, there was a fall of 1 in 183 followed by a rise of 1 in 180.

The terminus at Newcastle was in the south east corner of Carliol Square, Manors, though the intention was to end the line in Pilgrim Street, about 200 yards further west. It consisted of a temporary booking office and waiting room. For several months after the line was opened the platforms and passenger areas had no roof. There were two lines of track each of which had an engine-turning platform at the end, one being just over fourteen feet in diameter and the other just under. They were built by the company for £30 each. This station was lit by seven gas burners at night, indeed it was Mr Nicholson's hope that gas drawn from mine workings could be used to light the whole line, a novel idea! At North Shields – where the platforms were in a cutting sixteen feet deep – better facilities were provided for passengers. There was a booking office and waiting rooms with water closets and urinals for first class and second class travellers. The two platforms were sixteen and eighteen feet wide and the whole length of the station was 570 feet. Both platforms ended with a separate turntable, as at Newcastle, but there were also sidings, a goods shed and a carriage shed. A landing where road carriages could be loaded or unloaded was also provided. A feature of the North Shields station was the triple-arch timber roof also built by lamination. Intermediate stopping places were at Walker, Wallsend, Willington Township and Percy Main.

On the celebration day of Waterloo, 18 June 1839, the line was officially opened. Two trains made two trips each along the line, one of ten carriages and the other of eight. Of those, eleven were covered and seven open. The engines hauling them were *Wellington* and *Hotspur* built by the firms of Robert Stephenson and R & W Hawthorn, both of Newcastle. After alighting at North Shields the passengers formed a procession and walked along the road to Tynemouth, which was gaily decorated for the occasion, where they joined numerous other visitors in a carnival atmosphere. In the late afternoon about 700 guests of the company sat down in a huge marquee to enjoy food and entertainment. Unfortunately, the happy occasion was interrupted by a long, violent thunderstorm. Speeches were 'drowned' by the rolling thunder and most people felt they had been drowned by the downpour! The trains set off to Newcastle at 6.30 pm loaded with drenched passengers and returned for the remainder as soon as possible.

The company bought a small engine manufactured by Edward Bury of Liverpool from the Leeds & Selby Railway in 1838. This was the *St. Vincent* but it was sold in 1840 no doubt because it was too light for the duties required of it. Another loco was the *Exmouth*.

In the early days the stock of carriages consisted of eight first class of which four had been purchased from the Liverpool & Manchester Railway, two mail coaches with three compartments holding six passengers each, and fourteen second class which were open from the waist up though some had curtains at the side. (What purpose did they serve?) The earliest third class was a large carriage truck 20 feet long which could carry 60 passengers on ten seats arranged char-a-banc style. There were eight passenger luggage trucks, one of which formed part of each train. It is recorded in the company's Minutes that first class carriages were painted crimson, maroon, or in one case "a rich, light scarlet claret edged with yellow". Some time after 1841 the first class vehicles were changed to red and second class to claret. Like other railway companies of the time the N & NSR named some of its coaches, examples being *Times, Herald, Director*, *Victoria* and *British Queen.* The last two, together with mail coaches, also displayed the royal crest on their panels. Some first class coaches could be recognised by pictures (an idea copied in France more than 60 years later). One had four chamois, others had four gazelles, antelope or reindeer. Most of the original carriages had the fare painted on them, one shilling first class and sixpence second class, as an additional means of identification. Smoking in trains was banned after some of the best stock had been damaged when people had lit cigars or cigarettes from phosphorous boxes. Later, however, in 1856 first class passengers had the use of a smoking saloon on this branch, twelve years before railway companies were required by law to provide smoking areas on every train containing more than one carriage of each class unless exempted by the Board of Trade.

Signalling on many early railways consisted of circular boards up to four feet in diameter but more usually only about half that size. When turned to face an engine it meant 'stop'; or 'proceed' when turned end on. These were followed later by semaphore signals. In 1840 the Newcastle & North Shields Railway had disc signals at each terminus connected to the point switches to show drivers whether they were set correctly. This was quite an innovation in those days. It was one of the companies which used railway policemen to control the movement of trains. They had twelve of them in 1839 who were paid seventeen shillings (85p) a week, plus one inspector who earned 30 shillings (£1.50).

Apart from railway police and permanent way men, the railway employed one Secretary, one engineer, two booking clerks at each terminus, four collectors at intermediate stations, one locomotive inspector, three engine drivers and firemen, two cleaners, three guards, two brakesmen (who rode on carriages and helped to brake the train) five porters and four station men at Newcastle, and six porters at North Shields.

Return tickets were introduced in October 1841 costing the same as two single tickets but more convenient. They were referred to as *double tickets* or *tickets to clear the trip both ways.* It is recorded that this company made ticket holders pass through a turnstile in the same year. In 1843 small metal tickets were introduced, oval in shape and lettered Newcastle, North Shields & Tynemouth Railway round the edge.

The Newcastle & North Shields Railway worked passenger and goods traffic on the Seghill Railway from 25 June 1844. The following year the company was amalgamated with the new Newcastle and Berwick Railway. Subsequently, on 31 March 1847, this line was extended one mile to Tynemouth.

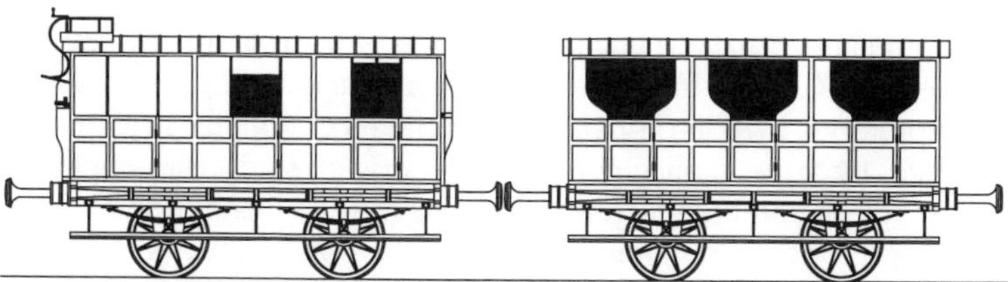

Two types of third class carriage used on the Newcastle and North Shields Railway.
GRM

NEWCASTLE & NORTH SHIELDS RAILWAY WINTER RUNNING.

THE Directors beg to announce that on and after Monday, the 16th November Instant, the TRAINS will leave NEWCASTLE *every Hour*, commencing at Eight in the Morning, and ending at Eight in the Evening; and NORTH SHIELDS *Half after every Hour*, commencing at Half after Eight in the Morning, and ending at Half after Eight in the Evening. On Sundays the Eleven and Twelve o'Clock Trains from Newcastle, and Half-past Eleven and Half-past Twelve o'Clock Trains from Shields will be omitted.

The Trains will call at the Stations at the following Hours

FROM NEWCASTLE.	FROM NORTH SHIELDS.
At Walker, 8, 10, 12, 2, 4, 6, 8.	8½, 10½, 12½, 2½, 4½, 6½, 8½.
Carville every Train.	Every Train.
Howdon (West Lane) every Train.	Every Train.
Percy Main, 9, 11, 1, 3, 5, 7.	9½, 11½, 1½, 3½, 5½, 7½

FARES:—

From either Terminus, the whole or any intermediate Distance,

First Class, 1s.; Second Class, 9d; Third Class, 6d.

From any of the intermediate Stations,

First Class, 9d; Second and Third Class, 6d.

Railway Office, Pilgrim-Street, Nov. 6, 1840.

From an Advertisement in Port of Tyne Pilot 14 Nov. 1840.

THE SEGHILL RAILWAY (1840-1847)

Before describing the Seghill Railway it is necessary to understand the background to the complex system of waggonways taking coal to the river Tyne.

One of these was constructed to Hayhole at Percy Main (later known as the Northumberland Dock complex) to convey the output of collieries around Backworth. It was along this steeply graded route that the first shipment of coal from Backwork A pit travelled in September 1818. From 1821 part of the most difficult stretch was worked by rope haulage from steam-driven stationary engines. These were sometimes referred to as winding engines. A waggonway from the Cramlington area some two miles away joined the Backworth waggonway at Murton Row until the traffic from each company was diverted to its own staith on the bank of the river. When Seghill colliery began producing coal in January 1826 it had to rely on an agreement with the Cramlington collieries to use their line a short distance away. The charge agreed was three shillings and sixpence (17½p) each for up to 22,500 chaldron loads a year, reducing to three shillings (15p) for anything in excess of that number. This meant that coal from Seghill was also travelling on the Backworth waggonway for about four miles before being switched to the new Seghill staith at the end of the run.

To this increase in traffic flow, together with more coal from the Cramlington area as additional shafts were sunk, was added a new line from Seaton Delaval pit to Cramlington waggonway in 1839, hence it was not surprising that the Backworth waggonway became grossly overloaded. Loaded chaldrons often clogged the sidings at Percy Main while waiting for ships consequently there was a shortage of empty waggons at the pits. Understandably, the Backworth collieries would give priority to their own needs but it caused so much frustration that the owners of Seghill colliery built their own line to the river. The route was surveyed for them by Robert Nicholson, engineer of the Newcastle & North Shields Railway. After earthworks had been completed and track laid, the Seghill Railway was opened for mineral traffic on 1st June 1840 and for passengers in August 1841. A station was built at Percy Main for this purpose. Goods and passenger services were provided by the Newcastle & North Shields Railway from June 1844. The Cramlington collieries also removed their traffic from the Backworth waggonway in 1839 by building their own line from Murton Row. At first waggonways carried only coal whereas railways also transported passengers and goods, but the former name gradually dropped out of use.

From Seghill to Prospect Hill near Allotment there were rising gradients varying from 1 in 61.5 to 1 in 228; after Prospect Hill the line dropped steeply in parts to Percy Main, the most severe being 1 in 25. Two locomotives, *Samson* and *John,* worked between Seghill colliery and Holywell. A stationary engine drew loaded waggons from there to the apex of the route after which they ran to Percy Main by gravity. Similarly, empty waggons were hauled up the bank before running freely back to Holywell, in charge of brakesmen.

Further north other companies were considering whether it was feasible to install a railway system to link their collieries around Blyth and Bedlington with staiths which would be erected near the mouth of the river Tyne, but after analysing the various options it was decided to swing the line sharply round at New Hartley to merge with the existing tracks from Seaton Delaval colliery. It was agreed also that the connection with the Cramlington waggonway would be severed and the line joined to the Seghill Railway instead. It was suggested that the enlarged system should be called the Blyth & Tyne Junction Railway.

The line from Percy Main to Seghill was thus extended through Seaton Delaval to New Hartley in 1846 where Hester pit was rail connected and could then despatch coal either from the Tyne or from Seaton Sluice. By March 1847 collieries at Blyth could take advantage of the shipping facilities offered at Percy Main. Passenger trains ran into the first station at Blyth on 3 March of that year. The advertised winter timetable commencing on 1st October 1847 was headed BLYTH, SEGHILL & PERCY MAIN RAILWAY but on the amended edition showing alterations to be introduced from 3 December the title was shown simply as the BLYTH & TYNE RAILWAY.

In the year ending 31 December 1851 Seghill colliery despatched 70,750 chaldrons to Hayhole on the river Tyne and 1,433 to Seaton Sluice. The combined shipments from collieries at Seghill, Hartley, Cowpen, Bedlington, Barrington and Netherton were as follows:-

from River Tyne	133,644 chaldrons
from Blyth	64,194 chaldrons
from Seaton Sluice	18,661 chaldrons

Miles travelled by loaded waggons 1,380,869.

At the end of 1852 the Blyth & Tyne was running twelve locomotives, nine 0-6-0s, two 2-4-0s and one 0-4-0 (Bury's design).

THE NEWCASTLE & BERWICK RAILWAY (1845-1847)

Schemes put forward for early railways were frequently challenged by those who preferred a different route. There were lively battles in meetings as experts tried to convince business men and entrepreneurs of the merits of their various plans. The policy of 'you scratch my back and I'll scratch yours' led to compromises but in the end it was Parliament that made the final decisions. Some proposals were rejected out of hand; some which were approved foundered because the necessary capital could not be raised; other schemes were sanctioned in their entirety though in some cases the companies decided to modify their plans and did not complete the full programme of development.

Even in 1824, while the world's first public railway was being built and other schemes around the country were being frantically discussed, the mayor of Newcastle upon Tyne had received a proposal communicated by a Mr William Bell of Edinburgh for a railway connecting the Scottish capital with London via Newcastle. The Tyne Mercury newspaper dismissed the idea as irrational and absurd. However desirable, it could never have been carried out completely at that time because of the lack of know-how and, of course, the cost. It was necessary at first for smaller companies such as the Newcastle & Berwick Railway and the Newcastle & Darlington Junction Railway to fulfil various local aspirations.

George Hudson, once a draper in York and later its Lord Mayor, supported a number of railway schemes by investing heavily in shares and he became chairman of several companies including the Newcastle & Darlington Junction which he broadened into the York & Newcastle Railway. By extending and protecting his empire from rivals he sought to establish rail links from York to London and Edinburgh. Known as The Railway King, his energy and enthusiasm secured a unity of administration and policy from Berwick to Rugby whereby he quickly brought together and strengthened the railway interests of Northumberland, Durham and Yorkshire.

In Northumberland the proposed railway through the county would pass through the estate of Sir Matthew White Ridley. His agent called in Isambard Kingdom Brunel, engineer to the Great Western Railway, to see whether in his opinion the route suggested by George Stephenson should be altered. In a letter dated 15 October 1844 Mr Brunel stated:-

My dear Sir
I have walked over the line pointed out by you last evening for consideration beyond Jesmond House. With every desire to give full consideration to any suggestion made I feel it would be deceiving Sir Matthew White Ridley if by even taking the section of that line I should lead him to believe that there were any probability of its being adopted or that its adoption could be at all a question of levels. The ground appears to me anything but favourable – but even if the section were perfectly unobjectionable – and if the line were not three quarters of a mile longer involving thereby an expense of £10000 or £12000 – the interference with private residential property is such that I should never feel justified in recommending such a course in preference to that which I had selected – indeed I am really surprised at your having thought it feasible in comparison with the other – I should compare it with the passing thro Blagdon instead of to the East of the Turnpike road.

Will you have the goodness to communicate this letter to Sir M.W. Ridley.

I am Dear Sir
Yours very faithfully
I.K. Brunel.

A copy of this report was duly sent to Sir Matthew the following day with an accompanying letter thus:-

Killingworth White House
Octr. 16th 1844.

Sir Matthew,
Mr. Brunel has made an examination of the line proposed to him for some distance out of Newcastle & as will be seen by his letter to me, a copy of which I enclose, he considers it both more unfavourable in the character of the ground & more objectionable as interfering with residences. There is nothing left for you now but to give every support in your power to Stephenson's line if you find it kept as I expect considerably to the east of Down Hill.

I have received my copy of the Railway Act of the present session but it relates entirely to the regulating of other matters than those connected with the obtaining of new lines.

As soon as I learn any thing certain of Stephenson's line I shall inform you, & as he is to be here this week I shall probably be able to see him.

I remain Sir Matthew
Your very obedient Servant
Henry Turner.

The Act which authorised the building of the Newcastle & Berwick Railway was passed on 31 July 1845. The length of the line was to be 95½ miles with capital to be raised by shares or loans fixed at £1,866,666. One of the seven directors appointed by the Act was Nicholas Wood, a well respected coal owner and railway engineer who had worked closely with George Stephenson in earlier days. The first chairman was the indomitable George Hudson. In that same year the Newcastle & North Shields Railway was amalgamated with the new company but it was to be managed as an independent line at least until part of the Newcastle & Berwick Railway was opened for traffic.

As the line was being constructed it was carried across the rivers Blyth, Wansbeck, Coquet and Aln on temporary wooden structures. They also served as construction platforms during the building of the permanent bridges which were a series of brick arches with stone facings supported on stone piers. Five smaller bridges were built on the slew principle.

This company provided large and impressive station buildings even in the rural areas of the county. They were designed by Benjamin Green.

The first part of this vital link in the main line to Scotland, the 14½ miles from Heaton to Morpeth, was opened on 1st March 1847. From Heaton to Newcastle use was made of the line from North Shields, together with the terminus in Carliol Square. Shareholders of the company were invited to a special meeting at York the following week at which George Hudson, MP, was in the

Chathill station, originally built by the Newcastle & Berwick Railway, was still in limited use in 1998. For at least fifteen years after the closure of the North Sunderland Railway the nameboards proclaimed 'Chathill for Seahouses'. (J A Wells)

chair. The purpose was to consider drafts for bills to be put before the current session of Parliament, the first of which was to propose branches that included Blyth and Seaton Sluice. It was reported that in the week since the railway opened to Morpeth it had carried more than 2,000 passengers, all local traffic. The section from Berwick to Chathill, a further twenty miles, was due to open almost immediately and the company would run omnibuses between Morpeth and Chathill. Bad weather, which had almost prohibited outside work for three months, had caused some delay but the Newcastle & Berwick Railway was in a very satisfactory position and they could hardly estimate the amount of traffic they would be carrying.

The northern section was opened on 29 March and the central section on 1st July 1847. From that date trains could run through from Newcastle to Tweedmouth. As there was no railway bridge between Newcastle and Gateshead at that time passengers and their luggage were conveyed by omnibus between the two places. The coming of the railway spelt the end of stage coaches and the last mail coach from Edinburgh arrived at the Queen's Head Inn in Newcastle on 5 July 1847.

At the above meeting proposals for the construction of the Cramlington and Percy Main branches were discussed and agreed. Finally, a bill would be laid before Parliament seeking an amalgamation of the Newcastle & Berwick Railway with the York and Newcastle. This merger was approved from 9 August 1847 and the new company was designated the York, Newcastle & Berwick Railway.

NEWCASTLE & BERWICK RAILWAY
TRAIN SERVICE FROM MONDAY 29th MARCH 1847

FROM NEWCASTLE	FROM MORPETH
7.45 am	9.00 am
10.45 am	2.00 pm
3.45 pm	6.00 pm
6.45 pm	8.00 pm
Sundays 8.15 am	9.15 am
5.45 pm	7.00 pm

NEWCASTLE & BERWICK RAILWAY
CHEAP FARES on GOOD FRIDAY and
EASTER MONDAY.

RETURN TICKETS will be issued on the above named Day at all the Stations between NEWCASTLE and MORPETH. Tickets issued on Good Friday will be available on that Day only; those issued on Easter Monday will be available for returning either on Monday or Tuesday.

By Order.
JAMES ALLPORT, Manager.
Newcastle-upon-Tyne, March 20th, 1847

THE YORK, NEWCASTLE & BERWICK RAILWAY (1847-1854)

The amalgamation of the York & Newcastle Railway with the Newcastle & Berwick on 9 August 1847, only a matter of weeks after the east coast main line was opened through Northumberland, was a logical step to strengthen the position of both companies. There was, however, a major problem which was how to bridge the formidable gap of the river Tyne, a question which demanded an urgent answer if through running was to be achieved.

Several crossing places were suggested each of which could have changed the development of railways around Newcastle and through the county. George Stephenson had regarded the linking of the east coast route as a matter of national importance, particularly as there were plans to connect Berwick-upon-Tweed with Edinburgh. In his opinion the best location was between Castle Garth, Newcastle, and Greenesfield, Gateshead, and this was accepted. Robert Stephenson was appointed consulting engineer responsible for the design and erection of the High Level bridge which would be funded jointly by the (then) Newcastle & Darlington Junction and the Newcastle & Berwick railway companies. A temporary wooden stage erected alongside the developing bridge was opened for rail traffic on 29 August 1848. The permanent approaches included the fine elliptical arch towering over Dean Street with a span of 80 feet. The bridge itself, 1,337 feet in

A 1914 postcard showing part of the High Level bridge at Newcastle, and the Swing bridge in the foreground. (Author's collection)

length and 112 feet above high water, was declared "a harmonious combination of cast iron arches, pillars and diagonal bracing". There were six arches each having a span of 125 feet. The first segment was put in place in mid July 1848 and the last key was fixed less than a year later. The weight of iron was 5,050 tons and the cost, excluding compensation and land, was £243,000. It was a two-deck construction having railway tracks above and a roadway with pavements below. To complete this magnificent bridge in such a short time was a very notable achievement. A government official inspected it on 11 August when several weighty trains passed across. He expressed himself perfectly satisfied with the nature and security of the work and the railway was brought into use on 15 August 1849 when the morning southbound mail was the first public train across. It was officially opened by Her Majesty Queen Victoria on 28 September as she was returning from Scotland. The roadway was opened the following February, tolls being charged for its use. This rail link was designed by Robert Stephenson with loads of 100 tons in mind yet it is still carrying trains of well over 1,000 tons plus strings of very heavy lorries, a tribute indeed. (It is not widely known that on Sunday, 24 June 1866 a very serious fire at a mill below the High Level bridge put the bridge itself in danger of being destroyed. So great was the threat that T E Harrison, chief engineer of the North Eastern

Railway, ordered a special train from London to rush him to Gateshead.)

Robert Stephenson also designed the stately 28-arch Royal Border bridge across the estuary of the river Tweed at Berwick, the foundation stone of which was laid on 15 May 1847 and the key-stone of the last arch was fixed on 26 March 1850. The bridge was formally opened on 29 August 1850. Whilst it was being built trains used a temporary wooden viaduct which was brought into use in October 1848.

It is interesting to trace the journey of Queen Victoria through the County of Northumberland and the city of Newcastle upon Tyne in September 1849 on her return from Court at Balmoral. It had been planned that an overnight stop at Perth would be made but because of an outbreak of cholera there, and at Stirling, arrangements were made instead for the Royal party to spend the night at Howick Hall, the residence of Earl Grey. Word had quickly spread that Her Majesty, Prince Albert and their daughters, the Princess Royal and Princess Alice would be passing through Berwick during the evening of 27 September, on their way to Windsor. It seemed that the whole of 'the good town of Berwick-upon-Tweed' turned out to give them a tumultuous welcome. A pilot engine, decorated in front with a large crown of evergreens and flowers, dashed into the station at 7.35 pm, followed by the Royal train which stopped to change engines. Church bells rang, bonfires were lit, people cheered and waved hats, handkerchiefs or flags in a huge, crushing throng. A loyal address was handed in unread for formalities were kept to a minimum as the train prepared to move off. There were seven first class coaches, the plush Royal saloon belonging to the London & North Western Railway, and a number of flat trucks carrying the posting carriages.

The Directors of the York, Newcastle & Berwick Railway, who had boarded the train at Berwick, presented the Queen with "a beautiful, illustrated map of the railway, printed in gold on enamel paper, mounted on rich white watered silk, elegantly bound in purple morocco, with antique boards indented in the centre, beneath which the royal arms executed on crimson velvet" (Newcastle Journal). It was greatly admired.

Little Mill, at that time a private station for Earl Grey (similar to one at Fallodon for Sir George Grey) had been fitted out with great taste and elegance to welcome the Royal party. After formal greetings they were escorted to Howick Hall. The Royal saloon was taken to Gateshead for the night. Shortly after 11 am the following morning numerous people from towns and villages had turned out to show respect for their monarch as the train passed. From Heaton, at the edge of the city, bridges and buildings were adorned with greenery and flowers; there was a large triumphal arch with VR on both sides, and Argyle Street bridge was draped with WELCOME TO NEWCASTLE AND GATESHEAD. Other banners proclaimed 'York, Newcastle & Berwick Railway', 'Stephenson', and 'Civilisation'.

As the train slowed down there was a 21-gun salute from the old castle mingled with peals of bells from the cathedral and music from a military band. Thousands of people thronged every point from where they could catch a glimpse of the Royal train; windows of buildings were choked with excited onlookers – yet it was not certain that the train would stop on the bridge as Her Majesty had previously intimated she did not wish to be delayed on the journey. The lines from Heaton and Gateshead met in a **Y** junction at Newcastle and as the train pulled up a new engine was coupled on to the rear. A special stop *was* made in the middle of the bridge where a spacious platform had been erected for officials. Although Queen Victoria and Prince Albert did not leave the train as it was raining they showed great interest and waved from both sides of the Royal saloon and received an address from the mayor, aldermen and burgesses of Newcastle and from the mayor and corporation of Gateshead. Another lofty triumphal arch made from iron, profusely decorated and surmounted by an elegant crown made from dahlias, was emblazoned with VR and WELCOME TO BOTH SIDES OF THE TYNE. The Queen's first visit to Tyneside proved the devotion of her people in the north east. As the train continued on its journey south the local officials of the railway would breathe a sigh of relief!

Two of the company's locomotives usually allocated to Royal train duties between York and Berwick were number 190 and number 77, both Stephenson engines. Loco 190, a 2-2-2 weighing 22 tons, was known as a patent express engine. It was used between York and Newcastle when Queen Victoria opened the new Central station. On 11 October 1850 No. 77 took the Royal train from Berwick to Newcastle at an average speed of 57 mph, excluding a five minute stop.

The company owned 199 locomotives in December 1849 with another ten on order. They classified them according to the duties they would normally perform, as shown in the diagram below.

YORK, NEWCASTLE & BERWICK RAILWAY: LOCOMOTIVE STOCK (1849)

Class number	Description of engine	Engines & tenders in working order	Engines requiring considerable repair	Engines rebuilding	Trifling repairs	Engines at work but requiring entire rebuilding	Total
1	Local coal traffic	23	3	2			28
2	Through passenger	48	3		1		52
3	Local passenger	17	3	1	5		26
4	Branch & pilot	19	1	1	2		23
5	Through coal & goods	46	5		2		53
6	Hartlepool Old Stock	4	1		3	9	17
	Totals	157	16	4	13	9	199
	Nasmyth's Gaskell & Co. have 10 goods engines to deliver of their contract at £2,550 each.						10
							209
	Total miles run during the half year July to December 1849						1,612,437

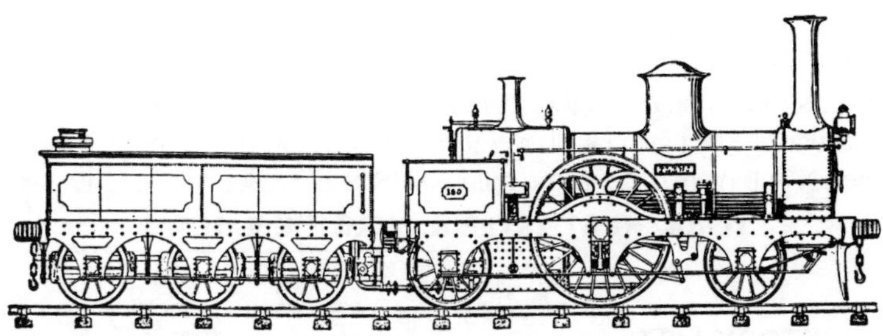

York, Newcastle & Berwick Railway 2-2-2 Locomotive No. 180 "Plews", built in 1848 by R & W Hawthorn. A similar engine, No. 57 "The Queen", was built the following year for the North British Railway.

The number of passengers carried in the second half of 1849 was 1,613,123 compared with 1,709,971 in the same period of the previous year. These figures were included in a Report issued to Shareholders at a meeting on 7 March 1850. It was explained that before the High Level bridge was opened a passenger travelling from, say, Berwick to Durham had to buy three tickets, one to Newcastle, another from there to Gateshead and the third for the journey to Durham. This counted as three passengers in the statistics, hence the apparent reduction in numbers once the bridge was in use.

1848	July to December		1849	July to December	
	Number of Passengers	Revenue		Number of Passengers	Revenue
1st Class	115,928	£30,041-9-8	1st Class	109,928	£29,815-14-10
2nd Class	582,579	£45,641-2-0	2nd Class	491,087	£42,936-19-6
3rd Class	922,491	£32,923-4-3	3rd Class	911,807	£32,885-17-0
Government	88,973	£12,317-2-11	Government	100,301	£13,502-8-2
Totals	1,709,971	£120,922-18-10	Totals	1,613,123	£119,140-19-6

NOTE: In old currency 12 pence, or pennies, (d.) = 1 shilling
20 shillings (s. or sh.) = £1. (1 shilling = 5 new pence)

The list of rolling stock owned by the company gives a good indication of the number of carriages needed to provide passenger services. It also reveals the scope of freight operations, emphasising the importance of coal haulage by having well over 9,000 wagons for that purpose. In 1847 the YN & B owned 213 route miles, in 1848 222 miles and in 1849 248.

YORK, NEWCASTLE & BERWICK RAILWAY

STOCK LIST DEC. 1849	In Working Order	In Good Order: under repair	Rebuilding	Number to Rebuild	Newcastle & North Shields Old Stock	Total
1st class coupé carriages	23	5				28
1st class carriages	48	3			10	61
Composites	24	3	1	5		33
2nd class carriages	123			1	6	130
3rd class carriages	64		1		14	79
Mail vans	2					2
Luggage vans	26					26
Carriage trucks	26	2				28
Horse boxes	32	2	1			35
Stores vans	2					2
Break (i.e. brake) vans	10		2			12
6-ton coal wagons	1,216	26				1,242
Coke wagons	707	40				747
Timber wagons	134	8				142
Cattle wagons	245	6		3		254
Sheep or box wagons	142	4				146
Goods wagons	1,088	20	1	53	37	1,199
Corn wagons*	238	10				248
Chaldron coal wagons	8,022	95	14	70		8,201
Ballast wagons	54	2				56
Stone wagons	102					102

* 82 Corn wagons have had additional stays put on them and the doors made to slide.

Bradshaw's General Railway Directory showed that in 1849 the Chairman was George Hudson, MP, and his senior staff were:-

Engineer in Chief	Robert Stephenson
Engineer	Thomas E Harrison
Superintendent of Locomotive Dept.	Edward Fletcher
Manager of Passenger & Goods Traffic	James Allport

James Allport introduced the first cranes in the country to have hydraulic power for railway use. These were installed at Trafalgar goods station, opened in 1850 near Manors, and proved very reliable.

The Central station at Newcastle was also opened in 1850. In June of that year W W Tomlinson records that electric lighting was exhibited there by a Mr W E Staite who subsequently submitted to the directors a tender for lighting the station.

YORK, NEWCASTLE, & BERWICK RAILWAY.

CHEAP TRAIN TO EDINBURGH, on MONDAY the 31st of JULY, 1848.

A SPECIAL TRAIN will leave NEWCASTLE for EDINBURGH at 7 A.M. on *Monday the 31st July*, calling at MORPETH, LESBURY, and BELFORD; and returning from Edinburgh at 2 P.M. on Friday the 4th, and on Monday the 7th of August.

FARES THERE AND BACK.

	1st Class.	2d Class.	3d Class.
Newcastle and Morpeth	15s. 0d.	10s. 0d.	7s. 6d.
Lesbury and Belford	12s. 0d.	8s. 0d.	6s. 0d.

Passengers from the intermediate Stations can proceed to Morpeth, Lesbury, and Belford, by the Train leaving Newcastle at 6·30 A.M.

By Order, JAMES ALLPORT, Manager.

Newcastle-upon-Tyne, 20th July, 1848.

YORK, NEWCASTLE, & BERWICK RAILWAY.

CHEAP TRAIN TO LONDON, *on Friday the 14th July*, to return from London on the Evening of Wednesday the 19th, or Monday the 24th July, 1848.

On Friday the 14th July, a SPECIAL TRAIN will leave GLASGOW for LONDON at 3 P.M. arriving at Edinburgh about 5·30 P.M. at Berwick about 8 P.M. and calling at Belford, Lesbury, and Morpeth, arriving at Newcastle about 11 P.M.

The Train will leave GATESHEAD about 11 P.M. calling at Belmont, for Durham, Darlington, Northallerton, Thirsk, Alne, and York.

Passengers from the different Branches will have to proceed by the ordinary Trains, paying the usual Fares to the above-mentioned Stations, where they will be able to procure Tickets for London.

Sunderland and Shields to Gateshead by 9·15 P.M.
Hartlepool..........to Darlington......by 6·0 P.M.
Richmond ....to Darlington......by 6·30 P.M.
Bedale.............to Northallerton by 5·40 P.M.
Boroughbridge......to York .... by 5.40 P.M.

Passengers from Durham will join the Train at Belmont by the 11·25 P.M.

FARES THERE AND BACK.

	1st Class. £. s. d.	2d Class. £. s. d.	3d Class. £. s. d.
Tweedmouth, Belford, Lesbury and Morpeth	3 0 0	2 5 0	1 10 0
Newcastle and Durham	2 15 0	2 0 0	1 5 0
Darlington, Northallerton, Thirsk, and Alne	2 10 0	1 15 0	1 0 0

Tickets may be had on and after Tuesday the 11th July, and an early Application for them after that Date is requested.—By Order,

JAMES ALLPORT, Manager.

Newcastle-upon-Tyne, July 5th, 1848.

PRESS ANNOUNCEMENTS OF SPECIAL TRAINS

Notice the co-operation with other companies in running a train between Glasgow and London even in those early days.

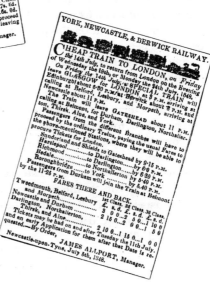

Two press reports of general interest:–

As the mail train upon the York, Newcastle and Berwick Railway was proceeding north one night last week, and when near to the station at Cramlington, a party of horned owls, being disturbed in their roost by the noise, made a furious attack upon the engine and those in charge of it. The fireman, while seated in the locomotive, was furiously assailed, and before he could discover the character of his foe, was seriously pecked in the face, and had one of his teeth forced out of its place.

Newcastle Journal 23 Dec. 1848

(Note: These birds may have been Long Eared Owls)

Thursday, May 22.

(Before R. Airey, Esq., and Mr. Ald. Dunn.)

ROBBERY IN A RAILWAY TRUCK – WM. CUMMINGS and WM. ROWLEY were charged with stealing a blanket, a quantity of tobacco, and other articles, in a railway truck belonging to the York, Newcastle, and Berwick Railway Company. It appeared that about two o'clock this morning, in consequence of hearing a noise proceed from a truck, which had a short time previously arrived from Darlington, with goods, one of the watchers at the central station lifted up the cover of the truck, and found, to his surprise, the two prisoners, when he immediately fastened down the cover to keep them secure, called in assistance, and gave them into the custody of sub-inspector Clark. On a further examination of the truck it was found that two barrels of tobacco contained in it had been opened; a parcel containing a blanket and some linen was also found open. A quantity of tobacco was also found in the pockets of the prisoners, who, on being questioned, said they got into the truck at Ferry Hill. As the precise extent of the robbery could not be ascertained till some inquiries were made as to the state in which the truck left Darlington, the prisoners were remanded till Monday.

Newcastle Weekly Chronicle
23 May 1851

YORK, NEWCASTLE, & BERWICK RAILWAY.

STATIONS.	UP TRAINS FROM BERWICK TO YORK.										SUNDAYS.								FARES.			
	1	2	3	4	5	6	7	8	9	10	11	12	13	14	15	16	17	18	1st clas	2nd clas	3rd clas	4th Class
				Expr:		Mail				Mail				Mail				Mail				1d.m.
LEAVE			A.M.	a.m.	a.m.	a.m.			p.m.	p.m.			a.m.	a.m.			p.m.	p.m.	s. d.	s. d.	s. d.	s. d.
Glasgow	....	....	....	8 0	....	....	....	....	....	4 0	....	....	....	....	....	....	....	....	....	....	....	....
Edinburgh	....	....	....	9 45	8 0	11 0	....	....	....	6 0	....	....	....	11 0	....	....	....	6 0	....	....	....	....
			1 2 3 Cl a.m.	1 Class a.m.	1 2 3 Class a.m.	1 2 Class a.m.			1 2 3 Cl p.m.	1 2 Class p.m.			1 2 3 Class a.m.	1 2 Class p.m.			1 2 3 Cl p.m.	1 2 Class p.m.				
Berwick	....	....	7 15	11 20	10 45	1 15	....	....	5 30	8 35	....	....	7 0	1 15	....	....	5 15	8 35	....	....	....	....
Tweedmouth	....	....	7 17	....	10 47	1 17	....	....	5 32	8 37	....	....	7 2	1 17	....	....	5 17	8 37	0 6	0 3	....	0 2
Scremerston	....	....	7 22	....	10 52	....	....	....	5 37	....	....	....	7 7	....	....	....	5 22	....	1 0	0 8	....	0 6
Beal	....	....	7 32	....	11 2	....	....	....	5 47	....	....	....	7 17	....	....	....	5 32	....	1 9	1 3	....	0 9½
Belford	....	....	7 48	....	11 18	1 43	....	....	6 3	9 2	....	....	7 34	1 43	....	....	5 49	9 2	3 6	2 0	....	1 4¼
Lucker	....	....	7 55	....	11 25	....	....	....	6 8	....	....	....	7 41	....	....	....	5 56	....	4 0	2 6	....	1 6¾
Chat Hill	....	....	8 2	....	11 32	....	....	....	6 15	....	....	....	7 48	....	....	....	6 3	....	4 6	2 9	....	1 9¾
Christon Bank	....	....	8 7	....	11 37	....	....	....	6 21	....	....	....	7 54	....	....	....	6 10	....	5 0	3 3	....	2 0¾
Longhoughton	....	....	8 24	....	11 54	....	....	....	6 36	....	....	....	8 11	....	....	....	6 27	....	6 6	3 9	....	2 6¼
Lesbury, Alnwick	....	....	8 29	11 55	11 59	2 15	....	....	6 42	9 32	....	....	8 17	2 15	....	....	6 33	9 32	7 0	4 3	....	2 8½
Warkworth	....	....	8 42	....	12 12	....	....	....	6 54	....	....	....	8 30	....	....	....	6 46	....	7 6	4 9	....	3 0¾
Acklington	....	....	8 52	....	12 21	2 30	....	....	7 4	9 47	....	....	8 40	2 30	....	....	6 56	9 47	8 6	5 0	....	3 3¼
Widdrington	....	....	9 3	....	12 33	....	....	....	7 14	....	....	....	8 52	....	....	....	7 8	....	9 6	5 9	....	3 8½
Longhirst	....	....	9 11	....	12 41	....	....	....	7 23	....	....	....	9 0	....	....	....	7 16	....	10 0	6 3	....	3 11½
Morpeth	....	....	9 19	12 25	12 49	2 55	....	....	7 33	10 10	....	....	9 9	2 55	....	....	7 25	10 10	11 0	6 9	....	4 3
Netherton	....	....	9 28	....	12 58	....	....	....	7 43	....	....	....	9 18	....	....	....	7 34	....	11 6	6 9	....	4 5½
Cramlington	....	....	9 40	....	1 10	....	....	....	7 53	....	....	....	9 30	....	....	....	7 46	....	12 0	7 3	....	4 9¾
Killingworth	....	....	9 50	....	1 20	....	....	....	8 2	....	....	....	9 41	....	....	....	7 57	....	13 0	7 9	....	5 2
ARRIVE AT Newcastle	....	....	10 15	1 5	1 45	3 30	....	....	8 15	....	....	....	10 0	3 30	....	....	8 15	10 45	14 0	8 9	....	5 7½

Timetable circa 1850

The York, Newcastle & Berwick Railway was one of three companies which amalgamated to form the North Eastern Railway from 31 July 1854.

THE DAVISON RAILWAY (1850-1855)

On 12 June 1850 the Bedlington Coal Company opened a private line from Bedlington colliery to Newsham, a distance of 2$^{3}/_{4}$ miles. There it was connected to a railway from Blyth to Percy Main. Sometimes referred to as the Davison Railway, it crossed the river Blyth on a high viaduct. Passengers were carried from August 1850. It was bought by the Blyth & Tyne Railway in 1855 and formed part of the route to Morpeth.

THE BLYTH & TYNE RAILWAY (1852-1874)

In the section on the Seghill Railway it was stated that the extended company was using the title *Blyth & Tyne Railway* by December 1847 (page 29) and it is from then that the development of this notable business continues.

At that time there was a rail connection from Blyth through Newsham, Hartley, Seaton Delaval, Seghill, Holywell and Prospect Hill to Percy Main station or the staiths. Collieries feeding on to this line had much better facilities on the Tyne but some coal was taken through the small harbour of Seaton Sluice. Blyth was very limited too as the port there had not been developed. Colliery owners around Bedlington were not slow to recognise the tremendous advantages of rail transport and constructed a line to join the Blyth & Tyne at Newsham. As stated, this involved the erection of a substantial wooden viaduct over the river Blyth. Designed by Robert Nicholson, it was 80 feet high, 770 feet long and was not replaced for over 70 years.

The opening of this connection brought much more coal traffic to the railway but the Bedlington Coal Company also wanted passenger trains which would help them to recruit miners from a wider area. The B & T calculated it would cost £1,522/15/6 (£1,522.77$^{1}/_{2}$) for a locomotive, one first class and two second class carriages plus a luggage van and various lamps. They also estimated £306/13/4 (£306.67) to run the trains for a year. Any loss incurred would be made up by the collieries concerned. The service was introduced in August 1850 with small stations at Bedlington and Cowpen Lane (renamed Bebside about 1862).

With the threat of other mining companies wanting to thread their own tracks to the Tyne and other groups hatching schemes for lines through Northumberland which might restrict future expansion, an application was made for Parliamentary powers of incorporation in 1851. The Royal Assent was given on 30 June 1852 to take effect from 1st January 1853. Robert Nicholson was appointed engineer. The Blyth & Tyne Railway Company then had to take decisive, aggressive action to keep out rival concerns. This they did by extending their system first to Morpeth where they sited their station and large goods shed only a road width from the former Newcastle & Berwick Railway. The Act giving permission for this was passed in August 1853. The line did not officially open for coal traffic until 1st October 1857 though there is evidence to suggest it was probably in use six months before that. The reasons for the delay were the late deliveries of components by suppliers, modernisation programmes which included the purchase of locomotives and rolling stock, and the cutting down of Prospect Hill to enable steam locomotives to be used on the entire route. When passenger and goods traffic commenced on 1st April 1858 the Blyth & Tyne main line was changed to run from Percy Main to Morpeth, with connections from Newsham to Blyth. Intermediate stations between Bedlington and Morpeth were provided at Choppington and Hepscott.

Once the Morpeth traffic was running the B & TR formed a junction at Bedlington and ran a line to North Seaton. This necessitated another large viaduct, over the river Wansbeck, reported at the time as being the largest timber structure of its kind in the kingdom. Trains began using this branch in November 1859. The company considered this line would eventually be extended to Warkworth but this idea was never fulfilled and it was taken instead to Ashington and Newbiggin in 1872. Coal was transported from North Seaton colliery and charged as under:-

Leading and shipping coal at Tyne 4sh.7d. (22½p) chaldron
(small coal 20% less)

Leading and shipping large or small coal at Blyth 2sh.4d. chaldron.

Permission was given on 3 July 1854 for a new line from Hartley to Tynemouth but it was some time before this Avenue Branch was built, part of it being on the trackbed of the old Whitley waggonway. It was finally opened for mineral traffic on 31 October 1860 but a severe winter caused landslips and it was 1st April 1861 before goods and passenger traffic were introduced. Through running of trains to and from Morpeth began at the end of May. The intermediate station, at Monkseaton, was called Whitley (see page 151).

The Blyth & Tyne officials were obviously aware of the number of passengers carried on the Newcastle & North Shields Railway route. A decision was taken to build their own line into the city from Whitley in order to capitalise on the potential passenger traffic. This in itself was a bold – even risky – decision. Apart from the expense of the infrastructure, track, stations and signals for example, there was the cost of additional locomotives, coaches and staff. Initial planning would take into consideration where stock would be stabled, coaling and watering facilities, gradients, timetabling, staff hours and what had to be provided at each station. These would be only a part of the many difficulties foreseen and unseen which, for a company formed primarily to transport mainly coal just ten years before, would present a formidable task. That it worked so well is a tribute to their efficiency. The line opened in 1864.

The terminus at Newcastle was New Bridge Street, the former Picton House. New stations were built at Jesmond, Gosforth, Long Benton, Forest Hall (for Killingworth), Hotspur Place, Cullercoats and Tynemouth. Subsequently the terminus at Tynemouth was moved nearer the town but while this was being built a temporary one not far away was used. This was renamed North Shields and the original station became North Shields Terminus. Hotspur was replaced by Backworth; then in 1871 a new station was opened at Benton (the present Metro) hence Forest Hall and Long Benton were closed.

In his book on the North Eastern Railway W W Tomlinson reported that in 1855 the Blyth & Tyne was "little more than a waggonway carrying a few passengers in low-roofed, springless carriages locally called bumler-boxes." This remark was actually made ten years later in a speech by the Chairman of the company but the idea of an insignificant, unimportant little mineral line in south east Northumberland has been perpetuated by some writers: others have chosen to ignore it. Tomlinson also recorded, however, that by 1860 "third class carriages were running of a type unsurpassed, perhaps, in the Kingdom. Designed in 1854, they had given such general satisfaction that neither the directors of the line nor the public desired a change of type." These were built by Joseph Wright & Sons of Birmingham.

For a year from May 1851 there was a through train from Seaton Sluice to Percy Main and back on Tuesdays and Saturdays. Also, in August and September of that year four excursion trains were advertised in the press as running from Percy Main for people to visit the gardens at Seaton Delaval Hall. For this purpose passengers would probably have used The Avenue halt near to where the waggonway to the harbour crossed the road from Seaton Delaval to the Hall.

In 1858 there were three trains in each direction between Morpeth and Percy Main on weekdays and two on Sundays. Between Blyth and Morpeth there were four trains each way and three on a Sunday. Timetables showed connections with other companies' trains. In the six months ending December 1859 B & T engines ran 31,942 miles on passenger trains. The timetable from March 1871 indicated eight trains in each direction between Newcastle and Tynemouth every day of the week. On Friday nights only, a late train left New Bridge Street at 11 pm. There was a similar service from the coast with only one intermediate stop, at Whitley. All but the late trains had accommodation for 1st, 2nd and 3rd class. From Newcastle there were four through trains each weekday to Morpeth and one from Blyth to Morpeth, plus an extra market train every Saturday. A similar provision was made in the Up direction and there were connections to Blyth. Day return tickets were available but not from all intermediate stations. Market train tickets and those for weekend travel were also mentioned in the notes. Passengers had to be in good time as the booking offices were closed five minutes before departure times to ensure punctuality. Children under three were carried free.

Passenger receipts in 1873 exceeded £50,000. It is significant that at the end of that year the company owned 49 3rd class carriages, four 1st class, six 2nd and eight composites. The B & T often provided excursion trains to race meetings, pantomimes, plays, operas and flower shows which were advertised on colourful posters.

An agreement with the North British Railway and its allies allowed for an interchange of traffic, carriages and trucks, together with through rates and fares.

Locomotives were supplied from a variety of manufacturers including Timothy Hackworth, Robert Stephenson, Coulthard's, R & W Hawthorn, E B Wilson and R B Longridge. The B & T also built and repaired their own at Percy Main. Early engines carried names of well known Northumbrian families such as *Hastings, Ridley* and *Sidney.* Others were called *Albert, Swift* and *Spofforth Castle.* A return covering the second half of 1854 revealed that the engines *Percy, Carr* and *Charles* had covered 11,785, 12,885 and 14,000 miles respectively. The company favoured 2-4-0 tender engines for passenger and goods work and 0-6-0s for moving coal. They were all fitted with a distinctive cab which sloped forward towards the boiler and gave crews much better protection than that provided by many contemporaries. The boiler of *Wasp,* a 2-4-0 tank loco, exploded in Blyth station in February 1861.

Some of the signals on the B & T were of the circular board type mounted on posts. They were fitted with coloured lamps for use at night or in foggy weather. By 1858 they were also using semaphore signals fixed on posts which were similarly illuminated. If the arm was concealed in a slot in the post, or showed a white light, it signified all clear; displayed at 45 degrees or giving a green light meant proceed with caution; the signal to stop was the arm at right angles to the post, or a red light. There was also a time interval of five minutes between trains.

A comprehensive Rule Book was issued to staff, certainly by 1858, which gave precise instructions on all aspects of the railway covering, for example, punctuality, keeping station areas clean, unpaid fares, the speed of trains, use of detonators, and the good maintenance of track.

Records exist of accidents on this railway, although these were by no means frequent. In June 1868 a passenger train leaving Newsham for Blyth was diverted on to a colliery line where the points were controlled by a point-lever and not interlocked. It smashed into a stationary coal train causing injury to eighteen passengers and both drivers. At Backworth in January 1874 a passenger train ran into the rear of another one standing in the platform. Twelve people were injured. Details of these, and others, are given in "Railway Accidents at Newcastle upon Tyne and in Northumberland".

Towards the end of its independent life an indication of rolling stock requirements to handle coal, coke, general merchandise and livestock can be gained from the following figures:-

chaldron waggons	3,155
coke trucks	27
goods wagons	61 (only five covered)
timber trucks	54
cattle trucks	9

As with most companies the B & T had its share of 'characters' – such as the station master at Tynemouth who hired out top hats to mourners at funerals – but that is another story!

The Blyth & Tyne Railway always paid good dividends, as high as 12½%. It grew rapidly into a well organised, compact system with a route mileage of 43 miles, surrounded by the North Eastern Railway and competing very successfully against this much larger company. It was the last independent line between the Tweed and the Humber and the NER was anxious to acquire it. Offers were made in 1872 but rejected. Final negotiations were completed and amalgamation was concluded on 7 August 1874 – even so the route is still referred to as the Blyth & Tyne. Fortunately, excellent records exist at Northumberland County Record Office and the Public Record Office, Kew.

(For subsequent history see page 147)

BLYTH AND TYNE RAILWAY.

ON AND AFTER

1ST JUNE, 1873,

THE FOLLOWING

ADDITIONS

TO THE

TRAIN SERVICE

OF THIS COMPANY WILL TAKE EFFECT:—

TYNEMOUTH BRANCH.

WEEK DAYS.—Additional Trains will leave Newcastle for Tynemouth at 9·30 a.m. and 1·30 p.m. Additional Trains will leave Tynemouth for Newcastle at 10·45 a.m. and 2·30 p.m.

MAIN LINE.

WEEK DAYS.—An additional Train will leave Morpeth at 9·10, Newbiggin at 9·5, and Blyth at 9·25 p.m. for Newcastle, Shields, and Tynemouth (*via* Avenue Branch).

An additional Train will leave Tynemouth for Blyth at 10·5 p.m. (*via* Avenue Branch).

For further Particulars see the Company's Time Tables.

Newcastle, 12th May, 1873. J. CABRY, GENERAL MANAGER.

Printed by M. & M. W. LAMBERT, 50, Grey Street, Newcastle-upon-Tyne.

BLYTH & TYNE RAILWAY.

CAUTION.

JOHN BOLAM,

HOLYWELL VILLAGE,

Was summoned before the Magistrates at Tynemouth, on the 11th inst., charged, under the 12th Clause of the Company's Bye-Laws, with wilfully Breaking the Window of a Third-Class Carriage at Seaton Delaval Station, on Saturday, the 25th ult.; for which offence he was convicted and fined in the mitigated penalty of

10s., and £1. 11s. Costs, together with 10s. 9d., the amount of damage; in all, £2. 11s. 9d.

Newcastle-upon-Tyne,
12th February, 1873.

J. CABRY, GENERAL MANAGER.

Printed by M. & M. W. LAMBERT, 50, Grey Street, Newcastle-on-Tyne.

THE NORTH EASTERN RAILWAY (1854-1922)

The North Eastern Railway was formed by the amalgamation of three rival companies namely the York, Newcastle & Berwick, the York & North Midland, and the Leeds Northern. The crest of the new organisation included the shields of those three major constituents which themselves had developed from companies going back to the 1830s and 1840s, but by the end of 1922 no less than 60 other railways had been absorbed. These included the Newcastle & Carlisle Railway (1862), the Stockton & Darlington (1863) and the Blyth & Tyne (1874). It became the fourth largest railway company in Great Britain covering with a virtual monopoly an area from the river Tweed to the Humber east of the Pennines and with three other routes stretching further west. In the County of Northumberland the NER owned the main line from Newcastle to the north of Berwick, the whole of the north Tyneside area with lines leading to numerous collieries, the west line to Carlisle with branches to Allendale and Alston; also the Alnwick, Amble, Coldstream and Kelso branches.

The company also had the extensive marshalling yards at Heaton, carriage and wagon works at nearby Walkergate, plus the huge goods complex at the Forth. There were engine sheds at Heaton, Percy Main, North and South Blyth, and Tweedmouth together with several smaller ones. Another major depot was at Gateshead in Co. Durham just across the river Tyne from Newcastle.

From 1854 the Locomotive Superintendent was Edward Fletcher who in his younger days was apprenticed to George Stephenson and was involved in the trials of the *Rocket.* Most notable of his designs were the class 901 2-4-0 passenger engines and his class 398 0-6-0s. Some of his 0-4-4 tank engines which were rebuilt between 1900 and 1921 as 0-6-0 shunters for work on staiths lasted well into the 1950s. One of these was at South Blyth, classified by the LNER as class J77.

T W Worsdell (Loco. Superintendent from 1885 to 1890) and his brother Wilson Worsdell, who was in charge between 1890 and 1910, produced attractive designs for efficient and reliable engines, noted for their smart appearance and good-sized cabs. The double cab windows on tender types was also a distinguishing feature. Wilson Worsdell introduced powerful 4-6-0s, the first in the country with that wheel arrangement for passenger work. For freight and mineral work there were the ubiquitous 0-6-0s many of which remained until steam was withdrawn in 1968, a fitting tribute!

Vincent Raven (later Sir Vincent) had worked closely with Wilson Worsdell and succeeded him in 1910. He developed the very powerful T2 class, two-cylinder 0-8-0 and the three-cylinder T3, both highly successful performers. For express work he designed class Z and Z1 4-4-2s which were acknowledged as magnificent in appearance and accomplishments. Towards the end of the NER era his two 4-6-2 'Pacifics', with their long, uncluttered boiler were introduced and were followed by three more built by the LNER. Vincent Raven created the first means of sounding an audible warning in locomotive cabs if a distant signal was showing caution, an innovative safety aid which was particularly useful in foggy weather. The device was first fitted to main line engines in 1896.

The basic colour chosen by the NER for its locos was a light green but a company lasting almost 70 years inevitably had changes of liveries and there were many variations in detail, particularly the lining. From 1894 to 1904 all engines were painted Saxony green with two-inch black bands edged with white picking out panels below the cab windows, on the tender sides and ends and on the splashers where appropriate. Buffer beams and buffers were vermilion and underframes were black, lined red. This style replaced a more elaborate livery of Saxony green with borders of crimson lake and more ornate lines, introduced in 1886 by T W Worsdell. From 1904 all goods engines were painted black with fine, red lining, then from 1917 mixed traffic locomotives were also black.

To work the various types of traffic eventually needed a fleet of 2,000 engines, with older ones being replaced as new styles appeared. Locomotives were classified by the North Eastern by numbers alone when the class would be designated by the first member of that particular class (eg 901), then by a letter in alphabetical sequence or by a letter and a number.

Engine drivers in 1907 earned an average wage of £2 9 shillings and 3¾pence (less than £2.50) per week.

From the early carriages, which looked like three stage coaches together on a railway chassis, evolved the more orthodox form of short four-wheeled passenger vehicles that were used for many years even on express trains. In the early 1870s most of the coaches on the NER were still of this type, but longer six-wheeled stock introduced in 1872 were built in large numbers. From 1895 bogie coaches were seen on the system. Most of these were 52 feet in length but with variations in detail, and those produced in the first ten years – numbering more than 1,200 – had a clerestory roof. After that they appeared with an elliptical roof. Within the ten years all passenger stock in normal service consisted of bogie vehicles which gave a much smoother ride, nevertheless a large fleet of six-wheelers was maintained for special traffic and excursions.

In its history the world famous *Flying Scotsman* train running between London and Edinburgh had consisted of four, six, then eight wheeled stock, reflecting evolution and progress, but in 1900 much superior coaches including dining cars made their debut, all running on 6-wheeled bogies. Restaurant cars had been used on important expresses since 1893 thereby eliminating a twenty minute stop at York for refreshments.

All east coast expresses passed through the territories of the Great Northern Railway from King's Cross to York, the North Eastern between York and Berwick, and the North British between Berwick and Edinburgh. Under the agreement of 1862 NER crews were permitted to take their locos right through to Edinburgh but this was not implemented until 1st June 1869, a few months after the introduction of East Coast Joint Stock between the two capitals. These wooden coaches were in the varnished teak livery of the Great Northern Railway and lettered ECJS. Inevitably some would find their way on to other routes from time to time and through trains would often include stock of the three individual companies. The first sleeping car to be used on the east coast main line was built by the North British in 1873. It was a six-wheeler used between Glasgow and King's Cross three times a week in each direction. The first North Eastern bogie sleeping car produced in 1894 was 52 feet long with four single berth and two twin berth compartments, a smoking compartment, two toilets, and a pantry with a gas cooker where the early morning cup of tea was prepared.

For years brakes on locomotives had to be supplemented by others worked by hand from brake vans which were included in each train formation. In the interests of safety, important experiments were carried out from 1874 in attempts to find the most effective system of slowing down and stopping trains. It was after trials between Tweedmouth and Newcastle on 18 March 1877 that the Westinghouse air brake was adopted as standard even though GN stock was fitted with vacuum brakes. Passenger and some goods engines therefore had to be equipped with both systems.

The great competitive rivalry between east coast and west coast companies for passengers travelling from London to Edinburgh in June-July 1888 resulted in such inducements as shorter travelling time, cut fares and greater comfort. There was another series of Railway Races in July-August 1895, this time to Aberdeen, which caught the imagination of the public. People turned out in large, enthusiastic numbers to give cheering, vocal support along the routes. On the night of 19 August trains left King's Cross and Euston simultaneously at 8 pm. The west coast train arrived in Aberdeen first, having beaten the east coast express to Kinnaber junction where the tracks converged. Two days later the GNR produced some spirited running between King's Cross and Grantham and from there to York though they lost time changing engines. The smart NER class M 4-4-0 number 1621 (preserved in the National Railway Museum) took the train to Newcastle where sister loco 1620 in charge of driver Bob Nicholson and fireman Tom Blades took up the challenge and made the sparks fly. Alnmouth (34.8 miles) was passed in 33½ minutes; Belford (51.6 miles) in 48 minutes and Berwick (66.9 miles) in precisely one hour. It is said that when the spectators at that station saw the speed the train was travelling from Tweedmouth – apparently ignoring a severe speed restriction – they scattered! The 124½ miles from Newcastle to Edinburgh was covered in 113 minutes, an average speed of over 66 mph. For the record the 523½ miles to Aberdeen took 8 hours 40 minutes on this occasion.

The advent of trams in the Newcastle area took considerable numbers of passengers away from the railway. In response to this the NER electrified the north Tyneside lines in 1904 then provided a frequent and reliable service between Newcastle and the coast. Outgoing trains from the city travelled via Wallsend, Tynemouth and Benton before terminating at New Bridge Street – about a mile from 'the Central' – prior to the return trip. From the beginning of 1909 the terminus was moved to Manors North, then from March 1917 all electric trains started from and finished their journeys at the main station. The 1904 stock, powered from an elevated rail supplying 600 volts, were light and airy saloons with open seating. A distinctive characteristic was the vertical match-board panels below the waist line. Two motor parcels vans were built at the same time to convey parcels, newspapers or fish in boxes. There were also two electric locomotives for use on the steeply graded branch from Manors to the Quayside. Servicing facilities were built at Walkergate but in a disastrous fire in August 1918 34 cars were

A dip in the track at Cullercoats and a heavy downpour combined to cause flooding from time to time. One such occasion was in 1900, when this photograph was probably taken. Some of the local fishing community were not slow to prove they had rowed along a railway track! (J Kirsopp collection)

destroyed and many others suffered severe damage. Replacement vehicles were built between 1920 and 1922, without the clerestory roofs of the original fleet. They had better seating and more modern electrical equipment. They were painted in the rich crimson lake, a distinct contrast to the older cars which were bright scarlet below the waist and cream above. These electric trains were very popular, carrying, for example, over ten million passengers in 1913.

On branch lines particularly, the North Eastern introduced *autocars* in 1905 where the locomotive was coupled between the

Horses were frequently conveyed in horse boxes attached to passenger trains. Each vehicle could carry three horses in separate padded stalls. There was also a compartment for accompanying grooms and a storage area for kit and food. (K Taylor collection)

coaches and could be used in either direction. The leading coach had a small compartment for the driver and was fitted with circular lookout windows. If traffic was light only one coach would be used. This system saved the engine having to run round its train at each terminus.

North Eastern Railway class 93 number 658 was built in 1867 by Robert Stephenson & Co. of Newcastle upon Tyne. It was sold to the Seaton Delaval Coal Company and worked also for the Hartley Main Collieries and the National Coal Board until 1959. (J A Wells)

Although passenger traffic on the main line and numerous branches was vital to the NER, goods and mineral haulage brought in over 60% of the revenue at one time. Apart from general merchandise wagons and covered vans there was a large fleet to handle livestock, agricultural machinery, steel, coal, meat, fish, fruit and timber. Special wagons were available to convey huge boilers, girders, boats, transformers, tree trunks – in fact almost anything. On Tyneside much of the steel plate and castings used in shipbuilding were consigned to rail, often as out-of-gauge loads. In 1914 the freight stock was 118,000 but of this total nearly 60,000 were for the transportation of coal and minerals, far in excess of other companies.

The standard hopper wagon to carry 20 tons of coal was introduced in 1902 and built in huge numbers. Some were still running in the late 1950s. Bogie hopper wagons with a capacity of 40 tons were built about the same time for use between the Ashington collieries and the shipping staiths at Blyth.

For goods traffic it was an advantage to have *through* trains running from one centre to another – say from Newcastle to Carlisle – with fully loaded wagons. For this sort of train the NER often used bogie vans each capable of carrying 25 tons. *Road vans* were used to convey goods to several stations on the same section of line, and *tranship vans* transferred sundries to tranship centres such as Gateshead for re-sorting. This was a well organised arrangement which worked very well, nevertheless a large proportion of goods traffic was in single wagon loads usually handled by trains shunting at the various stations or sidings on their route.

Some of the 25-ton covered vans were fitted with beds and stretchers in 1914 to convey wounded soldiers by ordinary passenger trains from north east coast ports to hospitals in nearby towns. In addition some 15-ton road vans were kept on standby at certain stations to be used as Rest Vans for servicemen who were feeling unwell when travelling on any of the numerous troop trains.

From 1917 wagons with a carrying capacity of up to twelve tons, belonging to the various railway companies, were used all over the country and were regarded as common property. The Railway Clearing House had an enormous staff to ensure that each company was properly paid for carrying another's goods or for wagons detained unnecessarily for loading or unloading. This created jobs for numerous number takers. A similar scheme applied to passengers travelling over different companies' lines in the course of their journeys.

Some sample figures relating to goods and mineral traffic may be of interest, bearing in mind they refer to the whole NER system.

Year	**Goods Traffic (tons)**	**Goods Train Mileage**	**Mineral Traffic Coal & Coke (tons)**	**Mineral Train Mileage**
1890	**9,385,730**	**7,538,523**	**26,266,510**	**7,653,369**
1900	**11,814,741**	**9,576,325**	**33,316,191**	**8,012,440**
1910	**14,807,960**	**6,303,957**	**40,390,130**	**5,022,381**

The North Eastern Railway operated almost 600 stations whose style and size reflected not only the numerous amalgamations of previous years but also the personal preferences of different architects.

The York, Newcastle & Berwick and the Newcastle & Carlisle Railways shared the expense of constructing the Central station at

Newcastle upon Tyne which was designed by the prominent local architect, John Dobson and opened in 1850 by Queen Victoria and Prince Albert. It complemented Dobson's outstanding buildings in the streets and was the finest example of railway architecture in the country. Even though the original design was modified, it was an imposing structure with a triple-arched train shed using curved wrought iron girders to support the roof, the first of its kind. The covered carriageway was added in 1863 by Thomas Prosser. Enlargements to the station took place in 1871 and 1877, with the final extension – which included the Royal Station Hotel and the east end concourse – being completed in 1894. There were then fifteen platforms twelve of which were bays.

Benjamin Green, who had designed stations for the Newcastle & North Shields Railway in 1839, produced some very distinctive Tudor style buildings for the Newcastle & Berwick Railway among which Chathill and Warkworth deserve special mention. Another neo-Tudor station was Jesmond, built by the Blyth & Tyne Railway in 1864.

Hexham station, on the Newcastle-Carlisle route, was extended and altered according to traffic requirements, as of course were

Old postcards of stations often contain a wealth of detail, as in this view of Acklington. Apart from the 4-wheeled coaches, notice the lamps, goods shed, loading benches, cattle dock and the end dock for unloading carriages, etc. The tender was possibly being used as a temporary water supply. (A E Ford collection)

many others. There, the fully glazed canopy with a double row of supporting columns was Thomas Prosser's design.

The impressive through station built by the NER at Tynemouth in 1882 was actually the fifth one there, being preceded by one terminus belonging to the Newcastle & North Shields Railway and three to the Blyth & Tyne. It was the work of the company's Chief Architect, William Bell, who opted for a very spacious building with an extensive hipped roof and a large area of glass. Tynemouth was used by many thousands of commuters, day trippers from Newcastle, people on holiday and others from packed excursions to the seaside. This officer was also responsible for the second station at Whitley Bay, a small but noteworthy structure opened in 1910 featuring an eye-catching Baroque tower.

A photograph by J T Barnard of Ashington endorsed 'Blyth Railway Group'. Details are not known but the station is probably Ashington, pre-1923. (Author's collection)

The two-platform terminus at Alnwick, with its stylish double-arched roof and attractive stonework, was obviously built to impress important visitors to Alnwick castle, the home of the Duke of Northumberland. All along the branch line to Cornhill was a series of elegant stone-built stations such as Edlingham, Wooperton and Wooler, all designed by William Bell who was noted for his use of half-hipped roofs.

From this brief mention of some of the county's (and former county's) stations can be seen the great variety that was common to the NER. The company had a good publicity department but relied also on its self-advertising presence in the standardised chocolate and cream station name boards, signs and notices, posters, seats and lamps. Stations such as Morpeth and Tynemouth had large wall maps approximately six feet square made from white tiles which showed the whole NER rail system. In most small goods yards there were the inevitable goods shed, cattle dock, weigh cabin, hand crane, coal cells and a loading gauge.

Signals were lower quadrant semaphores with some additional ground signals, often called 'dollies', for shunting. Each route was divided into *sections* some quite long others short, but using the absolute block method which assumed a line was blocked until it was proved to be clear. Each section was controlled by a signal box and trains were passed from one to another in safety. Again, there was some variation in the style of signal boxes; some were mainly of brick, others of stone or timber but with ample windows for good all round viewing. Locations where space was at a premium would probably have the 'box elevated on a gantry of girders with trains passing underneath'.

This, then, is a 'thumb-nail sketch' of the North Eastern Railway in Northumberland, without doubt the foremost company in the country in its time. It won considerable admiration as a well run and progressive organisation, particularly in the early 1900s, with strong management and business efficiency. Its high standard of locomotives and stock gave a reliable service second to none.

The NER became part of the London & North Eastern Railway on 1st January 1923.

FOOTNOTE: The North Eastern Railway Association has an incredible amount of detailed records relating to this company, much of which has been researched by experts in their particular subject.

TYNESIDE ELECTRIC LINES ROUTE DIAGRAM

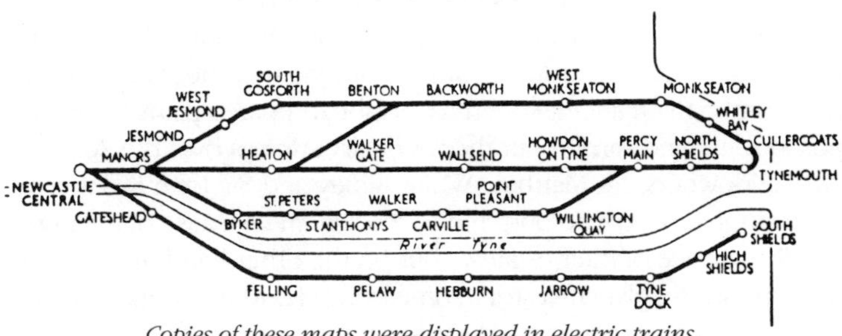

Copies of these maps were displayed in electric trains.

North Eastern Railway Class 686

North Eastern "Atlantic" Class Z1
Drawings by G. R. Mitcheson

THE BORDER COUNTIES RAILWAY (1854-1860)

Railway lines were built as businesses to make as much revenue as was reasonably possible from the transportation of people, minerals, goods and livestock. There was also another consideration which, basically, was to prevent rival companies from doing just that; therefore some routes were laid or extended and companies taken over as a defence measure to keep out the opposition from a certain area.

Promoters of the Border Counties Railway planned to lay a single track line with passing places from a mile west of Hexham in order to extract coal from land owned by the Duke of Northumberland around Plashetts, and ironstone from Bellingham. The well known Northumbrian engineer, Robert Nicholson, prepared plans of the proposed route and carried out the necessary surveys over the 26 miles. Two landowners, Sir Matthew White Ridley and Sir John Swinburne, were among those who objected to the scheme because of the possible disturbance of their estates – but on the other hand many others did support the plan. Investors, some from a London group, may have been tempted by promises of lucrative returns based on the estimates of the quantities of minerals available. Parliament accepted the proposals on 31 July 1854 but the Act stipulated that the work should be completed in five years, the usual time span.

A view of the station buildings and signal box at Kielder. The name was changed to Kielder Forest in 1948 shortly after nationalisation. (Courtesy of Beamish, the North of England Open Air Museum)

Although it was not the only contender, the North British Railway Company wanted to build a line from Hawick in Scotland to Carlisle, and the Border Counties company planned from the outset to make a connection with it. Their chosen route for this extended through the beautiful countryside of Kielder, Deadwater and Saughtree to what was later Riccarton Junction. The route in total would then be 42 miles. Significantly the cost of this project would be shared with the NBR. Approval was given at the second attempt in August 1859 and at the same time an extension of two years was granted to complete the North Tyne section.

The Border Counties encountered severe difficulties from the beginning. When Robert Nicholson died in 1855 his partner and nephew, John F Tone, took over the project as engineer. An acute shortage of cash meant that his main contractor, William Hutchinson, was not paid as work progressed yet he had to find the funds to pay those who worked for him. It is clear from the research of G W M Sewell (see bibliography) that there were many disputes between the engineer and Mr Hutchinson, the latter being forced to the verge of bankruptcy on several occasions. After four years the only part of the railway completed was the four miles from Hexham to Chollerford. One ongoing problem was the proposed skew bridge over the river at Border Counties Junction. It was to be sited not far from the confluence of the North and South

Tyne where the water levels could rise dramatically. The bridge had to be redesigned thus holding up progress for a year.

Permission was granted by the Newcastle & Carlisle Railway for Border Counties trains to travel on their tracks as far as Hexham, an arrangement which would be of mutual benefit. There was a passing loop and a short siding near Wall, and a temporary terminus was made at Chollerford pending construction of the next section. This part of the route was opened to the public on 5 April 1858, probably with hired trains, and proved very popular. There were four trains on weekdays and two on Sundays, the time taken for the journey being quarter of an hour.

The next major piece of work was the mile long cutting at Chollerton after which the line progressed steadily towards Bellingham. As the next phase neared completion Wark was chosen as the temporary terminus for passengers. On 1st December 1859 the directors arranged a special train of 20 carriages to run through from Newcastle. This of course was strictly illegal as the route had not been officially inspected and approved for passenger traffic beyond Chollerford.

Under the Act of 1859 the North British Railway was permitted to organise traffic arrangements which, together with their input of funds gave the company virtual control over the Border Counties Railway. Inevitably the two were amalgamated, on 13 August 1860. The line was developed and completed under new management. J F Tone was retained as Engineer and the main contractor remained the same. It is acknowledged that the work done by William Hutchinson was of a very good standard. The line to Riccarton, where it joined the Waverley route, was opened in 1862.

(For subsequent history see page 155)

BORDER COUNTIES RAILWAY: TOTAL RECEIPTS & PERCENTAGES				
	1874	1878	1882	1886
PASSENGERS	£13,831 4%	£12,336 5%	£10,595 5%	£10,583 5%
GOODS	£61,869 18%	£55,163 24%	£52,817 29%	£49,586 24%
MINERALS	£103,455 31%	£60,641 27%	£53,857 30%	£86,333 42%
COAL	£156,960 47%	£100,131 44%	£65,467 36%	£59,907 29%
TOTALS	£336,115	£228,271	£182,736	£206,409

Extracts from Traffic Returns. (Courtesy Northumberland County Library)

THE WANSBECK RAILWAY (1859-1864)

In October 1858 a Prospectus was launched in connection with the Wansbeck Railway. It offered 12,000 £10 shares with a deposit of £1 5 shillings per share. A provisional Committee included Sir W C Trevelyan, Bart., Chairman, of Wallington Hall, the Earl of Carlisle who had an estate at Morpeth, and Richard Hodgson, Esq., Chairman of the North British Railway who lived at Newbiggin-by-the-Sea. Details of the proposition were as follows:-

"It is proposed by means of this Railway to form a connection between the town of Morpeth, the eastern parts of the county of Northumberland, and the Ports of the Blyth and Tyne, on the one hand, and the districts traversed by the Border Counties and the North British Railways and the Western Ports, on the other; and at the same time, to develope the mineral and agricultural resources of the country in and adjoining the Valley of the Wansbeck.

The proposed Line will be 26 miles in length. It will leave the Blyth and Tyne and North Eastern Railways at Morpeth, and pass on the south side of the river Wansbeck by Coldsides and Meldon; thence crossing the Wansbeck below North Middleton, it will proceed by the north side of Cambo, Hartington, near Kirkwhelpington, Ray, and Woodburn, and will join the Border Counties Railway at Reedsmouth; with Stations at Morpeth and Morpeth Common, Meldon, Angerton, Middleton, Cambo, Kirkwhelpington, Woodburn, and Reedsmouth, besides Sidings at places best adapted for local accommodation.

The important agricultural districts of the Wansbeck and its tributaries will be opened out by this Line, and access given to the valuable beds of the Carboniferous or Mountain Limestone and Clay Ironstone, which are both abundant and of a very superior quality, lying in the western portions of the country accommodated by it. Coal of excellent quality, for all purposes, can be brought upon the Railway, from Plashetts on the West, and the great Newcastle Coal Field on the East.

As the Line will be connected immediately with the Railways before referred to, it will afford a direct outlet for the traffic of the central districts enumerated, to the Ports of the Blyth and Tyne on the east, and the Solway on the west.

It has been ascertained that the route selected is exceedingly favourable for the formation of a Railway of unobjectionable gradients, and that its cost will not exceed £4,500 per mile as a single Line, with Land and Bridges for a double Line.

The very moderate calculation of £10 per mile, per week, of Traffic Receipts, after deduction of £55 per cent. for Working, Taxes, and Local Burdens, affords a return of above £5 per cent. on the estimated cost, viz., £117,000.

The following Railway Companies have already signified their readiness to interchange their Traffic, Carriages, and Trucks, with the Wansbeck Railway Company, viz., the Blyth and Tyne, the Border Counties, the Port Carlisle and the Silloth Harbour and Railway, and the North British.

Nearly the whole of the Landowners, whose property will be affected, have already expressed their cordial approbation of the project, and no opposition is anticipated.

The necessary proceedings are in progress for applying to Parliament in the next Session for an act to authorize the construction of the Line."

The Bill was presented to Parliament in 1859 and was passed on 8 August of that year. The usual five years was given for the railway to be completed. As it was accepted that this would be a link line the North Eastern, North British, Blyth & Tyne and Border Counties railways were all given authority to make arrangements with the new company for the interchange of traffic. The NER did not show a lot of enthusiasm particularly when it was decided that at Morpeth the line would be carried over the east coast main line south of the station to connect with the Blyth & Tyne towards Bedlington. When the route became operational it meant that passenger trains from the Wansbeck valley had to reverse into the B & T station. The locomotive then had to run round its train and push it out of the platform to clear the junction before setting off along the branch towards Scotsgap.

John F Tone was appointed Engineer as he had previously been asked to survey the most suitable route and submit a report. Construction commenced at the Morpeth end in 1861 and the Blyth & Tyne conveyed materials to the site of operations as the tracklaying progressed. The first eleven miles, as far as Scotsgap, were opened on 23 July 1862, using North British locomotives and stock. Scotsgap remained a temporary terminus until October 1863 by which time the line had reached Knowesgate. The station there was then used temporarily as the end of the line. The railway continued to Reedsmouth and the whole route was in operation from 1st May 1865.

The Wansbeck Railway could not have survived without the North British who had invested heavily in the project. Amalgamation was inevitable and in 1864 the Wansbeck Railway became part of the North British system, some months before the section between Knowesgate and Reedsmouth was completed.

(For subsequent history see page 176)

WANSBECK RAILWAY: MORPETH		
	NUMBER OF PASSENGERS	RECEIPTS
1874	22,823	£1,488
1878	19,381	£1,361
1882	17,424	£1,235
1886	17,755	£1,259

Extract from Traffic Returns.
(Courtesy Northumberland County Library)

WANSBECK RAILWAY: TOTAL RECEIPTS & PERCENTAGES								
	1874		1878		1882		1886	
PASSENGERS	£3,826	7%	£4,043	8%	£3,735	10%	£3,876	11%
GOODS	£12,618	23%	£9,313	20%	£9,193	25%	£7,728	22%
MINERALS	£24,139	44%	£24,770	53%	£19,420	52%	£17,668	49%
COAL	£13,961	26%	£8,851	19%	£5,119	13%	£6,371	18%
TOTALS	£54,544		£46,977		£37,467		£35,643	

Extracts from Traffic Returns. (Courtesy Northumberland County Library)

NORTH BRITISH RAILWAY COMPANY.

THE WANSBECK VALLEY RAILWAY will be OPENED THROUGHOUT, on MONDAY, 1st MAY, on and after which date TRAINS, affording Communication between NEWCASTLE, TYNEMOUTH, MORPETH, &c., and HEXHAM, HAWICK, GALASHIELS, EDINBURGH, &c., will be Run as under :—

	WEEK DAYS ONLY.		
	1	2	3
	A. M.	A. M.	P. M.
Newcastle (Central) N.E. Ry.... *Dep.*	—	11·45	5·5
Newcastle (New Bridge) Blyth and Tyne Railway ,,	8·30	11·30	3·45
Tynemouth, B. and T. Railway ,,	8·30	11·30	3·45
CLASSES	1. 2. 3.	1. 2. 3.	1. 2. 3.
	A. M.	P. M.	P. M.
Morpeth .... *Dep.*	9·45	12·40	5·50
Meldon ,,	10·2	12·57	6·7
Angerton ,,	10·10	1·5	6·15
Middleton ,,	10·15	1·10	6·20
Scots Gap (for Cambo) ,,	10·21	1·16	6·26
Knowes Gate ,,	10 32	1·28	6·38
Woodburn ,,	10·49	1·46	6.56
Reedsmouth Junction .... *Arr.*	11·5	2·5	7·15
Hexham .... *Arr.*	11·53	—	8·2
Bellingham ,,	—	2·15	—
Hawick ,,	—	3·43	—
Melrose ,,	—	4 21	—
Galashiels ,,	—	4·30	—
Edinburgh ,,	—	5·40	—

	1	2	3
CLASSES.	1. 2. 3.	1. 2. 3.	1. 2. 3.
	A. M.	A. M.	P. M.
Edinburgh .... *Dep.*	—	6 40	—
Galashiels ,,	—	8·14	—
Melrose ,,	—	8 24	—
Hawick ,,	—	9·8	—
Bellingham ,,	8.5	11·1	—
Hexham ,,	7·30	—	1·27
	A. M.	A. M.	P. M.
Reedsmouth Junction .... *Dep.*	8·15	11·10	4.10
Woodburn ,,	8·28	11·23	4·23
Knowes Gate ,,	8·47	11·42	4.42
Scots Gap ,,	8·58	11·53	4·52
Middleton ,,	9·4	11·59	4·57
Angerton ,,	9·9	12·4	5·2
Meldon ,,	9·17	12·12	5·10
Morpeth .... *Arr.*	9·40	12·35	[illegible]
Newcastle (Central) N.E. Ry. *Arr.*	—	1·30	6·53
Newcastle (New Bridge) Blyth and Tyne Railway ,,	11.5	3·20	7·5
Tynemouth ,,	11·5	3·20	7·5

The "Classes" refer only to the North British and Blyth and Tyne Companies' Trains.

Passengers, Parcels, Goods, Minerals, &c., will be Booked at Moderate Through Rates between the North British and Blyth and Tyne Railways by the above Route.

For Rates and other Information, apply to W. M. Bell, North British Railway, Morpeth, W. Hardie, North British Railway, Edinburgh, or to

THOMAS K. ROWBOTHAM,
General Manager.

Edinburgh, April 26, 1865. 352

Press notice announcing the opening of the Wansbeck Railway

THE NORTHUMBERLAND CENTRAL RAILWAY (1863-1872)

About the same time as the Wansbeck Railway became operational as far as Scotsgap some of the influential members of its committee – notably Sir Walter C Trevelyan, Earl Grey and Richard Hodgson (by then an MP) – decided to support a proposal for a railway from Scotsgap to Cornhill via Rothbury. John F Tone, who was born at Capheaton, was engaged to make a survey of the suggested route. As a result of his recommendations a Bill was laid before Parliament and passed without opposition on 28 July 1863. All the leading supporters either lived in Northumberland or had important interests in the area: some of them were in prominent national positions, too.

Nevertheless, from the outset there were problems in raising the necessary finance. Subsequently, some meetings were so badly attended that there was not even a quorum, at others shareholders angrily expressed their frustration when no progress had been made after two years. When the London company engaged to construct the line withdrew in 1865 the work was given to Dawson's, a local contractor, instead. At that stage it was decided to abandon the scheme beyond Rothbury but the date for completion of the line was extended by Parliament. Although preparatory work was commenced at Scotsgap in the spring of 1866 it was halted before the end of 1867 and held in abeyance until early in 1869. By that time some of the earthworks had collapsed, particularly the foundations of an embankment at Forestburn Gate. Work resumed under the supervision of George Bruce after John F Tone had been replaced.

The line was complete and ready for inspection in August 1870, seven years after the railway was authorised. The inspection was undertaken by Lt. Colonel C S Hutchinson who insisted that certain unfinished details should be completed before he would allow the railway to open. After these were rectified the line was opened to the public on 1st November of that year.

The company had wanted the successful Blyth & Tyne Railway to operate the route for them, or, if not, the North Eastern Railway but as neither had been granted running powers between Morpeth and Scotsgap it was the North British Railway which provided the service, somewhat reluctantly. From Scotsgap the stations were Ewesley, Brinkburn and Rothbury all of which were built to basic, minimum standards. Rothley was a small station for the private use of the Trevelyan estate at Wallington.

The completion of a railway, or significant parts thereof, in the nineteenth century inevitably resulted in lavish dinners at which self-congratulatory speeches, toasts and formal replies were the accepted ritual. The Northumberland Central Railway was no exception. A great number of invitations had been sent out and a special train left Morpeth at 10 am on 31 October. A visitor to the lunch at the Rothbury Hotel would have heard toasts to The Queen, the Prince & Princess of Wales and other members of the Royal family; the Army, Navy and Volunteers; the Lord Lieutenant and Magistrates of the County; the Northumberland Central Railway; the Duke of Northumberland; the Town & Trade of Morpeth & Rothbury ... It caused laughter when one speaker said it was hoped the Northumberland Central Railway would do better than the Wansbeck line which ran two trains a day – one very early in the morning and the other very late in the evening and no day train "except two that stop before they get to the terminus". Replying to one toast, the Rev'd. G S Thompson, vicar of Acklington, enthused that he had looked forward for years to "that auspicious moment when the town of Rothbury should be connected with the world by means of the railway whistle!"

The Newcastle Daily Chronicle not only described the events of the day but gave graphic details of the scenery and features of the route. Undulating moorland with the Simonside hills conspicuously in view, glimpses of the silvery Coquet, the beautiful landscape at Rothley lake and the commanding view from Rothbury station to the grounds of Sir William Armstrong's country residence at Cragside clearly inspired the writer. He also placed on record that the steepest gradient was 1 in 60, the tightest curve had a radius of twelve chains (264 yards) and the highest point of the line (near Rothley) was 694 feet above sea level. The embankment leading to the bridge over the river Font at Combhill was 155 feet long and the bridge itself had twelve arches each with a span of 30 feet, sixty feet above the water. During its construction, stone had to be taken in carts for two miles across stark moors on very rough roads. The embankment at Forestburn consisted of about 100,000 cubic yards of earth.

Brinkburn was expected to attract visitors to the countryside and the priory. Across the valley from the station was the large works built some years before for smelting iron – but as it had lacked adequate means of transporting the pig-iron it was a non-viable project from the beginning. Just before reaching Rothbury there was a formidable cutting 280 feet long and 88 feet deep, near the Thrum Mill.

As the actual cost of the railway had greatly exceeded the estimates, the NCR continued to have financial problems in spite of injections of cash from the Duke of Northumberland. There were accusations of inadequate management and despite changes to the Board disharmony prevailed at meetings. This unsatisfactory state of affairs could not continue and by Act of Parliament the Northumberland Central Railway was amalgamated with the North British company on 1st February 1872, less than two years after it was opened for traffic.

(For subsequent history see page 186)

NORTHUMBERLAND CENTRAL RAILWAY: TOTAL RECEIPTS & PERCENTAGES								
	1874		1878		1882		1886	
PASSENGERS	£3,231	25%	£2,673	12%	£2,741	15%	£2,632	15%
GOODS	£5,672	44%	£5,956	26%	£5,495	31%	£6,189	36%
MINERALS	£1,461	12%	£2,428	11%	£5,119	29%	£2,192	12%
COAL	£2,483	19%	£11,568	51%	£4,383	25%	£6,288	37%
TOTALS	£12,847		£22,625		£17,738		£17,301	

Extracts from Traffic Returns. (Courtesy Northumberland County Library)

THE NORTH BRITISH RAILWAY (1844-1922)

On 22 June 1846 the first Anglo-Scottish passenger train left Berwick-upon-Tweed for Edinburgh, less than two years after the NBR was formed.

The North British Railway was based in the Scottish capital. From its early days it was very anxious to establish roots in Carlisle and stretch its fingers to Newcastle, independent of the east coast route. The company's growth and development in Scotland is beyond the scope of this book but in Northumberland it was really an ambitious interloper which eventually owned about 80 route miles either by taking over small, independent railways or by being the 'power behind the throne' when new lines were proposed.

In order to compete against another Scottish company it may have been an advantage if the North British and the North Eastern Railways had amalgamated but discussions in 1857 and 1858 between representatives of both Boards ended in deadlock when the NB rejected the terms being offered. About that time their Chairman was Richard Hodgson who was known as a shrewd tactician. It was in 1857 that the Blyth & Tyne Railway reached Morpeth which gave a direct connection from there to Percy Main. Passenger traffic was introduced on 1st April 1858. To the west was the Border Counties Railway, so if the two were connected there would be direct access to the Tyne and – who knows? – eventually a route into the North Eastern stronghold of Newcastle! This was the reasoning behind a decision to build a railway through the sparsely populated Wansbeck valley, one which would generate little traffic.

After the Border Counties Railway had passed into NB hands in August 1860 the site of the proposed station at Reedsmouth was moved to the west in order to drop the trackbed by about ten yards in anticipation of the future junction. The river Rede was crossed by a five span stone bridge instead of the timber viaduct proposed by Robert Nicholson. Work meanwhile was proceeding on other sections and the line was in use as far as Falstone in September of the following year. The viaduct at Kielder was a seven span structure with parapets built to represent the battlements of a castle and is now a listed building. Finally the line to Riccarton was completed, examined and approved in May 1862, ahead of the route between Carlisle and Hawick.

By amalgamating with the Border Counties Railway the North British had gained access to Hexham: it also prevented the North Eastern from taking over that company which would have strengthened its hold in the area. The North British also wanted to stop the NER from absorbing the Newcastle & Carlisle Railway but was unsuccessful. The Act of 1862 however did give the NBR running powers between Hexham and Newcastle with attendant facilities for coal, water, engine turning and goods. In return the North Eastern was allowed to run its trains through to Edinburgh without having to change engines at Berwick. Thereafter the urgency of reaching Newcastle by a long, devious route from Edinburgh faded. In 1872 North British trains began using a platform at Morpeth's North Eastern station adjacent to the main line and connected to it.

Once the Bill authorising the Wansbeck Railway was passed in August 1859 the North British sought to lay a railway to link Rothbury with Morpeth, a scheme first considered in 1855. The intention was to extend this line northwards to Cornhill (renamed Coldstream in 1873) via Alnham and Wooler. The Northumberland Central Railway act was passed in July 1863 (page 69) and the line was constructed between Rothbury and Scots Gap where it joined the Wansbeck Railway. Both quickly became part of the NBR. The extension to Coldstream was never built, instead the North Eastern Railway provided the link from Alnwick in 1887.

Engine sheds were built at Howford, Rothbury and Reedsmouth. Howford was the Border Counties depot which was beside the junction with the Newcastle & Carlisle Railway. Rothbury normally housed only two engines but Reedsmouth, a larger depot, was a two-road through shed where maintenance and repairs were carried out. For major overhauls their locomotives were sent to Cowlairs. Through passenger trains from Scotland changed engines at Reedsmouth and were taken forward to Newcastle by small 4-4-0 tank engines. There were also 4-4-0

The Drummond 4-4-0 tanks were introduced by the North British Railway in 1880. The first of the class, number 72, carried the name ***Morpeth*** *and is shown here at Scotsgap. (A E Ford collection)*

tender engines and the ubiquitous 0-6-0s. An engine in the fleet at one time was known to local enginemen as The Dipper. It was number 224 which had plunged into the water when the Tay bridge collapsed in 1879. It was recovered and repaired but Scottish crews did not want it back! Some of the 4-4-0 locos which worked on the Border Counties line carried the names of characters in the novels by Sir Walter Scott – *Wandering Willie, Jingling Geordie, Caleb Balderstone, Ellengowan...*

After the 1862 Agreement the North British ran three trains in each direction between Newcastle and Edinburgh, the journey taking just under five hours, or 6½ hours if changing trains at Riccarton Junction. There were trains also between Newcastle and Riccarton or Hawick. Extracts from the 1910 timetable relating to the Border Counties section, together with the Morpeth branch, are given as examples. In the early days the NBR, like other companies, progressed from four-wheeled coaches to six-wheelers then bogie suburban stock. Passenger trains also conveyed milk in churns, parcels, newspapers and along the north Tyne route mail and large baskets full of bread.

The NBR was also authorised to run two freight trains a day in each direction between Hexham and Newcastle. Southbound, these originated at Edinburgh and Glasgow and were usually loaded to capacity. They travelled via Riccarton and Reedsmouth before joining the Newcastle & Carlisle route. A pick-up goods

Bellingham, one of the stations on the Border Counties Railway leading to Riccarton Junction and the Waverley route to Edinburgh is shown circa 1906. The building is currently used as office premises by Northumberland County Council Highways Department. (Courtesy of Beamish, the North of England Open Air Museum)

worked stations and sidings between Hexham and Riccarton and, later, the Rothbury engine ran to Reedsmouth where there was an exchange of traffic. In Northumberland local goods trains on the North British conveyed coal, stone, lime, timber, straw, hay, animal feed, agricultural machinery and general merchandise. The anticipated huge reserves of coal at Plashetts did not reach expectations but what was mined was taken to Scotland, mainly for domestic use. This would be supplemented as necessary by loads originating on the Blyth & Tyne or the North Eastern railways. Moving cattle brought considerable revenue but sheep and horses were carried, too, the latter travelling to or from Ireland in some cases.

All North British wagons carried a quatrefoil on each side as a means of identification additional to the prominent **NB** letters. There was a small crescent enclosing two figures which indicated either the year of manufacture or the last major overhaul. At the end of 1922 the North British Railway had the fifth largest wagon fleet.

In earlier days the single line of the Border Counties branch was worked on the Staff & Ticket system. The Staff was a length of brass, approximately twenty inches long and with a diameter of over an inch. It was engraved with the names of the two stations to which it applied. A driver had to be in possession of this to travel over that particular section of line. If however there was more than one train in the same direction the driver was *shown* the Staff and he was given a coloured ticket to authorise him to proceed. The Staff was given to the driver of the last train who handed it over when he had completed the run through that particular section. It was then available for any train or trains in the opposite direction. This system was flawed in that trains could be despatched on a time interval of five minutes and if one should break down or was delayed it could be run into.

This happened at Wall on 12 September 1877. The 10.35 am Newcastle to Edinburgh goods stopped at Acomb siding to make up its train by attaching fifteen full trucks of coal. Its load was then nineteen wagons of coal, seven full goods trucks, five empty ones plus the brake van – which the engine struggled to move. It had travelled slowly for less than a mile when it was struck in the rear by the 11.35 am passenger train from Newcastle to Hawick which had left Hexham at 12.28 pm. On a line with numerous curves and cuttings a driver had little chance of seeing danger ahead. The passenger train was not fitted with continuous brakes and was travelling about 20 mph when the accident occurred. Fortunately, only three people were slightly hurt.

Less than two years earlier, on Saturday 3 July 1875, a passenger train from Rothbury stopped at Longwitton, the former Rothley. Mixed trains were quite common and on that occasion the engine left its coaches in the platform in order to pick up eight empty stone wagons and take them with the coaches to Scotsgap, the next station. As it was travelling down an incline of 1 in 60 on an embankment 30 feet high at approximately 26 mph the coupling between the first two wagons was pulled out of its socket when a cotter pin snapped. This caused the coupling hook, which was being dragged along, to catch under a rail and for the rest of the train to become derailed before plunging down the embankment. A connecting train to Reedsmouth was despatched from Scotsgap to the scene and took some of the injured to Morpeth. Four people were killed, ten were severely injured and fifteen others were hurt.

An Act of Parliament passed in 1889 forced railway companies to introduce much safer working procedures including the absolute block system and the interlocking of points and signals. The need for such measures throughout the country was illustrated on 15 October of that year at Wark where there was no signal cabin and no interlocking. There was a single platform with a passing loop and a further loop gave standing room for trucks. A goods train which had left Sighthill, Glasgow, at 9.25 pm the previous night for Newcastle arrived in the loop at 7.21 am when it was just daylight. In the course of shunting, the engine needed to run on the main line for fifty yards or so in order to reverse on to three wagons of cattle at the loading bank and push them on to its train. The porter working the points allowed the guard to make this move even though a passenger train was due. There was a head-on collision in which the engines became buffer locked and four coaches suffered damage to their ends, injuring five of the seven passengers. Such events were reported at length in the press and the North British was usually accused of being parsimonious.

On 31 December 1922 the 120 individual railway companies ceased to exist. They were amalgamated into four main companies, namely:

the London & North Eastern Railway (LNER),
the London Midland & Scottish Railway (LMS),

the Great Western Railway (GWR) and
the Southern Railway (SR).

This was known as The Grouping, and the North British Railway became part of the emerging LNER.

THE HEXHAM & ALLENDALE RAILWAY (1865-1876)

The importance of coal traffic to the railways of Northumberland cannot be overestimated but another natural mineral was to be found in an area of the north Pennines around Alston, Allendale, Weardale and Teesdale, namely lead ore.

Lead mining in the Allendale district was under the control of the Sir William Blackett estate for 200 years. In later years their successors were the Blackett-Beaumonts. Pack horses were used to transport the ore for smelting at Allendale, Allenheads and Langley, after which it was taken to Haydon Bridge for transfer to rail. The ore was carried in two bags each containing eight stones (ie one hundredweight), one on each side. The horses travelled in *packs* or *companies* of up to 50 at a time. The combined loads of four animals was known as a *bing*. By about 1805 some carts were in use, each carrying one bing. In the mid-nineteenth century the price of lead reached a peak of £32 per ton but when cheaper lead started to come in from abroad efforts had to be made to reduce local costs. The feasibility of laying a railway line from the North Eastern Railway at Hexham to Allenheads was considered somewhat belatedly.

It was proposed that the first part of the system would go from Border Counties Junction, west of Hexham, through to Langley and Allendale, a distance of thirteen miles. As funds permitted this would be followed by a seven mile extension to Allenheads. There were no objections when the Bill was laid before Parliament and it was given the Royal Assent on 19 June 1865. The engineer was Thomas J Bewick and the first chairman was Wentworth Blackett-Beaumont. The North Eastern Railway signalled its support by subscribing £10,000 towards the initial cost.

Spanning two valleys involved the company in some expensive engineering work. The first section of 7¾ miles as far as Langley was opened for goods, livestock and mineral traffic on 19 August

1867. By mid-January of the following year the line had reached Catton Road, a further 4½ miles. It will be noted that the line was ¾ mile short of the intended length though it was in close proximity to the smelter which was served by a siding. The Hexham & Allendale Railway could not afford stations at first therefore passenger traffic was deferred until 1st March 1869. There was a bay platform at Hexham for this branch, services being provided by the NER.

From the junction with the main line trains faced a long, steep climb to Langley, 800 feet above sea level, before dropping to Staward then a gradual descent to the terminus midst more attractive scenery.

Goods on this branch included lead products, general merchandise for the villages, timber, stores and materials for industry, and some agricultural traffic. The Revenue Account for the half-year ending 30 June 1868 was very modest:-

Income from	goods traffic	£697
	minerals	£331
	livestock	£2
	parcels	£2

Like several other railway companies, this one had cash flow problems. It struggled for less than a decade before being bought out by the North Eastern Railway on 13 July 1876 who paid £6 for every fully paid £10 share. The section to Allenheads was never built and as it was obvious that the line would never be extended beyond Catton Road the name of the terminus was subsequently changed to Allendale in 1898. Passenger services were withdrawn on 22 September 1930.

(For subsequent history see page 133)

THE SCOTSWOOD, NEWBURN & WYLAM RAILWAY (1871-1883)

Newburn was a well populated, industrial district dominated by coal mining, brickworks and glassworks but to reach a railway the residents had to go to Scotswood or further west to Wylam. During the 1860s pressure grew for a railway giving a direct link to the town. By 1870 the course for a line westwards from Scotswood had been surveyed. The two main difficulties encountered were a ridge of high land between Scotswood and

Opened in 1876, Wylam bridge carried the Scotswood, Newburn & Wylam Railway across the river Tyne. Like all bridges it was subjected to stringent tests before being authorised to carry rail traffic. It is now part of a walkway and in 1997 was painted in the original colours of off-white vellum and mouse grey. (J A Wells)

Lemington and erecting a suitable bridge across the river Tyne at West Wylam. The promoters of the scheme decided to include a new dock at Scotswood from where large quantities of local coal could be shipped, making a profitable railway and dock. The scheme was designated the Scotswood, Newburn & Wylam Railway & Dock Company. The Bill authorising this was passed on 16 June 1871 and the main earthworks were in progress the following year.

The projected cutting through the sandstone ridge soon caused problems when it was discovered that the clay and sand in the strata were unstable. It was then agreed to build a tunnel but this, too, proved troublesome and before it was finished part of it collapsed. At the other end of the line progress on the Wylam bridge was impeded by frequent heavy floods.

The first section, from Scotswood to Newburn, a distance of 2¾ miles, was opened on 12 July 1875 with traffic being worked by the North Eastern Railway. The route was extended, initially as a single line, from Newburn to Wylam – a further three miles – and this was opened in May 1876. The second line of rails alongside was completed and ready for use on 24 August. Because of overspending the dock project was abandoned.

Just before the junction with the NER's main line between Newcastle and Carlisle lay "the beautiful little wrought iron bridge which, with a single span of 240 feet, carried the line over the Tyne at West Wylam" (Tomlinson). It was described in the local press as a novel design, perhaps the only one of its kind in the country at that time. The railway was suspended from the bow-string girders whereas on the High Level bridge they supported it. The structure looked so flimsy and frail that many people living in the area were sure it would collapse – indeed there were some experts in the construction of railway bridges who shared this view. Nevertheless it was inspected by Colonel Hutchinson of the Board of Trade in October 1876 and subjected to severe tests. Those in attendance included the construction engineers Messrs W G & H Laws, the resident engineer for the northern district of the NER, and the assistant locomotive superintendent of that company. The Newcastle Daily Journal of 7 October 1876 recorded that the first test was to take an engine and tender on to the centre of the bridge on the Down line. The same locomotive and a tank engine were then taken on to the bridge but it showed no signs of canting over. Other tests were applied, one being six tender engines weighing 350 tons, coupled together, running on to the bridge at a good speed. This was repeated several times with little or no deflection being observed. The final test was for three locomotives at each end to start simultaneously then stop in the centre of the bridge. Again this proved perfectly acceptable and the Inspector was totally satisfied with the results which reflected great credit on the builders. Perhaps the officials of the SN & W Railway had wisps of doubt during the whole process as all the NER drivers were invited to a dinner that evening at the Turf Hotel, Collingwood Street, Newcastle, because they had been so brave in the face of danger!

The remaining 3/4 mile between Wylam and The Hagg was opened once the bridge had been declared safe. In October 1879 Scotswood station buildings were destroyed by fire. No dividends were ever paid by this company and because of increasing liabilities this 6 1/2 mile railway was bought out by the NER in 1883.

(For subsequent history of this branch see page 179)

Scotswood, Newburn and Wylam Railway

OPENING

OF THE LINE TO

WYLAM

ON SATURDAY, MAY 13TH

The portion of this Line between Newburn and Wylam will be opened for Traffic, and the Service of Passenger Trains from and after that date on Week Days, will be as under:-

	A.M.	P.M.	P.M.
Leave Newcastle	8.20	1.0	5.45
" Scotswood	8.29	1.9	5.54
" Lemington	8.35	1.15	6.0
" Newburn	8.40	1.20	6.5
Arrive North Wylam	8.47	1.27	6.12

	A.M.	P.M.	P.M.
Leave North Wylam	9.0	1.40	6.25
" Newburn	9.7	1.47	6.32
" Lemington	9.12	1.52	6.37
" Scotswood	9.17	1.57	6.42
Arrive Newcastle	9.30	2.10	6.55

On SATURDAYS, an Additional Train will leave New - castle at 4.25 p.m., returning from North Wylam at 5.10 p.m.

BY ORDER

Newcastle May 1876

Printed by John Bell & Co. Railway Bank, Pilgrim Street, Newcastle

Copied from original document

THE NORTH SUNDERLAND RAILWAY (1892-1951)

In 1890 it was recorded that 300 small fishing vessels were using the harbour at Seahouses. Just four miles away, at Chathill was the North Eastern Railway's main line which could put more profitable markets within reach of the boat owners. Roads in the area were not good – so why not a railway? A public meeting was held in April 1891 following which a private Bill was laid before Parliament the following year and received the Royal Assent.

It was agreed with the NER that the new company, the North Sunderland Railway, could use a platform at Chathill thus saving the expense of a separate site. The line was to be single track with a run-round loop outside Chathill station and with one intermediate stop at North Sunderland. Goods traffic commenced on 1st August 1898 but following a Board of Trade inspection passenger trains were delayed until 14 December of that year by which time alterations to signalling, correct interlocking and the fitting of continuous brakes to coaching stock had been completed and approved.

A hire purchase agreement enabled the company to buy its first locomotive, a new Manning Wardle 0-6-0 saddle tank which the directors named *Bamburgh.* It was painted green, lined with broad black bands edged with white, and with red buffers, buffer beams and connecting rods. Five second hand, four-wheeled carriages were purchased from the Highland Railway and arrangements were made with the NER for the loan of some wagons.

The first timetable for the North Sunderland Railway provided seven passenger trains each way on weekdays. Fares initially were set at 3d., 2d., and 1d. for 1st, 2nd and 3rd class respectively. In 1914 there were seven trains on weekdays but with an extra one in both directions on Saturdays. The service had dropped to five each way in 1934-35 which was repeated in May-July 1938 but with the addition of a 9.40 pm departure from Chathill. This timetable showed up to six services to and from Chathill on Sundays, which may have been an experiment. 1936 indicated four return trips on Sundays by bus. Up to 1937 some excursions were run through to Seahouses by the North Eastern Railway and LNER.

During the First World War when the line was under Government control mixed trains of passenger and goods were run. At that time the company possessed only the engine and two coaches. When hostilities were over the country paid £1,267 as compensation which enabled *Bamburgh* to have a thorough overhaul. Another coach was bought from a Tyneside firm in 1924.

Lack of capital resulted in very little maintenance being carried out to stock, track and infrastructure on this four mile line. The condition of the engine and coaches deteriorated, track became overgrown with weeds and the loop at Chathill was barely usable. When it was impossible to use this run-round facility trains were backed out of the station. The engine gave the coaches a tug to get them moving forward, it was then quickly uncoupled and ran ahead on to a different line, the points were deftly changed and – all being well – the train ran back into the platform. This was known as fly-shunting but, as one official wrote, "It is the kind of operation you may risk if you have no alternative!" An LNER goods train was derailed in 1927 when rotting sleepers caused the track to spread. Three years before that four wagons were being propelled from North Sunderland to Seahouses during shunting. When the locomotive braked it was realised with horror that the leading three wagons had not been coupled to the fourth one and they continued to run forward. Gathering speed, they crashed through the engine shed beyond the platform, smashed through a wall and crossed a road.

An engine and coaches were hired when necessary until in 1937, three ex-Great Eastern Railway coaches were bought from the LNER. Debts, however, continued to snowball until in 1939 the company asked the LNER to run the branch on its behalf. More stringent safety measures were quickly introduced.

Steam locomotives used on the line at various times were NER and LNER 0-4-0 and 0-6-0 tanks. There was also an ex-LMS 0-4-0 saddle tank number 11217 (known as a Pug) which was originally from the Lancashire & Yorkshire Railway. It remained for a short time in 1948. In the early 1930s Messrs. Armstrong Whitworth, who were pioneering diesel electric traction, loaned a small shunting engine of 95 hp weighing 15 tons to the NSR for six months. The company bought a similar machine in 1934 named *Lady Armstrong* but after four years of service it suffered several breakdowns.

In 1951 the 1939 agreement with the LNER was rescinded by British Railways causing the closure of this little line. The last train, carrying about 40 passengers, chugged out of Seahouses hauled by a Y7 0-4-0 tank engine number 68089 displaying *Farne Islander* on a headboard. Onlookers waved hankies as detonators exploded under the train. Demolition started in 1953 and the station yard at Seahouses is now a car park. Apart from a credit balance of less than £47 in its first year, the North Sunderland Railway only twice made a profit – £305 in 1943 and £65 in 1944.

Further information can be found in "The North Sunderland Railway" by A Wright.

THE LONDON & NORTH EASTERN RAILWAY (1923-1947)

At the beginning of the First World War all railway companies were put under Government control. During the hostilities – in which the railways played a vital part – maintenance of track, stations, locomotives and stock was reduced to an absolute minimum so that by 1918 many problems needed to be addressed. Motor transport had developed and much of the traffic that had previously been carried by rail was transferred to the roads. Costs of renewing or repairing the railway system had escalated and as income was decreasing an Enquiry was set up to seek the best way forward. In 1921 the decision was that the number of railway companies should be reduced to four, each consisting of several of the larger organisations (called the Constituents) and various smaller ones which were referred to as the Subsidiary companies.

The LNER group had seven Constituents, including the North Eastern, the North British and the Great Northern, and 26 subsidiary companies. In general terms it covered the eastern side of the nation in an area from London to Harwich, Yarmouth, Leeds, Bradford, Carlisle, Edinburgh, Glasgow and Aberdeen though there were certain anomalies where territories overlapped. In Northumberland the LNER took over the main line from Newcastle to just north of Berwick, the Newcastle and Carlisle route and all other sections previously owned by the North Eastern Railway and the North British; nevertheless it is essential to look further afield to appreciate the overall picture.

Each of the former companies had its own methods of working with definite sets of rules and regulations. Locomotives, coaches and wagons with their individual parts differed from those of others. Where companies previously had been business competitors they had to be welded together to become the new FORWARD-looking railway of the future. The enormity of this formidable task of standardisation should not be underestimated – but it was done.

At the Grouping there were no fewer than 236 different classes of locomotive from the various companies which passed into the LNER. Initially the engines kept their old numbers but had the new company's initials placed on the tender or tank side followed by a suffix letter, D for NER stock and B for North British. As renumbering continued, former North Eastern engines retained their original number (probably because they were on oval plates) whereas the North British had 9,000 added. To simplify classification each different wheel arrangement was designated by a letter. For example all 4-6-2s, whether tender or tank engines, were A; 4-6-0s were B, 0-6-0s were J and the later 2-6-2s were V. This was followed by a number to identify the various styles.

Herbert Nigel Gresley (Sir Nigel from 1936) was appointed chief mechanical engineer to the LNER following his success on the Great Northern Railway where he had introduced the class A1 4-6-2 locomotive for fast main line expresses. This aesthetic and successful design was continued by the LNER and from it was developed the A3 class to which all but one of the A1s were subsequently converted. Engines with this wheel arrangement were known as *Pacifics.* Many of them were built at Doncaster and carried the names of famous racehorses as a tribute to the well known horse racing area. Their names, perhaps, would also convey the impression that these locos were racing thoroughbreds too! In the 1930s the railways continued to fight back against losing traffic to the roads with a determined quest for more speed and comfort for passengers. On 5 March 1935 the A3 No. 2750 *Papyrus,* hauling a special train weighing 217 tons from Newcastle to King's Cross, attained a speed of 108 mph when travelling down Stoke bank towards Peterborough. This was authenticated by the dynamometer car. In 1903 the Great Western Railway claimed one of its engines was the first to reach 100 mph but this was subsequently challenged as being inaccurately timed by a stopwatch between two distance posts.

From May 1928 the summer timetable showed The Flying Scotsman express between King's Cross and Edinburgh was scheduled to run non-stop between the two capitals. To achieve this five Pacifics were fitted with special corridor tenders to enable the crews to be changed en route. The driver and fireman not on the engine 'rode the cushions' in a reserved compartment at the front of the train. The service from London was inaugurated by No. 4472 *Flying Scotsman* which was destined to

LNER A4 class number 2510 ***Quicksilver*** *leaving Newcastle with 'The Silver Jubilee' express. The service was introduced in September 1935 and reached London in four hours. (D Patten collection)*

become the world's most famous engine. No. 2580 *Shotover* ran the corresponding train from Edinburgh. Each set was made up of eleven coaches including a triplet dining unit and a coach containing a hairdressing saloon. The departure from King's Cross was witnessed by an enormous crowd and was attended by the Lord Mayor of London and Nigel Gresley himself. These non-stop runs were the first time that expresses did not call at Newcastle.

One problem faced by drivers, particularly on high-speed trains, was smoke and steam obstructing their view. What was needed was a design which swept the exhaust clear of the cab. Nigel Gresley's answer was the streamlined A4 Pacifics which were an immediate success. The first one of this class was No. 2509 *Silver Link,* built in September 1935. 2510 *Quicksilver* was completed at the same time, to be followed before the end of the year by 2511 *Silver King* and 2512 *Silver Fox.* All were finished in silver and grey livery to haul a new, fast service, The Silver Jubilee. On 27 September 1935 a demonstration run from King's Cross to Grantham was arranged for railway officials and the press. It was an experience never to be forgotten as the train covered the first seventeen miles in seventeen minutes and reached a maximum of 112½ mph twice. For 43 consecutive miles the *average* speed was 100 mph. Grantham (105½ miles) was covered in 1 hour 28 minutes with a load of 230 tons gross. The public service between Newcastle and King's Cross was commenced three days later, leaving Newcastle at 10 am and arriving in London at 2 pm to an enthusiastic welcome. The journey back to the north east left at 5.30 pm, arriving in Newcastle exactly four hours later. 2509 ran this return service on her own each weekday for three weeks. The silver and grey coaches were designed to reduce air resistance. They consisted of a twin articulated brake-third, a triplet restaurant car, and another twin articulated first and third class. The three catering vehicles on this and other expresses were carried on four bogies as one unit. All were double-glazed.

The highest speed ever recorded by a steam hauled passenger train in normal service in the British Isles was on 27 August 1936 when *Silver Fox* touched 113 mph on the Up Silver Jubilee with a load of 270 tons. Running at 100 mph

FROM	To	Vehicles in order from Engine.	Class.	Weight Tons.	Seats. 1st.	Seats. 3rd.	UP WORKING.
		"THE CORONATION."					
	4.0 p.m. from	King's Cross	Saturdays excepted.				
	(Will not run	August 4th and 7th).					
King's Cross	Edinburgh .... (arr. 10.0 p.m.)	Brake Third (North End)	F1718	63		24	4.30 p.m. from Edinburgh.
		Open Third	F1717			42	
		Kitchen Third	F1716	74		12	
		Open Third	F1715			42	
		Open First	F1714	66	24		
		Open First	F1713		24		
		Kitchen Third	F1712	75		12	
		Brake Third (South End)	F1711			30	
		Observation Car (Luggage Locker North End)	F1719	34	*16* (unclassed)		
	Leaving	King's Cross....		312	48	162	
	4.0 p.m. from	King's Cross.					
King's Cross	Newcastle .... (arr. 10.8 p.m.)	Brake Third	K 1236	32		24	10.40 a.m. from Newcastle.
		Third	C 1800	38		42	
		Pantry Third	K 1227	39		*39*	10.40 a.m. from Newcastle Week-days, 11.0 a.m. Sundays.
		Rest. First.	K 1599	44	*18*		
		Compo	K 1064	34	15	30	10.40 a.m. from Newcastle.
		Brake Compo	K 42777	34	12	24	
Bournemouth dep. 11.2 a.m. T. W. Thurs. 11.16 a.m. M. F. & S.O.		Brake Compo H	N.E. or S.R.	32	12	24	8.20 a.m. from Newcastle.
Bristol .... (dep. 2.12 p.m.)		Third G L	L.M.S.	30		48	8.20 a.m. from Newcastle.
		Brake Compo G	L.M.S.	30	12	24	
Leaving	York M.F.O.			278	51	168	
"	" M.F.S.X.			245	51	126	
"	" S.O.		....	308	51	216	
"	" M.F.O.	(when note H	applies)	246	39	144	
"	" S.O.	(" " "	")	276	39	172	
West Riding portion to be formed next to engine leaving King's Cross. For remainder of formation see page 42 G.N. Section Carriage Working.							

C—Mondays, Fridays and Saturdays only. F—Actual vehicles alternating with vehicles marked F page 86. G—Attached at York. H—Not attached Fridays and Saturdays, July 8th to September 2nd, and Mondays, July 31st and August 7th. K—Actual vehicles alternating with vehicles marked K page 66.

Loading of Luggage, Parcels, Parcel Post and Mails.

"The Coronation"

<u>4.0 p.m. from King's Cross (Sats. exc.)</u>

Will not run August 4th and 7th.

FRONT BRAKE THIRD.
Luggage from King's Cross to Edinburgh.

REAR BRAKE THIRD.
Luggage from King's Cross to York and Newcastle.
Luggage and mails from York to Edinburgh.
Mails Newcastle to Edinburgh.

LOCKER COMPARTMENT OBSERVATION CAR.
Luggage and mails from King's Cross to Edinburgh.
Loading of General Parcels traffic totally restricted.

<u>4.0 p.m from King's Cross.</u>

Gangways to be kept clear for passengers dining en route.

NEWCASTLE BRAKE THIRD.
North End. Luggage from Grantham and Lincoln.
South End. News and Parcels York, Darlington, Durham and Newcastle.

NEWCASTLE BRAKE COMPO (Guard).
North End. Luggage and Mails for York and transfer and Newcastle.
South End. Luggage for York, Darlington and Durham.

General Parcels loading from :—	To be restricted to :—
Leeds portion	
King's Cross	Beyond Wakefield.
Peterborough	
Grantham	
Newark	
Retford	
Doncaster	
Newcastle portion	
King's Cross	York and beyond.
Peterborough	
Grantham	
Newark	
Retford	
Doncaster	
Selby	Totally restricted.
Cleethorpes portion	No restriction.

Carriage working for two expresses from King's Cross, 1939.

on certain sections became quite common with LNER Pacifics.

The LNER introduced two more fliers, one to the West Riding of Yorkshire and the other to Edinburgh in July 1937. The latter was the Coronation, named in honour of King George VI. It consisted of a nine coach train weighing 325 tons. The last vehicle – used in the summer months only – was an observation car with a streamlined end known as a beaver tail. The whole train was harmoniously finished in light blue above the waist and garter blue below. The A4 engines for this service, a masterpiece of design, were also in the attractive garter blue livery with red wheels. From an East Coast Carriage Working document of July 1939 the make up of this train is shown below together with the arrangements for loading luggage, parcels and mail. By contrast, part of the other 4 pm departure from the capital is shown as an example of conveying through coaches from the LMS and Southern.

Most of the A4s were named after birds and it must be recorded that No. 4468 *Mallard* – a regular visitor to Newcastle and Northumberland – achieved a speed of 126 mph with the reserve Coronation set on 3 July 1938 during brake trials. This unbeaten world speed record for steam was accomplished while descending Stoke bank where the gradient was 1 in 200. An average speed of 120.4 mph was maintained for five miles.

Another Gresley innovation was the 2-8-2 P2 class which were the first eight-coupled passenger engines in Great Britain, designed to work heavy trains on the steeply graded lines in the north of Scotland. When Sir Nigel Gresley died in 1941 his place as chief mechanical engineer was filled by Edward Thompson. He decided to rebuild the six P2s into Pacifics but with the cylinders between the leading bogie and the driving wheels. Critics said this gave them an unbalanced look and that they were not very successful. As a prototype for a new class, he ordered that the original Gresley Pacific *Great Northern* should also be rebuilt. When it returned to traffic in its new form, which included a double chimney and smoke deflectors, many railway engineers and enthusiasts were said to be appalled. His B1 class 4-6-0, however, was a useful mixed traffic locomotive often seen in Northumberland.

Edward Thompson's last design was another 4-6-2, the first one of which bore his name. It was completed just as he retired in June 1946. The style was altered by his successor, A H Peppercorn, and those A2s carried names such as *Blue Peter, Sun Chariot* and *Hornets Beauty.*

The LNER inherited engine sheds at Gateshead and Blaydon on the south side of the Tyne and at Heaton, Percy Main, North and South Blyth, Tweedmouth, Alnmouth, Rothbury, Hexham, Alston and Reedsmouth.

The standard livery for express passenger engines was apple green lined out with black and white – the former Great Northern colours. Freight engines were black lined with red. Letters and numbers were yellow, gold and red, shaded.

For general main line use, and on certain secondary routes like the Newcastle & Carlisle, the LNER constructed the distinctive Gresley coaches in teak. These were well varnished and were enhanced by a white roof which sloped at each end. The standard length was 61½ feet. They were joined at each end by means of a gangway from where the vestibule led to a side corridor running the length of each coach. This gave access to separate compartments, all of which had an external door. There were fewer doors on the corridor side. There was a toilet at one or both ends of the vehicles depending on the type. The screw coupling used by most companies kept the buffers of adjacent coaches together but the actual length of the buffers meant that the gangways had to be long enough to bridge the gap, hence the concertina appearance. Buckeye automatic couplers were used on the GNR in the early 1900s and these were adopted as standard on Gresley coaches. The buffers were retractable, giving a much shorter distance between the carriages. These couplings were also much safer by helping to hold the train upright in the event of a derailment. People often asked why the buffers of these coaches were flat at the top. It was probably to overcome the difficulty of coupling them to those Royal Mail vans which had the gangways off centre. New first class sleeping cars were built between 1924 and 1927. Like other vehicles riding on the excellent Gresley bogies, they ran very smoothly and quietly.

Pullman trains, privately owned by the Pullman Car Company, operated over certain important routes. They were luxury stock, very well constructed and with beautiful interior workmanship.

Serving the north east were the Tyne-Tees Pullman and the Queen of Scots. These, and most of the important expresses, carried roof boards on the coaches showing the name of the train, its main route, or both.

For suburban routes the LNER continued to use stock inherited from the North Eastern, the North British and other companies, some of which remained in service until replaced by diesel multiple units in the 1960s. On runs such as between Morpeth and Rothbury, the Alston branch, or between Manors and Newbiggin, the usual procedure was for the engine to be at the front of the train and for it to change ends at each terminus. This worked very satisfactorily but on shorter runs, say between Blyth and Monkseaton, it was much more convenient to use a push-and-pull unit where the engine remained at one end. When the train was being propelled the driver was in a special compartment in the leading coach which had port-hole windows or rectangular ones in the end, an idea developed from the NER's autocars which were first used in 1905. Where traffic on a branch was light, steam railcars were used. At first these were painted to represent teak livery but the colour scheme was changed first to bright red and cream then, later, to green and cream, the same as was used for main line tourist stock. By 1933 the LNER was operating 90 steam railcars of various designs. The firm of Armstrong Whitworth of Newcastle produced some early attempts at dieselisation and both locomotives and rail-cars were tried out on the LNER.

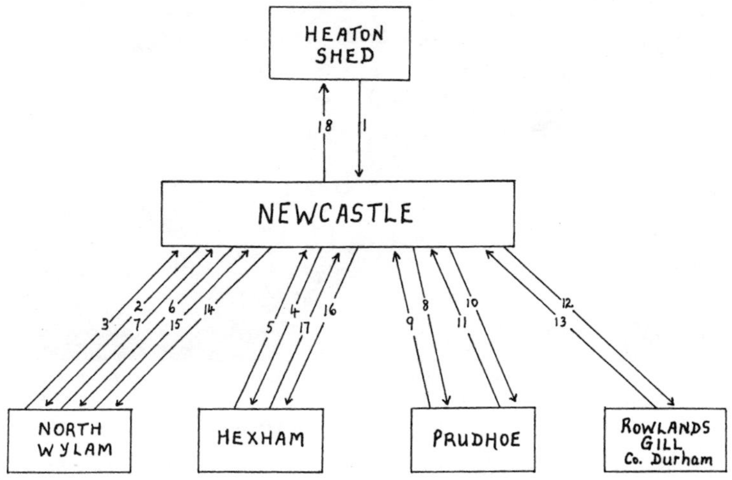

Diagram to show the working day of an LNER Diesel Railcar in 1937-1938

When the LNER was formed the wagon stock it inherited totalled 284,488. This included open wagons, covered vans, mineral trucks, cattle wagons, timber trucks, vehicles for special loads and brake vans, but not service vehicles. Some of them had already seen considerable use and were eventually scrapped but others survived throughout the 25 years of the company and continued into BR days. In general, former North Eastern stock retained the same numbers but those from the North British had 700,000 added to their existing number. It was several years before all former company initials disappeared from wagon sides. As they visited the Works, or new ones were produced, wagons and vans became more standardised.

At first the letters **NE** were prominently displayed with 18 x 12 inch white letters, unless it was a low-sided wagon when the size was reduced. The running number was usually painted in five-inch figures below the E. The carrying

The works of C A Parsons at Heaton consigned huge stators to rail as out-of-gauge loads. For exceptionally heavy objects it was necessary to spread the weight. Sometimes cantilever fulcrum wagons were attached at each end with counter-balance weights for this purpose. The weight of this particular load was 130 tons. (C A Parsons) (NB The company no longer holds copies of this photograph)

capacity, in smaller figures was displayed on the lower left side. If there was a code name this was printed above. The actual weight of the truck was painted on the underframe just to the left of the right side wheel. Also on the solebar would be stencilled the date it was painted or lifted off its wheels and there was a small panel on which could be chalked the date the wheels were oiled. Wagon codes, which were used as a convenient means of transmitting information briefly, often gave an indication of the wagon's purpose. They used, for example:

CONFLAT for a flat truck to carry containers, the various types being designated by a suffix letter;

PLATE for a long, flat wagon to carry sheets of steel;

TUBE a long, open truck for carrying pipes, etc;

TRESTROL trolley wagon with trestle;

MAC low centred wagon for high loads such as machinery.

The construction of new stock was determined by the demands of traffic. In order to speed up the conveyance of goods many wagons and vans were fitted with screw couplings and equipped with vacuum brakes which could be operated from the engine. These were known simply as *fitted* vehicles and usually had the letters XP on each side. The number of 'fitted' wagons behind the engine – from none to a full train load – determined the class of goods train and the maximum permitted speed. This was shown by the position of one or two lamps on the locomotive. Some of the 'fully-fitted' trains using the main line through Northumberland conveyed fish from Aberdeen and elsewhere to London. These were usually headed by a Pacific or one of the Gresley V2 2-6 2s to maintain a fast schedule. At times it seemed the smell of fish drifted along minutes after the train had passed!

Although the LNER had several styles of brake van from the different companies, the new standard type was one with a 16-feet wheelbase and platform ends. The guard could activate brakes throughout a 'fully-fitted' train in an emergency. Being longer, these vans rode better particularly on fast trains.

The livery for LNER freight stock was grey for non-fitted vehicles, red oxide for vacuum braked ones and white for meat and fish vans.

The principal goods stations at Newcastle were at the Forth and New Bridge Street, Manors. The Forth goods shed was over 600 feet long and nearly 400 feet wide. It handled heavy sundries traffic and, in the yard outside, container traffic, cement, bricks, glass, manure, meat, livestock and timber. New Bridge Street, designed by William Bell, was opened fully in 1912. It was one of the first reinforced concrete structures in the country, four stories high connected by wagon hoists, and with a cellar area for up to 40 wagons. Apart from other commodities the yard handled all the rail-borne fruit and vegetables for Newcastle. Train loads of bananas were brought to storage sheds, having been carried from ports in special vans steam heated from the engine to help the fruit ripen during the journey. Heaton was the main marshalling yard in LNER days. Nearby was the Carriage & Wagon Works which repaired and serviced rolling stock.

With the threat of war looming the railways began making preparations in 1937. A year later it was decided that the Ministry of Transport would take control and would appoint a Railway Executive Committee to liaise between the Government and executive officers of the railway companies. Among the preparations were the relocation of Control offices away from major cities, the reorganisation of marshalling yards and converting parts of railway workshops to produce munitions. Later, as more factories were needed to keep the war effort going, the railways carried the raw materials to build many of them. When war came in September 1939 the railways were ready.

Huge numbers of troops and their equipment were moved all over the country very often at short notice. After the evacuation from Dunkirk the four railway companies provided 620 special trains to carry 320,000 troops from various ports to reception areas all over the country. They then had to be regrouped in different locations. Train loads of tanks, bombs, food and supplies had to be given priority over normal traffic and prodigious amounts of coal had to be transferred to rail when it became too dangerous to use coastal shipping. Much of this was taken from different parts of the country to the bases of many fighting ships and merchantmen in northern Scotland. Some of these trains used the Border Counties branch to ease pressure on the main line. Stations, marshalling yards, goods areas and trains were all blacked out. One can only try to imagine the difficulties of backing a long train into a siding in the dark, or shunters trying to run with wagons to pin brakes down as they were being sorted in a marshalling yard!

The LNER made every effort to run modified passenger services and 20 or more coaches on a train packed with passengers and service personnel was by no means unusual. The pristine green livery of express engines was soon changed to drab wartime black with only **NE** on the tender. On all engines precautions had to be taken to make sure the glare from the firebox could not be seen from above by enemy aircraft.

In 1940 the north west curve at Benton was put in which enabled through running from the north of Northumberland on to the Blyth & Tyne line via Jesmond before rejoining the main line at Manors. It provided a by-pass away from the vulnerable Heaton yards and the high viaduct over the Ouse burn not far away. The vital bridge between Newcastle and Manors, and the Royal Border Bridge at Berwick, were both at high risk of being attacked by aircraft. If either had been destroyed the main line would have been irretrievably breached and traffic to and from Scotland would have had to travel via Carlisle. Although railways were frequently targeted by enemy bombers, Newcastle upon Tyne escaped relatively lightly. A bomb at Argyle Street and an unexploded bomb at Manors North did close the line for a few hours in the early days of the war. The worst event was in September 1941 when New Bridge Street warehouse was hit by incendiary bombs. At the time it was well filled with stores of flour, sugar, molasses, grain, linseed and cattle food, most of which cascaded to the ground as the building burned. The glow in the sky that night could be seen 35 miles away and it was several days before all the fires were extinguished. Some very heroic deeds were performed on that occasion, typical of what happened all over the country in those dark days.

Throughout the six years of war the railways took a beating. Only really essential maintenance work was done. Engines were flogged, rolling stock was overstretched, track was neglected and repairs to buildings were put on hold. Consequently, at the end of hostilities the four railway companies were in a mess but in true LNER style they all started afresh. Prewar liveries began to reappear ... a wholesale renumbering of locomotives took place in 1946 – but things could never be the same. From 1st January 1948 the railways were taken into public ownership (along with the collieries) and the noted London & North Eastern Railway passed into history and became part of British Railways.

PASSENGER SERVICES WITHDRAWN BY THE LNER

17 June 1929	South Gosforth to Ponteland and Darras Hall
7 July 1930	Chevington to Amble
22 Sept. 1930	Alnwick to Coldstream
22 Sept. 1930	Hexham to Allendale

HEATON MARSHALLING YARD (c.1947)

DOWN SIDE OR NORTH YARD *Handles traffic from the south and west of Newcastle for places north of Newcastle.*			UP SIDE OR SOUTH YARD *Handles traffic from the north of Newcastle for places south and west thereof, and local traffic.*
NEW YARD	*NORTH YARD*	*WEST SIDINGS*	
Capacity 400 wagons Approx. 400 handled each day.	*Capacity 400 wagons Approx. 700 handled each day.*	*Capacity 300 wagons*	*Capacity 700 wagons Approx. 800 handled each day.*
'Fitted' wagons made up into full train loads for Scotland.	*Shipment traffic for Scandinavian countries.*	*Traffic for Riverside and Blyth area.*	*Local traffic transferred to Down Yard for re-sorting.*
	Heavy traffic for shipyards.	*Special wagons for stators, etc.*	*Reception for empty wagons for collieries and works.*
	Local traffic for stations to Berwick.		*Carriage sidings 200 coaches put through washing plant daily.*

Wagons are also collected and sorted for the Forth and New Bridge Street goods station, and 'crippled' vehicles for Walkergate Carriage and Wagon Works.

BRITISH RAILWAYS (1948-1994)

After the Second World War the economy of the country took a long time to stabilise. The railways which again had contributed so much to the war effort faced an enormous up-hill battle towards recovery – but vast programmes were planned. The Government of the day, however, decided that public ownership was the only way forward and the railways were nationalised from 1st January 1948, together with all the collieries. A corporate identity was needed which would eventually standardise the different practices of the private railways. Initially, for administration purposes, the country was divided into six regions each characterised by a different background colour, mainly for signs and notices. Northumberland was part of the North Eastern Region whose colour was orange.

BR inherited just over 20,000 steam locomotives including the Ministry of Supply 'austerity' engines which were produced in numbers during the war and worked in various parts of the country. The words BRITISH RAILWAYS were painted on each engine over a period but this was replaced by first one lion-and-wheel emblem then another. A renumbering programme took some time to complete but, briefly, Great Western stock retained their original numbers, Southern engines had 30,000 added to theirs, the LMS 40,000 or 50,000 and the LNER 60,000. Locomotive exchanges took place to assess performance and efficiency, and different liveries were tried before Brunswick green was adopted as standard for main line stock and black for freight locomotives, though there were variations. The classes of the former companies were retained but BR also divided locos into passenger, freight and mixed traffic types with, ultimately, a power classification from 0 to 9, giving combinations such as 7P, 5F, 4MT, 8P/6F which were indicated on the cab sides together with a Route Availability (RA), again up to 9. Each route was assessed for curves, gradients, clearances and weights on bridges, then engines were restricted accordingly (as in LNER days). A substantial cast plate on the smokebox of each engine recorded its number, and a small, oval plate lower down showed its home shed, an idea which found great favour with train spotters. Gateshead, the principal shed for the area, was 52A; Heaton, together with Rothbury, 52B; Blaydon, with Alston and Hexham, 52C; Tweedmouth and Alnmouth 52D; Percy Main was 52E and North/South Blyth 52F. Locomotives shedded at Reedsmouth were sent to Cowlairs for major repairs. From

Alnmouth station in 1962 looking south. There is an interesting variety of trackwork – points, crossover, scissors crossing, double slips and 'jacks' (i.e. run-off points). (J Scott collection)

The popular Bellingham Show brought a number of special trains each year. Here ex-NER J21s 65110 and 65061 wait with their stock at Reedsmouth in September 1956. (Ian S Carr)

1951 standard classes were produced with number series in the 70,000-90,000s. The last steam engine built for British Railways was a 2-10-0 9F, number 92220 *Evening Star*. Unlike the rest of its class, it was painted in passenger livery as a mark of distinction. Although they were designed for heavy freight haulage, these engines were sometimes used on passenger trains and speeds of 90 mph have been recorded.

In the 1950s passenger traffic on all the local branches was similar to LNER operations but in 1954 the first lightweight diesel multiple units (DMUs) were introduced. These gradually found their way on to many routes: they were on the Blyth & Tyne in 1958 and they replaced north Tyneside electrics in 1967.

A4 No. 60030 ***Golden Fleece*** *makes light work of an express to Edinburgh as it crosses Plessey viaduct over the river Blyth circa 1960. (A Stalker)*

Non-stop running between King's Cross and Edinburgh was reinstated in the summer of 1948, on the Flying Scotsman express, and even with diversions via Kelso and St. Boswells to and from Edinburgh caused by storm damage, some drivers still managed to complete the whole journey without stopping. In the following year the non-stop schedule was re-allocated to a new train running ahead of 'the Scotsman' named The Capitals Limited. This became The Elizabethan in 1953 to mark the Coronation of HM Queen Elizabeth II, and in the following year it ran the 393 miles in 6½ hours. These fast trains were normally handled by Gresley's pedigree A4s, a duty to which they were ideally suited. Liveries of the passenger coaches in those early days were carmine and cream followed by maroon. It is worth recording that parcels trains of the 1950s were composed of a colourful variety of four, six or eight-wheeled vehicles of many different styles which had belonged to the four former companies.

Early in 1955 the British Transport Commission published its Modernisation Plan which envisaged that over a fifteen year period steam locomotives would be replaced by diesel or electric traction, with many more being fitted with an automatic warning device working in conjunction with colour light signals controlled from new power-operated signal boxes. There would be better track for faster speeds, new marshalling yards, the remodelling of freight services and refurbishment of stations and parcels depots.

There were, however, cutbacks, too, beginning with the withdrawal of passenger services from a growing number of stations on the main line. Newham (1950), Longhirst and Scremerston the next year, Lucker in 1953, were followed by a string of closures on 15 September 1958 namely Forest Hall, Killingworth, Annitsford, Plessey, Stannington, Chevington, Warkworth, Little Mill, Christon Bank and Goswick. Longhoughton survived until 1962, Tweedmouth to 1964; finally Beal and Belford were closed to passengers at the end of January 1968. Smeafield, between these two (which originally was a private station) had lost its service in 1930. Most goods facilities were withdrawn in the mid-1960s but some were earlier.

Diesel-electric locomotives were introduced in the 1960s. Those with two powered axles in each bogie were referred to as BO-BOs whereas three powered axles in each bogie were CO-COs. Some designs were built as CO-BOs. An unpowered or carrying axle was shown by including the figure 1, such as in A1A-A1A (ie two powered and one carrying axle in each bogie) and 1CO-CO1. Diesels were given a power classification from type 1 to type 5 but were later identified by a class number preceding the locomotive's number. One of the type 4 with a 1CO-CO1 wheel arrangement became class 40: these were frequently seen on main line work throughout the county. Much of the coal and freight was handled by class 37s which often required the assistance of a brake tender to help control the train. These were no longer needed once wagons had been fitted with automatic brakes controlled by the engine.

Quite a number of diesel classes were not of a satisfactory design or were unreliable and prone to failure.

On the passenger side it was the fast, powerful type 5, English Electric Deltics that caught the eye. From 1961, they put in sterling work on the east coast expresses for fifteen years. A total of 22 Deltics was bought for £200,000 each. They were powered by Napier engines giving 3,300 hp and could travel at 105 mph, usually clocking up an average of about 200,000 miles a year. Within a few years of their debut the average time for all daytime expresses between London and Edinburgh was less than 6 hours.

In the 1960s BR had to adjust to an expanding travel market in order to compete with airlines and coach operators. It was marketed under the name of Intercity. During that time Golden Rail holidays offered package tours to the mass market. Mark II passenger coaches were produced in 1964 but designs continued to improve

Steam cranes from Gateshead and Doncaster prepare for action following the derailment on Morpeth curve of 'The Aberdonian' sleeper on 7 May 1969, hauled by 55011 ***Royal Northumberland Fusiliers.*** *Six people were killed and 121 injured in this accident which was caused by excessive speed. (J A Wells)*

in style, comfort, better riding on the track, good heating and ventilation, double glazing for noise elimination and in on-board catering. It also became apparent that it was much better to run a well filled train than one almost empty, so special fare structures were announced.

Faster trains and tighter schedules meant that a great deal of work was required to bring track up to the highest standard on the main line. Curves were eased where possible, junctions relaid, tracks were realigned and strengthened to increase line speeds and long lengths of rail were welded together to give a smooth, quiet run. At Morpeth curve speed could only be increased from 40 to 50 mph. Semaphore signals and block working from signal box to signal box (which had a proud safety record) were rapidly swept away north of Newcastle leaving colour light signals controlled by power boxes at Newcastle, Heaton, Benton, Morpeth, Alnmouth and Tweedmouth.

The branches, of course, did not fare so well. Where there were few passengers, or a modicum of goods traffic, Dr. Beeching, Chairman of the British Transport Commission decreed that money could not be wasted on lines that were totally uneconomic. In that respect he was right, but socially ... we may never know. Would the extraction of millions of tons of timber from Kielder forest not be better travelling by rail rather than on the roads, and now that even more use is to be made of the army training areas around Otterburn should not all the equipment and supplies be conveyed by train? If the lines had remained the answer must surely have been 'yes'.

It was noted that in the 1960s engines from Gateshead shed taking over expresses were often in a dirty condition but at that time many steam engines looked neglected and run down as if pride had gone. Steam was withdrawn on 4 August 1968 though the world's most famous locomotive, the LNER's No. 4472 *Flying Scotsman* – by then privately owned – continued to make special runs in various parts of the country including Northumberland. The A4 *Sir Nigel Gresley* in striking garter blue livery also hauled charter trains. Others followed, as will be noted later in the book.

The next phase of development was high speed trains on the east coast main line. The prototype made its appearance in 1973, making frequent runs between Leeds, Newcastle and Edinburgh to prove its capabilities and for crew training. A speed of 143 mph

The prototype high speed train made a number of test runs between Newcastle and Edinburgh in July 1973. It is seen here dashing through Cramlington on its way north. (J A Wells)

was achieved on one test run. Continuing improvements to track and signalling permitted the dramatic acceleration of everyday running with speeds up to 125 mph. Another special HST consisting of two power cars and eight coaches set off from King's Cross in July 1977 with the aim of reaching Edinburgh in five hours. The trip was successful. The usual formation for HSTs on the main line was, and continues to be, a streamlined power car on each end, two first class coaches, a restaurant/buffet car and five standard class coaches. The first class accommodation is at the 'southern' end of the train so that its customers do not have so far to walk along the platform and can be first in the queue for taxis on arrival at King's Cross. From the beginning these trains proved they are capable of travelling safely at high speeds over long distances, with comfort and reliability. They are powered at each end by a 2,250 hp diesel engine giving a total output of 4,500 hp. Each first class coach has seats for 48 people and standard class can accommodate 76.

In order to appreciate the tremendous changes in freight handling it is necessary to look back to the 1950s when many trains conveyed a mixture of merchandise in ordinary open wagons and covered vans but often included individual wagon loads of

Compiled from photographs by Ian S. Carr

timber, chemicals, steel plates, pipes, fruit, agricultural implements, oil and foodstuffs, to name a few. Travelling from one part of the country to another meant a lot of sorting in marshalling yards along the way. Those goods trains often consisted of wooden bodied wagons with a short wheelbase and 'loose' three-link couplings. Express freights were used where the vehicles could be braked from the engine and be closer coupled. It was more economical when complete trains carrying, say, fish, meat, grain or cement could be worked through to their single destination.

The way forward was for wagons to be built from steel, with larger carrying capacity and tailored to customers' needs. Aiming for full train loads with all vehicles fitted with continuous brakes worked from the locomotive and travelling throughout as one complete unit meant eventually that fewer marshalling yards were needed, but some new, larger ones had to be built. Tyne Yard, near Gateshead, was one of those replacing flat sorting yards such as Heaton. In the 1980s freight passing along the main line north from Newcastle on weekdays included block loads of coal, petrol, pipes, steel, pet foods, alumina, fertilisers and cars. Trains carrying cars and vans from the Midlands to Scotland would often have on board over 200 vehicles. Seasonal flows of grain were conveyed in 58 tonne Grainflow polybulk wagons. In spite of the closure of most collieries, coal was still the most usual traffic, some travelling between Yorkshire and Scotland. These sets of wagons became known as Merry Go Rounds – MGRs for short. The usual rake was 36, generally but not always working between a colliery and a power station or port. When coal was sent from Ellington colliery to Ellesmere Port for forwarding to Ireland it was carried in Cawoods rail-mounted open containers in sets of 42. Once air brakes were fitted to all freight stock, brake vans and guards were no longer necessary.

British Rail introduced *sectorisation* in 1987 when freight was divided into four trainload sectors handling coal, petroleum products, metals and construction materials; together with Railfreight Distribution and Railfreight General. Each one had its own colourful symbol which brightened up the drab, grey livery of the locomotives to which they were applied. It was quite common to see one sector borrowing another's locos to haul its trains. British Rail used freight engines on passenger services, too, as it was found that if these were advertised it encouraged a considerable number of enthusiasts to use the trains. Locomotives by then were far-ranging. A Network South East diesel in its distinctive red, white and blue livery, having hauled a train to the north east at the end of the week would probably be utilised on a permanent way train at the weekend before its next scheduled run.

With the introduction of computerisation each style of wagon was given a three-letter code for identification. The system known as TOPS (Total Operations Processing System) was initiated in 1975 and stored details of every wagon and its last location. If travelling, full details of its load, destination and next working could be shown on the screen. The whole scheme has been broadened considerably during the last twenty years. The former method of giving Engineers' vehicles a code named after sea creatures was retained alongside the computer designation.

In an attempt to save taxpayers' money, management staff were appointed from industry to find ways of making the railways more self-sufficient. True railwaymen who knew the system thoroughly were replaced and with them many years of experience were sacrificed. Newcastle became an 'open' station and other stations became unstaffed stopping places, leaving them prey to vandalism and graffiti.

When steam was declared redundant in 1968 most people thought it was the end of an era stretching back as far as Richard Trevithick's creation of 1803, yet what happened afterwards was a phenomenon few thought possible. Individuals and groups bought up steam locomotives, often in a totally dilapidated state, and restored them with infinite patience to their original clean, sparkling condition. At the cost of thousands of pounds and many, many hundreds of hours of work these enthusiasts put them back into first class working order. They opened preserved railway lines in many parts of the country, restored rolling stock and created a new leisure industry. Not only that, but after passing stringent examinations and safety tests quite a number of these engines were allowed by BR to haul special trains on the main line. Some of these preservation groups were entrusted to put new life into locomotives in the national collection and put them back to work.

THE 1990s (to August 1998)

What was the picture in Northumberland towards the end of the long period of state owned railways? The most exciting development was the electrification of the east coast main line from London King's Cross to Edinburgh and Glasgow, a colossal undertaking which involved raising bridges and parapets, putting up masts, erecting overhead cables, supplying power, lengthening platforms and providing stock. At Morpeth the whole canopy, nearly 50 metres, on the Up line was moved back from the track by a metre, in one piece. The first train to be powered by a class 91 electric locomotive ran from Newcastle to London on 12 June 1991. The service commenced full operation on 8 July.

These locomotives, which are capable of travelling at 225 km/hr (140 mph) are normally on the north end of the train. A fixed, standard formation is an advantage for maintenance purposes but if a locomotive has to be replaced at the terminus, King's Cross, it is a lot simpler to do so rather than have to shunt the whole train. At the opposite end of the train is a similar looking vehicle but without a pantograph (the driving van trailer or DVT) and it is much easier to load heavy luggage or parcels at the business end of the station rather than at the far end of the platform. Each set has nine coaches in the formation – two first class each seating 46 passengers, the restaurant/buffet car and six standard class vehicles with seats for up to 74 passengers in each one. Arguably, these mark IV coaches are not as comfortable as the '125' trains which continue in use for destinations beyond Edinburgh that are not electrified, namely Aberdeen and Inverness. Non-stop journey times between Newcastle and Edinburgh were less than 1½ hours in 1996.

Class 90 electric locomotives are seen from time to time hauling expresses, mail trains or charters though they do not have the speed of the 91s. Class 86 electrics, normally used on the west coast main line, began hauling mail trains on the east coast route in February 1996 but occasionally a class 87 was used instead. New electric Royal Mail trains, class 325s, made trial runs on the main line in September of that year before being used regularly on the Capitals Mail.

Local services on the main line and the Carlisle route are provided by Regional Railways North East using Pacers, Sprinters, Super Sprinters or 158 units. The Pacers, having single axles at the ends of each coach, have caused many problems, reflecting the difficulties of trying to put a bus on to railway wheels! Up to January 1990 when the service to Liverpool from Newcastle was still loco hauled the Trans Pennine stock was sometimes used with a class 47 diesel between Newcastle, Morpeth and Alnmouth.

At Newcastle the station layout has been simplified as there are now more trains passing through rather than terminating there. Two additional through platforms for local traffic were brought into use on the south side in 1991, making five through roads and five bays. The former east end platforms are now a car parking area. There were many raised eyebrows when the new-style Travel Centre was opened. Comments were heard that it looked like some sort of gasworks because of all the blue 'pipes' on the outside! The remarks of others who thought it spoilt the appearance of a lovely station are not printable. The roof of this 1850 building is undergoing restoration because of its condition but it is a major task. It was supported by about 100,000 tons of scaffolding, said to be the largest construction of its kind in the country. Sparks from a welder's torch in 1995 caused further damage to the roof at the east end of the station.

Of all the stations on the main line, the only ones left open for passengers are Manors, Cramlington, Morpeth, Pegswood, Widdrington, Acklington, Alnmouth, Chathill and Berwick. Of these Pegswood, Widdrington and Acklington have only one local train a day northbound and two southbound including Saturdays, in the 1998 summer timetable. Manors has three in each direction. Chathill is used as the terminus for two trains a day before they return to Newcastle. All other local services run as far as Morpeth which explains why only two main line expresses in each direction stop there on weekdays. Alnmouth and Berwick have more. On the Carlisle line Wylam, Prudhoe, Stocksfield, Riding Mill, Corbridge, Hexham, Haydon Bridge, Bardon Mill and Haltwhistle in Northumberland are still used. The new station serving Gateshead MetroCentre, opened in 1987, provides not only a very good service from Teesside, Newcastle, Hexham and Carlisle but also has some trains from further afield. There are no stations on the northern section of the Blyth & Tyne catering for passengers, nevertheless the feasibility of reopening the branch has been considered several times. The line is used when required as a diversionary route between the main line at Benton quarry and Morpeth, apart from mainly coal traffic.

The train load of alumina from North Blyth to Fort William runs each weekday usually reversing at Bedlington and travelling via Morpeth north curve whereas the large aluminium ingots are loaded on to Freightliner flat wagons at Alcan's smelter, Lynemouth, then taken to Tyne Yard via Bedlington and Newsham before travelling to south Wales. Freight on the main line is still principally coal but of the 60 or so collieries in the county when they were nationalised only Ellington remains in production. It is now privately owned by RJB Mining. The west line carries coal, petrol, limestone, steel and gypsum. Motive power throughout the area in 1998 was largely class 56s, 60s and 37s, with very few class 31s being seen north of Newcastle.

The entire 393 miles from King's Cross to Edinburgh is currently controlled by just nine centres which include Newcastle, Morpeth, Alnmouth and Tweedmouth. The Newcastle Integrated Electronic Control Centre features the most sophisticated technology. The first section was brought into operation on 12 April 1991 but was quickly extended to cover 136 route miles as far as Plessey northwards, to Blaydon westwards and to Danby Wiske (north of Northallerton) to the south. Apart from interlocking and other safety features the computer stores the complete working timetable, sets up routes for regular service trains and is able to deal with trains running up to one hour early or three hours late. Operators (or signallers) oversee the computer's work, set up routes for special trains or diversions and earlier or later workings than the computer can store. The system is linked to the trackside by fibre-optic cables.

Some of the four-aspect colour light signalling between Newcastle and Tweedmouth was replaced in 1989-90 thereby removing the advance warning of a double yellow. To compensate for this signals were repositioned further apart to give drivers time to pull up. The opportunity was also taken to signal each line for bidirectional running, useful for emergencies or during engineering operations.

The signal box at Morpeth covers the section between Plessey and Acklington on the main line, the coal loading areas at Butterwell and Widdrington, and as far as Bedlington on the Blyth & Tyne. The electronic panel is a Solid State Interlocking system which is different from that at Newcastle. Each train is identified by a code consisting of a single number followed by a letter and two more digits. As a train enters the zone from an adjacent con-

Part of the interior of Morpeth control centre showing the track diagram, television monitors and the control panel. 1996. (D Patten)

trol centre, or from the signal box at Bedlington North, its code is shown on the panel and moves as the train progresses. Its actual position is indicated by a series of red lights on the track diagram but it can also be monitored on television screens as it passes level crossings. Morpeth controls nine crossings and another two are activated by the trains themselves. The controller can also call up on the screens actual track layouts which show the position and reference number of every point and signal. Red or green (not yellow) lights on the panel repeat the aspect of every signal on the track. The movement of every train over a 24-hour period is recorded on tape, so too are conversations between signalling staff and train crews. Hot axle box detectors, usually positioned about every 25 miles, are sited at Dam Dykes near Cramlington and at Chevington. These scan every train and record in the control centre its speed, the number of vehicles and the number of axles. A warning sound is emitted if a 'hot box' is recognised, and the actual axle is identified.

Apart from those already mentioned the only surviving signal boxes in use are Wylam, Prudhoe, Hexham, Haydon Bridge and Bardon Mill (emergency use only) on the west line. The former 'box at Haltwhistle has been decommissioned in favour of a much smaller unit in a Portacabin. On the Blyth & Tyne traditional signal cabins remain at Newsham, Bedlington South, Bedlington North, North Seaton, Ashington, Marchey's House, Winning and Freemans Crossing.

What has been hailed as the engineering achievement of the century, the Channel Tunnel, opened for traffic in 1994. It connected Great Britain and France for the first time since the Ice Age. In anticipation of direct services from Scotland and Newcastle to Paris or Brussels, alterations were made to platform

Maintenance of infrastructure and track are essential (though largely unseen) aspects of our railways. Modern machines work with great precision, such as this powerful tamper seen during alterations at the north end of Morpeth curve to accommodate the overhang of Eurostar trains. (J A Wells)

clearances to accommodate the overhang of Eurostar stock on curves. At Morpeth this work was completed early in 1996. The first Eurostar train, a set of sixteen vehicles, to travel on the main line through the county was hauled 'dead' by two class 37 locomotives on 3 June 1997. It was taken to Glasgow Central for confirmation of clearances before returning south three days later. The designated European Passenger Service's 'Nightstar' stock of high-technology sleeping cars, for use through the Channel Tunnel to destinations in Europe, made several test runs between Heaton and Dunbar in September 1996. Following changes of plan all the coaches were put into store until their future use has been determined.

When the Royal Train took HM the Queen to and from Morpeth in June 1993 it was 'topped and tailed' by two class 47s, *Windsor Castle* on one end and *SS Great Britain* on the other. By contrast, two months later 'The Canny Coalman' (a special train for railway enthusiasts) with a class 56 on each end, visited freight outlets such as Bates terminal at Blyth, Alcan at Lynemouth and Widdrington opencast loading area.

The 1990s have also seen a continuation of steam hauled specials or light engine movements. The LNER A2 60532 *Blue Peter* stopped on two occasions to take water in the Blyth & Tyne sidings at Morpeth, using a hydrant in the road alongside. The 2-6-0 K1 number 2005 together with 44767 *George Stephenson* (owned by Ian Storey of Morpeth) also took water on their way south with 'The Claymore' after working in Scotland. These occasions brought out crowds of photographers and sightseers. 44767 also ran a series of Santa Specials round the Blyth & Tyne in December 1994. In April 1995 60007 *Sir Nigel Gresley,* running in early BR experimental blue livery, was scheduled to haul a number of trains from Newcastle. Both of these engines were based temporarily in the former diesel depot at Cambois. *Blue Peter* passed through the west of the

An enthusiastic crowd welcomed LNER V2 No. 4771 **Green Arrow** *at Hexham on 6 July 1987 when it hauled the 'Darlington Bank Top Station Centenary Express'. The engine had travelled tender-leading from Newcastle and after running round its train was being made ready for its return journey. (J A Wells)*

county on its way to Carlisle and beyond in November 1996 and September 1997. 60007, the post war record holder at 112 mph, followed the same route in the autumn of 1997 and headed a special train throughout from King's Cross to Edinburgh in October. The former LMS Pacific, 46229 *Duchess of Hamilton* travelled from Glasgow to Newcastle and York in December 1996. Last, but not least, the restored Deltic D9000 (55022) *Royal Scots Grey* has made runs on the main line and through the Tyne Valley during 1997. It is painted two shades of green, the livery carried in its early BR days. In the country as a whole no less than 108 different steam locomotives have run on main lines between 1971 and 1996.

In June 1998 *Blue Peter* was conveyed by low loader from Doncaster to Ian Storey Engineering at Hepscott for retubing and boiler repairs after which it was taken to the North Yorkshire Moors Railway.

March 1994, May 1996 and September 1997 were three occasions when the beautifully restored Pullman cars which now form the British section of the Orient Express but which are also available for charter work, travelled over the main line. Another rake of luxury stock is painted in the striking pre-1923 livery of the London & North Western Railway.

The railway system has been decimated over the years with goods in particular being transferred to the roads. In 1953 24% of freight went by rail but in 1995 it was only about 5%. If a fraction of the money spent on motorways had been invested in the 'iron roads' we would have a system second to none. On the other hand if there had been co-operation with management by the unions instead of confrontation which punished those who supported the railways, many millions of pounds would not have been lost. Nevertheless early in 1996 it was revealed that the feasibility of relaying lines to Kielder was being studied with a view to extracting up to 330,000 tons of timber a year from the forest. Trains would probably be routed via Longtown and could be operational by the year 2000, if the plan is accepted.

British Rail, as we knew it, ceased from 1st April 1994 when changes were made to its structure, leading to Privatisation. Its final demise was early in 1997 by which time all the numerous aspects of its business had been sold.

Part 2

THE DEVELOPMENT OF MAIN LINES AND BRANCHES

THE EAST COAST MAIN LINE NEWCASTLE TO BERWICK

Opened in 1850 by Queen Victoria and Prince Albert, Newcastle Central station was extended over the years until finally in 1894 it had fifteen platforms, twelve of which were bays. The site then covered seventeen acres. It cannot be denied that having only three through platforms caused delays when some trains were running behind schedule but the layout remained until electrification. Main line trains ran to London, Bournemouth, Bristol, Carlisle, Cardiff, Swansea, and to various destinations in Scotland (among others) and the station served as the terminus for local trains from a wide area. In pre-Grouping days it was usual to see North Eastern and North British engines in the station but stock for certain expresses, say before 1914, gave a greater variety as they were made up from coaches belonging to the Lancashire & Yorkshire Railway, the Great Western, Great Central, London & South Western or the London & North Western, together with through coaches from the Midland Railway. At that time there would be at least 740 passenger trains a day but taking into consideration empty stock movements, excursions, goods and mineral trains passing through, and light engines, the minimum number of trains handled on a normal day would be 1,300. The estimated number of passengers on a day in summer would be about 100,000 but probably up to twice that number on a Saturday or bank holiday. In 1959 the number of tickets and season tickets issued at Newcastle was nearly 3½ million.

A view of the junction at the east end of Newcastle Central in 1967, taken from the keep. (Author's collection)

Three signal boxes at Newcastle Central, together with the one at Manors were replaced by a new power box in 1959. Initially it controlled 10 miles of track through 641 route switches and 132 point switches, 94 colour light signals and 87 ground signals. (Westinghouse Signals Ltd.)

At the east end of the station three lines from the south over the High Level bridge diverged to serve eight different platforms. They intersected with the four main tracks from the north and the east which gave access to ten platforms thus creating what was at one time the world's largest complex of diamond crossings.

The huge gantries with 330 semaphore signals which controlled train movements were replaced by colour lights in 1956-57. Two years later a new power box in the station superseded No.1, No.2, and No.3 signal boxes together with Manors, which between them had 538 miniature levers.

In the 1960s parcels continued to be dealt with mostly at the main platforms, particularly number 8. They averaged 11,000 a day which, together with large consignments of Royal Mail, presented the staff with a formidable task. Some readers will recall the long strings of barrows, piled high, snaking their way to and from the parcels office!

The tradition of having large Christmas trees in major stations was first introduced in 1932, at Newcastle.

Across the bridge, Manors is a Y-shaped junction where the quadruple tracks of the East side continue towards Heaton. Manors North was opened on 1st January 1909 after the line from Jesmond was extended to join the main line. Thereafter the passenger terminus was transferred to the new station from New Bridge Street which then became a coal depot serving merchants in the city. It was March 1917 before all electric trains on the north Tyneside circle started from and returned to the Central. A branch for goods traffic to and from the Quayside was laid by the NER in 1870. It was about half a mile in length but most of it was in a tunnel on a long, tight curve. In 1904 two electric locomotives with a central cab, numbers 1 and 2, replaced the steam engines. They picked up current from the live rail or from a pantograph. British Railways painted these in lined green and renumbered them 26500/1. The former is preserved in the National Railway Museum but its partner was scrapped in 1966 at Choppington.

At Heaton there were substantial marshalling yards, carriage sidings, an extensive carriage and wagon repair works and a large motive power depot – altogether a fascinating place. Steam engines have been shedded there since the end of August 1875, until June 1963. Nearby the engineering works of C A Parsons consigned huge stators to rail which required special wagons and careful movement orders for heavy, out of gauge loads.

Five miles out of Newcastle, Forest Hall was one of the places where the NER found it necessary to erect a small gantry signal box which gave the signalman a commanding view of the trains. At one time the level crossing was frequently closed to road traffic: it was eventually replaced by a flyover and a footbridge. Now a public house called *The Flying Scotsman* occupies the site. A little further

"The Flying Scotsman" public house, Forest Hall, built on the site of the former station. (J A Wells)

north are the *Rocket* and the *George Stephenson,* two of several in Northumberland with a railway connection.

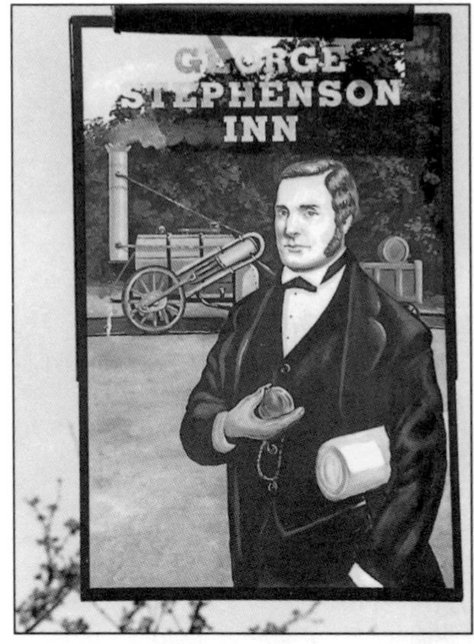

The sign outside the "George Stephenson" inn, West Moor in 1997 (J A Wells)

At Killingworth station, not far from George Stephenson's cottage at West Moor, was a number of bay platforms used by special trains to the Newcastle Races in Gosforth Park. All around here and for some miles further north were collieries with winding gear for the cages, screens, some washing plants and mountainous tips of waste clearly visible. This was coalfield territory!

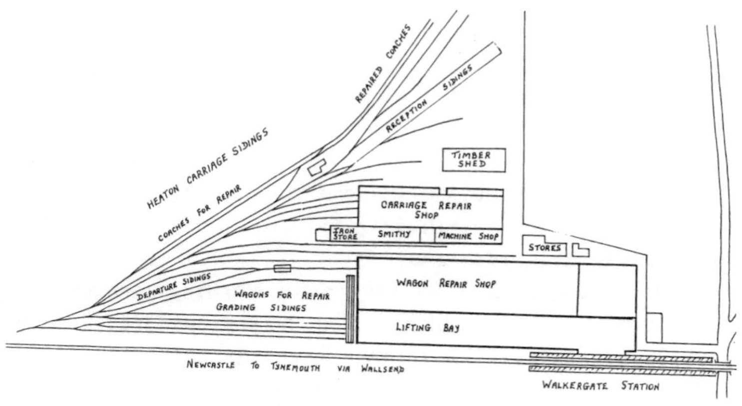

Carriage and Wagon Works, Walkergate, c.1950.

Plessey signal box in June 1977, four months before demolition. In those days its sole function was to control the level crossing (which has since been removed). The wheel and ratchet were used to work the gates. (J A Wells)

Dam Dykes, to the south of Cramlington, is associated with the acrimonious General Strike of 1926 when trains which were running with the help of volunteers were stoned. The Flying Scotsman express was derailed when a length of line was removed by striking miners. The engine, *Merry Hampton,* overturned and four coaches were thrown off the track amid yells and catcalls from the mob. Further back in time The Flying Scotsman service, together with another express carrying mail, were stranded in snowdrifts which had badly affected areas of the north east in 1888 and caused severe disruption. On that occasion the leading engine of 'the mail' was scooped up in the darkness by the four-engine snowplough train which had gone to its rescue.

The Newcastle & Berwick Railway opened the line through Morpeth in 1847; the Blyth & Tyne established their passenger terminus there in 1858 and the Wansbeck Railway arrived in 1862. At the Grouping in 1923 it was the North Eastern and the North British Railways which shared the station. The NER cast iron notices were removed only a few years ago but there are still the remains of a drinking fountain, an old pair of metal gates at the end of the subway and an NER tile map. Next to the for-

Special wagons were used to transport heavy out-of-gauge loads, in this case a transformer weighing 145 tons supported by cross and lateral beams and carried on four six-wheeled bogies. Routes were carefully planned with suitable clearances but where necessary the load could be moved sideways by a few inches on some wagons. (C A Parsons) (NB The company no longer holds copies of this photograph)

mer B & T station, which they had rented for ten years, Green's Agricultural Merchants erected a custom built warehouse the facade of which is in keeping with the Blyth & Tyne buildings.

A pair of J 39s, numbered 64868 and 64929 on shed at Alnmouth. This depot closed on 19 June 1966. (A E Ford)

The severe curve at the south end of Morpeth station has seen four major accidents involving three passenger trains and a set of vans carrying Royal Mail. The first, on 25 March 1877, was caused by a broken fishplate; the other three (May 1969, June 1984 and June 1993) were the result of drivers ignoring speed restrictions.

A view of Belford circa 1950 featuring an NER gantry signal box, level crossing gates, footbridge, semaphore signals, goods shed, cattle wagons and a cast iron trespass notice. (Author's collection)

In summer months the NER introduced special fares, particularly for families, to Warkworth and other attractive watering places.

On the approach to the station from the south passengers can catch sight of Alnmouth and its picturesque bay. The scenery has changed and a few miles further north there are some spectacular views of the sea from near the cliff-tops.

Between Lucker and Belford the first water troughs on the NER were installed in March 1898. This enabled larger engines to take up water at speed by lowering a scoop under the tender and was of particular benefit to those east coast trains which did not stop at Berwick. In 1970 Belford was one of the places which portrayed the old giving way to the new. The modern signal box, powered level crossing gates and colour light signals contrasted at that time with the elevated water tank and redundant water columns.

Goswick has been the scene of three major derailments. In August 1907 an express goods train ran far too fast through points when being diverted on to the slow line. The same thing happened to an express in October 1947 when 28 people were killed and 65 severely injured in Northumberland's worst railway disaster. The engine was the luckless *Merry Hampton*, victim of the 1926 vendetta. The third crash involved a Glasgow to Colchester train in which only one person needed first aid treatment.

Finally to Tweedmouth and the estuary of the famous salmon river, the Tweed, then across the 28 lofty arches of the Royal Border bridge to Berwick station, built on the site of a castle about 130 feet above sea level. The present station was completed in 1927. After another two and a half miles the east coast main line crosses the border into Scotland.

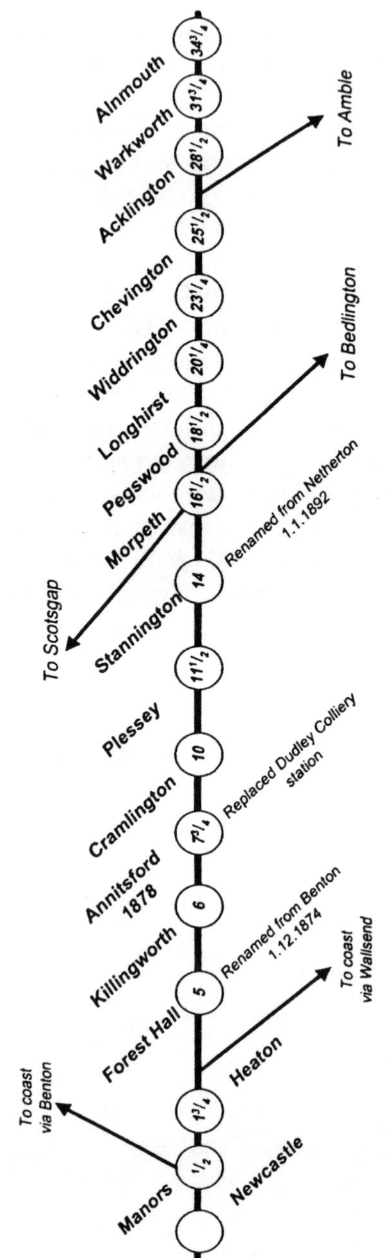
Newcastle
Manors
1/2
To coast via Benton
1 3/4
Heaton
To coast via Wallsend
Forest Hall
5
Renamed from Benton 1.12.1874
Killingworth
6
Annitsford 1878
7 3/4
Replaced Dudley Colliery station
Cramlington
10
Plessey
11 1/2
Stannington
14
Renamed from Netherton 1.1.1892
To Scotsgap
Morpeth
16 1/2
Pegswood
To Bedlington
18 1/2
Longhirst
20 1/4
Widdrington
23 1/4
Chevington
25 1/2
Acklington
28 1/2
To Amble
Warkworth
31 3/4
Alnmouth
34 3/4
Newcastle to Alnmouth

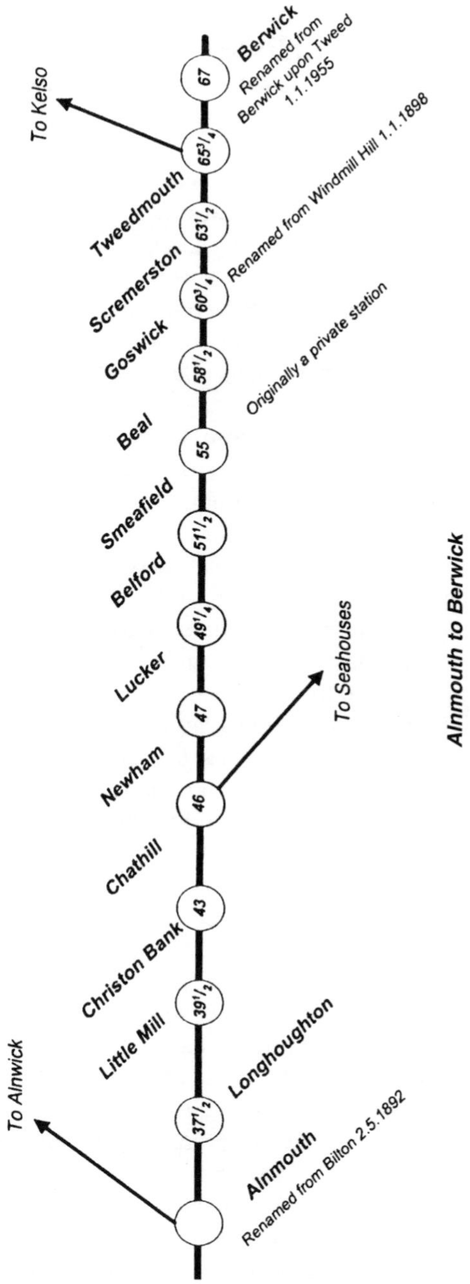

Alnmouth to Berwick
To Alnwick
Alnmouth
Renamed from Bilton 2.5.1892
37½
Longhoughton
Little Mill
39½
Christon Bank
43
Chathill
46
To Seahouses
Newham
47
Lucker
49¼
Belford
51½
Smeafield
55
Beal
Originally a private station
58½
Goswick
60¾
Scremerston
Renamed from Windmill Hill 1.1.1898
63½
Tweedmouth
65¾
To Kelso
67
Berwick
Renamed from Berwick upon Tweed 1.1.1955

THE MAIN LINE TO THE WEST (Newcastle to Carlisle)

The west end of the Central station was always a busy place. Apart from main line trains using the King Edward VII bridge there were services to and from Carlisle, Hexham, North Wylam, Blackhill in County Durham, Durham itself via Scotswood, and Riccarton Junction. From Central to the west of Forth Banks there were six running lines carrying between 50 and 60 regular passenger trains a day in each direction, plus numerous additional trains slotted into the normal timetable, and heavy traffic in goods and minerals. Congestion in NER days was compounded by all incoming trains stopping at Elswick so that tickets could be collected from passengers.

In April 1910 the first departure westwards was an express to Carlisle at 1.10 am which ran non stop. It consisted mainly of vans carrying milk, sundries and mail but there was a through carriage to Stranraer to connect with a steamer to Larne. A similar working left Carlisle at 1.5 am including Sundays and arrived in Newcastle at 2.30 am. There were fourteen trains to Hexham each weekday plus an extra one on Saturdays, and nine to Carlisle. There were also odd trains on weekdays from Newcastle to Stocksfield, Wylam or Haltwhistle, plus three from Hexham and one from Haltwhistle to Carlisle. Similar numbers of trains ran in the Up direction but with slight variations. (Very few trains stopped at Mickley but the timetable showed that the 7.10 pm departure from Newcastle did call there on the 9th and 23rd only!) By comparison, a short extract from the Working Timetable for the period October 1934 to April 1935 is shown on page 130.

The huge goods station at Newcastle Forth was opened in 1871 but was considerably enlarged in 1895 and 1906. There were three separate yards handling a large variety of loads. Infirmary Yard, near the old Newcastle Infirmary, had a large dock for dealing with showmen's vans, motors, large timber, hay and general full loads. The cattle dock could handle 52 wagons of livestock at a time, with an average of 1,000 loads a week in 1914. The Forth staff loaded or unloaded 800 trucks a day on average, working day and night. Shunting was done using locomotives or by capstans, not horses although no less than 348 were stabled in the various buildings in that year. Horses were used for deliveries and collections in the city. 150 carting staff, called rulleymen, were employed full time and another 80 or so were hired each week. Provender to feed all NER horses between Darlington and Glasgow – 1,386 of them – was stored at the Forth and distributed therefrom. At the end of the last century 25,000 delivery sheets might be used for the Received traffic each month with up to twenty separate parcels on each one. Invoices received each month would number about 32,000, with another 26,000 being despatched and some 75,000 consignment notes completed.

The firm of Armstrong Whitworth also built railway locomotives. Shown here is an order for India in the 1920s. At the end of World War II this company renovated large numbers of war department engines many of which were sent overseas. (Author's collection)

The Elswick Works of Armstrong, Whitworth & Co. Ltd. occupied the comparatively narrow space between the railway and the river but extended an enormous length towards Scotswood. It had its own halt for workmen's trains between 1915 and 1924 and again from 1941 to 1947. At Scotswood the junction to North Wylam diverged to the right then after the line had crossed the river Tyne a branch leading to Blackhill forked away to the left. The main line hugged the river on a ledge about twenty feet above the water before twining through the wooded Tyne Valley to Stocksfield, Riding Mill and Corbridge, all well favoured residential areas. It was near Stocksfield that a locomotive broke a connecting rod in August 1840. The driver sustained injuries from which he died the following day and his fireman was badly scalded.

Part of Hexham goods yard in 1978 with cement tankers. This has been the railhead for two coal merchants, two oil depots, military stores and equipment, resin for chipboard, wood pulp, sugar beet, track ballast and thousands of tons of rock salt. Timber traffic has now returned. (J A Wells)

Hexham, a charming country town of great antiquity and rich in history, had the two main platforms plus another for local trains and a bay for the Allendale service. The original engine shed was destroyed by fire in 1929 but was rebuilt and remained in constant use until its closure in 1959. What was probably the last traditional goods yard in the north east was closed there in July 1991. At Fourstones the railway follows

*A class 37, 37069, named **Thornaby TMD,** hauling an inspection saloon, passes a diesel multiple unit at Hexham in August 1988. (Ian S Carr)*

the wide sweep of the Tyne but beyond Bardon Mill the river, much narrower now, bounces over the numerous stones on its bed and the tranquil valley gradually gives way to expanses of heather-clad moorland, the home of red grouse, curlew and golden plover. Gradients on the line become more pronounced.

At Haltwhistle, manufacturing centre at one time of Hadrian Paints and later of Kilfrost, the goods yard was also an exchange point for traffic to and from the Alston branch. The platforms there are staggered and the high signal box was squeezed between two tracks before becoming wider higher up. The water tank (which is still standing) was built for the Newcastle & Carlisle Railway by Tate, Wylie & Co., Engineers, in 1861. Many passengers over the years have used Haltwhistle as a convenient starting point to explore Hadrian's Wall which stretched from Wallsend to the Solway. Those Roman soldiers must have found guard duty on some of the exposed sites a very chilly experience!

Over the years a varied selection of motive power has been deployed on the Newcastle to Carlisle route including A3, A8, B1, B16, C7, D17, D20, G5, H1, J21, J27, J39, K3, V1/V3, V2, BR standard classes and diesel locomotives.

Such an attractive, scenic route, has always been favoured for excursions and has been very popular for steam hauled runs some of which have continued over the Settle & Carlisle route from Carlisle. In June 1981, to celebrate the bi-centenary of George Stephenson's birth, 4767 *George Stephenson* travelled over the line. Out of 842 Black Fives built, only this one had Stephenson link motion and was given its name in 1975 during the 150th anniversary of the opening of the Stockton & Darlington Railway. Some months later this engine double headed a special with K1 2005. In March 1985 92220 *Evening Star* celebrated the 150th anniversary of the opening of the first section of the Newcastle & Carlisle Railway by making four return trips between Newcastle and Hexham. It was an ex Southern Railway type, 34092 *City of Wells,* complete with Golden Arrow insignia (why?) that was used when MetroCentre station was opened. Other locomotives on various duties during the 1980s have been:-

NEWCASTLE and CARLISLE—Weekdays

DOWN	28 PASSENGER	31 Light Engine MO	32 PASSENGER J	33 RAIL MOTOR	34 D Goods arr.	34 D Goods dep. Y	35 EXPRESS PASSENGER arr.	35 EXPRESS PASSENGER dep. A	36 Goods D	37 PASSENGER HC	38 PASSENGER
	a.m.	a.m.	a.m.	a.m.	a.m.	a.m.	a.m.	a.m.	a.m.	a.m.	a.m.
NEWCASTLE Central	7 15		7 35	7 50	—	—	—	8 20	—	8 43	—
NEWCASTLE Forth	..	—	..	..	—	—	..	..	—	..	—
Elswick	7 19	—	7 39	..	—	—	..	..	*	8 47	—
Scotswood	7 23	—	7 43	..	—	—	..	..		8 51	—
Blaydon Sidings	..	7 30	..	..	—	7 48	..	..		—	—
Blaydon	7 27	..	7 47	7 58	*	..	..	8 28		—	—
Ryton	—	..	7 52	..	*	..	..	..		—	—
Wylam	—	..	7 57	..	8 16	8 26	..	..		—	—
West Wylam	—	7 41	..	..	8 31	9 5	..	..	Acomb Colliery	—	—
Prudhoe	—	..	8 3	8 10	9 12	9 36	..			—	—
Mickley	—	..	..	..	9 40	9 50	..	..	—	—	—
Stocksfield	—	..	8 9	8 16	9 57	10 55	..	8 41	—	—	—
Riding Mill	—	..	8 14	8 21	11 1	11 15	..	..	—	—	—
Corbridge	—	..	8 19	—	11 25	12 45	..	..	—	—	—
Hexham	—	8 10	8 25	—	12 55	2 5	8 53	8 55	*	—	—
Border Counties	—	—	—	—	..	..	..	..	..	—	—
Fourstones	—	—	—	—	2 35	2 50	..	9 2	—	—	—
Haydon Bridge	—	—	—	—	2 59	3 30	..	9 9	—	—	—
Bardon Mill	—	—	—	—	..	..	..	9 17	—	—	—
Haltwhistle	—	—	—	—	4 0	—	9 25	9 26	—	—	9 32
Greenhead	—	—	—	—	—	—	..	..	—	—	9 38
Gilsland	—	—	—	—	Clara Vale Colliery 8.1—8.11	Warden Paper Mill Sdg. 2.15 D 2.30	..	..	—	—	9 43
Low Row	—	—	—	—			..	..	—	—	9 50
Naworth	—	—	—	—			..	..	—	—	9 54
Brampton Junction	—	—	—	—			9C42	9 46	—	—	9 58
How Mill	—	—	—	—			..	..	To Wall DD	—	10 5
Heads Nook	—	—	—	—			..	..		—	10 9
Corby Gates	—	—	—	—			..	..		—	—
Wetheral	—	—	—	—			..	..	—	—	10z13
Scotby	—	—	—	—			..	..	—	—	10 18
Durran Hill Jun.	—	—	—	—			..	..	—	—	..
CARLISLE *London Rd*	—	—	—	—			—	—	—	—	—
CARLISLE Citadel	—	—	—	—	—		10 3	—	—	—	10 24
CARLISLE Canal	—	—	—	—	—	—	—	—	—	—	—

DOWN	39 PASSENGER A	40 Goods C	41 RAIL MOTOR	44 PASSENGER A	46 EXPRESS PASSENGER SO arr.	46 EXPRESS PASSENGER SO dep. HC	47 EXPRESS PASSENGER arr. A	47 EXPRESS PASSENGER dep.	48 PASSENGER arr.	48 PASSENGER dep.
	a.m.	a.m.	a.m.	a.m.	a.m.	a.m.	a.m.	a.m.	a.m.	a.m.
NEWCASTLE Central	8 50	9 15	9 20	9 50	—	10 20	—	10 30	—	—
NEWCASTLE Forth	..	9y35	..	..	..	..	..	..	—	—
Elswick	8 54	..	..	9 54	..	..	..	..	—	—
Scotswood	8 58	..	..	9 58	..	..	..	..	—	—
Blaydon Sidings	..	9 45	..	..	..	..	..	..	—	—
Blaydon	9 2	—	9 28	10 2	SUSPENDED	10 28	..	10 38	—	—
Ryton	9 7	—	—	10 7			..	..	—	—
Wylam	9 12		..	10 12		..	..	..	—	—
West Wylam	..	Tyne Dock Bottom dep. 7.0 a.m.	..	—			..	..	—	—
Prudhoe	9 18		..	10 18			..	..	—	—
Mickley	..		..	..		..	..	..	—	—
Stocksfield	9 24		9 41	10 24			..	..	—	—
Riding Mill	9 29		..	10 29	..	..	..	..	—	—
Corbridge	9 34		..	10 34	..		..	..	—	—
Hexham	9 40		9f55	10 40	10 51	10 54	11 0	11 4	—	11 15
Border Counties	—		..	—	..	..	..	..	..	..
Fourstones	—		..	—	..	..	..	..	..	11 22
Haydon Bridge	—	p.174	10 6	—	..	..	..	11 16	..	11 29
Bardon Mill	—	—	—	—	..	..	..	..	..	11 37
Haltwhistle	—	—	—	—	11c16	11 20	11 30	11c34	11 45	11 47
Greenhead	—	—	—	—	..	..	..	..	..	11 53
Gilsland	—	—	—	—	..	..	..	..	..	11 58
Low Row	—	—	—	—	..	..	..	..	..	12 5
Naworth	—	—	—	—	..	..	..	..	..	12 9
Brampton Junction	—	—	—	—	..	..	..	..	..	12 13
How Mill	—	—	—	—	..	..	..	..	..	12 20
Heads Nook	—	—	—	—	..	..	..	..	..	12 24
Corby Gates	—	—	—	—	..	..	..	..	..	..
Wetheral	—	—	—	—	..	..	..	..	12c27	12 28
Scotby	—	—	—	—	..	..	..	..	..	12 33
Durran Hill Jun.	—	—	—	—	..	..	..	..	..	..
CARLISLE *London Rd*	—	—	—	—	—	—	—	—	—	—
CARLISLE Citadel	—	-	—	—	11 53	—	12 8	—	12 39	—
CARLISLE Canal	—	—	—	—	—	—	—	—	—	—

DOWN	49 B Goods SO arr. S	49 B Goods SO dep.	50 PASSENGER	51 B Goods arr.	51 B Goods dep. V	53 EXPRESS PASSENGER F	58 PASSENGER A	59 RAIL MOTOR SX	60 EXPRESS PASSENGER SO A	62 RAIL MOTOR SX HC	63 PASSENGER SO A
	a.m.	a.m.	a.m.	a.m.	a.m.	a.m.	a.m.	p.m.	p.m.	p.m.	p.m.
NEWCASTLE Central	SUSPENDED	—	10 50	—	—	11 25	11 50	12 20	12 20	12 25	12 25
NEWCASTLE Forth		—	..	—	—	..	..	..	..	..	..
Elswick		—	10 54	—	—	..	11 54	..	..	12 29	12 29
Scotswood		—	10 58	—	—	..	11 58	..	..	12 33	12 33
Blaydon Sidings		10 45	..	—	11 10	..	..	..	..	..	..
Blaydon		..	11 2	..	..	11 33	12 2	12 28	12 28	12 37	12 37
Ryton		..	11 7	..	..	..	12 7	..	..	12 42	12 42
Wylam	..	..	11 12	..	..	..	12 12	..	..	12 47	12 47
West Wylam	10	58	..	11	23	..	..	..	..	..	..
Prudhoe	..	..	11 18	..	11 40	..	12 18	..	..	12 52	12 53
Mickley	..	..	..	..	..	..	..	..	..	—	..
Stocksfield	..	..	11 24	..	..	..	12t25	12 42	12 42	—	12 59
Riding Mill	..	..	11 29	..	..	..	12 30	12 47	12 47	—	1 4
Corbridge	..	..	11 34	..	..	..	12 35	12 52	12 52	—	1 9
Hexham	11 27	12 20	11 40	12 9	12 26	11x57	12 41	1 d 0	1 d 0	—	1 15
Border Counties	12	25	—	12	31	12 0	—	..	..	—	—
Fourstones	1 15	1 21	—	12 54	1 2	—	—	1 7	1 7	—	—
Haydon Bridge	..	..	—	..	..	—	—	1 14	1 14	—	—
Bardon Mill	..	..	—	..	..	—	—	1 22	1 22	—	—
Haltwhistle	1 59	2 39	—	1 40	2 39	—	—	1u31	1u31	—	—
Greenhead	..	..	—	..	..	—	—	..	..	—	—
Gilsland	..	..	—	..	..	—	—	1 40	1 40	—	—
Low Row	..	4 0	—	..	..	—	—	—	..	—	—
Naworth	..	..	—	..	..	—	—	—	..	—	—
Brampton Junction	4 11	4b10	—	3b10	3 15	—	—	—	1a54	-	—
How Mill	..	..	—	..	..	—	—	—	..	—	—
Heads Nook	..	..	—	..	..	—	—	—	..	—	—
Corby Gates	..	..	—	..	..	—	—	—	..	—	—
Wetheral	..	..	—	..	..	Hawick 2.11 p.m.	—	—	..	—	—
Scotby	..	..	—	..	..		—	—	..	—	—
Durran Hill Jun.	4	38	—	3	37		—	—	..	—	—
CARLISLE *London Rd*	4 40	4 50	—	3 39	3 55		—	—	—	—	—
CARLISLE Citadel	—	—	—	—	—		—	—	2 11	—	—
CARLISLE Canal	5 4	—	—	4 3	—	—	—	—	—	—	—

A—"HC" to or from intermediate stations.
F—"HC" except for beyond Hexham.
J—"HC" except from Riding Mill for West of Darlington and South of York to be transferred at Hexham to No. 39 up.
S—Warden Paper Mill Siding 12.30—12.43 p.m. Warden dep. 1.8 p.m.
V—Warden Paper Mill Siding 12.36—12.49 p.m. On Wednesdays attaches live stock at Brampton Junction when required SO. Warden dep. 1.8 p.m.
Y—SO departs Corbridge 1.15 p.m. and arr. Hexham 1.25 p.m.

a—Arr. 1C50 p.m.
b—Brakes.
d—Arr. 12.58 p.m.
f—Arr. 9.53 a.m.
t—Arr. 12.23 p.m.
u—Arr. 1.30 p.m.
x—Arr. 11.55 a.m.
y—Arr. 9.20 a.m.
z—Arr. 10C12 a.m.

1934-35 (Extract)

NOTES: *MO = Mondays only* · *SO = Saturdays only* · *SX = Saturdays excepted* · *HC = Horse boxes and carriage trucks are not conveyed on this train* · *DD = Distribution Depot* · *C = Collect tickets* · ** = Stops when required*

LNER A3 4472 *Flying Scotsman*
LMS Princess Coronation class 46229 *Duchess of Hamilton* (making her first visit)
LNER A4 4498 *Sir Nigel Gresley*
LNER V2 4771 *Green Arrow* and
SR King Arthur class 777 *Sir Lamiel* with the Northern Belle.

In July 1988 the world record holder *Mallard* had several outings to commemorate the 50th anniversary of her unbeaten achievement.

It is worth recording that numerous redundant wagons have found their way on to farms. They have ranged from milk vans and horse boxes from pre-Grouping days to covered vans and containers. They have served a useful purpose for hen houses, as a stable, a lambing area or a store for foodstuffs, fertilizers and equipment.

The route to the west is now via King Edward bridge and Dunston. Between the latter and MetroCentre passengers could see the Gateshead Garden Festival which was held in 1990 and where a replica of *Locomotion* was to be seen running along a short length of fish-belly track. This cross country line remains an important diversionary link between east coast and west coast main lines in addition to its normal function.

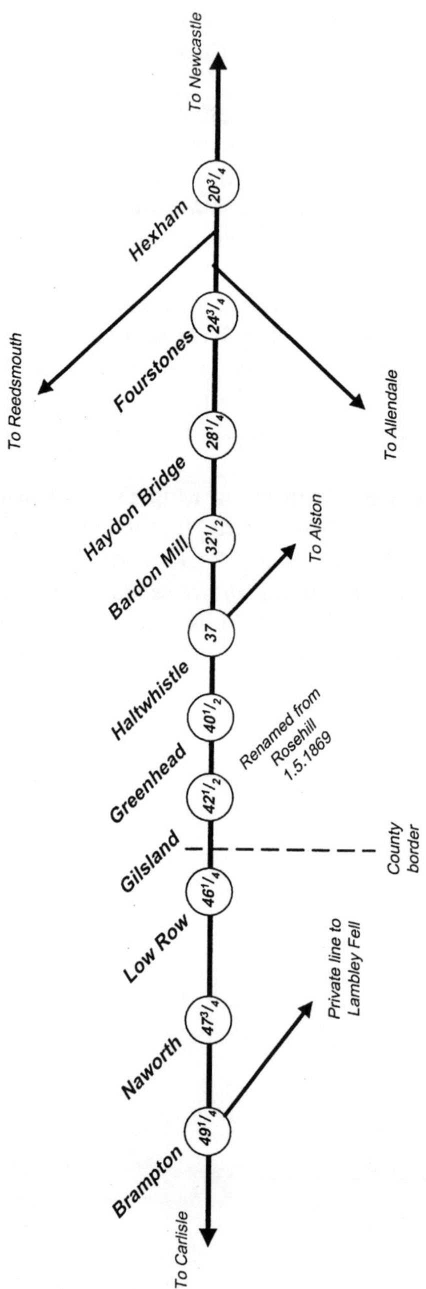

Hexham to Brampton
(Distances from Newcastle)

THE ALLENDALE BRANCH

From March 1869 passenger services to Allendale were provided by the North Eastern Railway which later bought out the private company, in 1876. The operation changed little over the years, the usual number of trains being three or four per day. Hexham shed provided the motive power with 0-4-4 or 2-4-2 tank engines, the latter being nicknamed 'double-enders' by loco men because of their wheel arrangement.

Allendale station, originally called Catton Road, was the terminus of the Hexham & Allendale Railway, later known as the Allendale branch. Goods traffic commenced in August 1867 but passenger services were not introduced until March 1869. (Courtesy of Beamish, the North of England Open Air Museum)

The station at Allendale, which had a single platform with a small turntable at the end leading also to a run-round loop, could handle passenger, parcels and goods traffic with facilities for unloading carriages, machines on wheels, livestock and coal. The hand crane had a capacity of two tons. Like many other rural stations, coal could be emptied quickly through the bottom doors of wagons into coal cells below rail level before being shovelled into sacks for distribution. The NER introduced the system of allowing station masters to be coal agents thereby supplementing their salary.

In 1923 the branch became part of the London & North Eastern Railway but passenger services were withdrawn in September 1930. Thereafter it remained open mainly for agricultural and general goods traffic including some timber. There was a creamery very near to the station which gave a useful amount of traffic to the railway. An example of how the line was worked can be illustrated by reference to Working Timetables. Between October 1934 and the end of April 1935 two goods trains left Hexham at unspecified times each morning, both of which stopped at intermediate stations only to detach. The first, running as a No.1 express goods, conveyed empty milk cans, parcels, newspapers and mail and was worked by the engine and men of the 5.30 am Blaydon to Hexham goods. On the return trip it stopped at these stations only to attach vehicles to take to Hexham if required. From Allendale it carried milk, parcels and livestock.

The second train, in both directions, was a slower class D goods running at about 20 mph which could also take parcels if required. It was worked by the engine and crew of a Hexham to Wall mineral.

In the evening there was another No.1 express goods which left Hexham at 6 pm, stopped if necessary, and reached Allendale at 6.45 pm. It, too, could carry parcels traffic. This train left again at 7 pm and was scheduled to stop at Staward, Langley and Elrington Halt for three minutes each before reaching Hexham at 7.39. It conveyed a milk van and parcels, also any empty vans from Staward and Langley. There was one express goods on Sundays which left Hexham at 4.10 pm and called briefly at each station before arriving at the terminus at 4.41. It then left at 5.5 pm to return to Hexham.

The milk churns used on the railways were of two types, the more common being ones which held ten gallons (80 pints). Many porters became very proficient at tilting these to an angle and rolling them along the platform sometimes at an incredible speed which made it look so easy! There was a larger, taller type, conical in shape used less frequently. It did not happen on this branch, but where the amount of bulk traffic warranted it milk was carried in special six-wheeled glass-lined tanker wagons which were often attached to passenger trains, even expresses.

There were no signal boxes on this stretch of line, only ground frames worked by the guard or porter. Only one train at a time was allowed on the branch and the driver had to be in possession of the Train Staff from and to Border Counties Junction.

The Allendale line was closed by British Rail on 20 November 1950. Staward station then became a holiday cottage for a time.

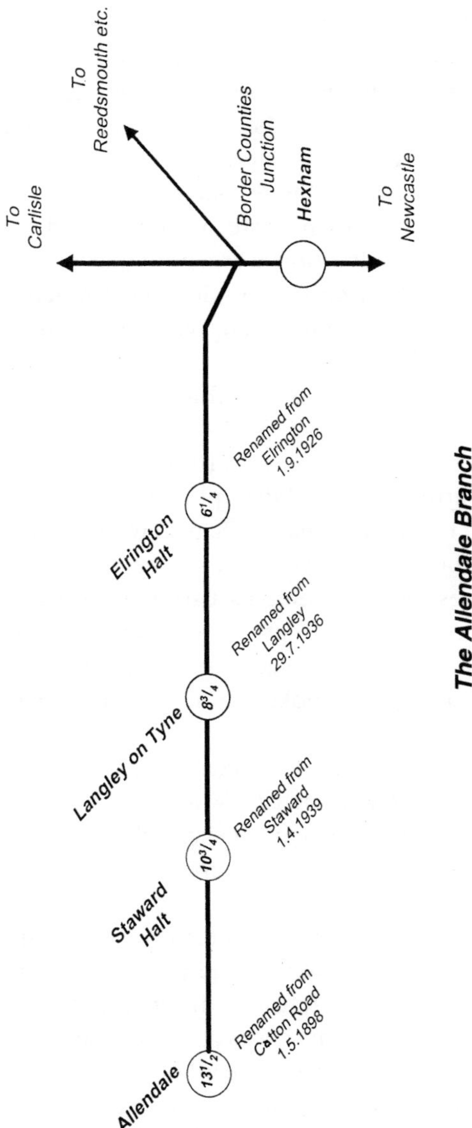

The Allendale Branch

THE ALNWICK BRANCH (Alnmouth to Alnwick)

When plans were being prepared for the main line through the county linking London with Edinburgh the Duke of Northumberland refused to have it running across his land. Traders demanded a rail link but had to be content with a rural branch line. This was opened for goods on 19 August 1850 and for passengers on 1st October. Permission to build this branch was included in the Bill which approved the construction of the Newcastle & Berwick Railway. In 1854 it became part of the North Eastern Railway and in that year four trains in each direction were provided on weekdays of which two Up and three Down had accommodation for 3rd class passengers. They ran at an average speed of 20 mph. Fares were as follows:-

1st class 8d., second class 6d., third class 4d., Government 3d.

On this three mile branch in 1910 there were twenty trains from Alnmouth each weekday plus two extra ones each Saturday, and eighteen (plus one Saturday only) from Alnwick. On Sundays there were seven trains in each direction. Horses in horse boxes and gentlemen's carriages conveyed on low sided flat trucks were one feature in the early days of the NER and this continued until the advent of the motor car. In 1911 the number of tickets booked from Alnwick was well over 77,000.

It is interesting to see the increased service timetabled for July to December 1914 – the year the First World War started. The accompanying page from the Working Timetable also indicates the provision for cattle specials and the conveyance of horse boxes by passenger train.

The railways gave employment in various capacities to numerous people. The high profile jobs most seen by members of the public were station staff, engine drivers, firemen and guards, but behind these was an unseen army to keep the trains running – signalmen, cleaners, platelayers, loaders, checkers, number-takers, carters, lampmen, shunters, fitters... All had an important part to play: each one had his own aspirations, interests and problems but together they were THE RAILWAY!

Safety was considered of paramount importance on any railway and their rule books reflected this. The weather was always a factor that could cause difficulties. During fog or falling snow platelayers were stationed at distant signals to help train crews. A distant signal showing a horizontal arm, or a yellow light at night, indicated that the next home signal was at danger. A detonator was then placed on the line so when a driver heard the bang as it exploded under his engine he knew he had to slow down and be prepared to stop. If the fogman heard the signal move to the clear position he would remove the detonator – but what a miserable, freezing job that must have been with perhaps only a small, upright box to shelter in.

A serious accident which happened in fog occurred between Alnwick and Alnmouth on 11 November 1898, though in this case the weather was not to blame. The new station at Alnwick (opened in 1887) had two platforms and two run-round loops under cover, plus various sidings nearby. A 2-4-2 tank engine and five coaches arrived in platform 2 at 8.33 pm. The loco ran round its train ready for its return trip at 8.50 pm. The driver gave a 'pop' on the whistle before edging the train further back under the overall roof. The signalman however thought the engine needed to be in the goods yard and pulled off the signal to allow it to leave the platform. As he was having his supper at the time he just left the signal as it was when the engine did not appear. Three minutes before the departure time he offered the train on the block bell to the signalman at Alnmouth as the next signal box along the line, Shilbottle Colliery, was closed. Alnmouth accepted the train and the signalman at Alnwick continued with his meal. As the train started to leave the station he realised to his horror that he had not changed the points to put it on the proper line but because of the interlocking there was nothing he could do. The driver meanwhile, on the assumption that he had a clear run, passed other signals at danger. The guard should have kept a lookout to see that all was well as the train left the terminus and could have used his emergency brake: instead he was sorting parcels in his van. Catch points to derail any runaway vehicles on the steep gradient did their job very effectively less than a mile away. The engine and first coach were flung on their side and all but the rear brake van were derailed.

In October 1934 there were sixteen passenger trains each weekday from Alnmouth to Alnwick, plus one on Saturdays only and another which did not run on Saturdays. Of these, six departed from Newcastle and two, including a rail motor, from Berwick. Two of those which ran from the Central station were signalled as expresses though they did stop at several places on the route. The eight Sunday trains ran between Alnmouth and Alnwick only.

In 1950, two years after nationalisation, there were still sixteen trains from Alnmouth (three of which ran from Newcastle) and eight on Sundays. There was a slight reduction in 1957 to thirteen on weekdays plus two extra on Saturdays but by then Sunday trains had been withdrawn.

This branch was one of the last steam hauled lines in the country. Passenger trains were often handled by D class 4-4-0s or J39s at one time then towards the end K1 2-6-0s or V1/V3 2-6-2 tanks were scheduled. On the last day of steam haulage, 17 June 1966, a massive 9F 2-10-0 was the motive power! Diesel units continued the service until 29 January 1968. Goods traffic was withdrawn on 7 October that year.

The good news is that there are definite indications that this popular line will reopen as Northumberland's own preserved Aln Valley Railway, perhaps as soon as 2001, when it will once again be "Linking Coast to Castle".

32 I.

ALNMOUTH and ALNWICK—Weekdays.

DOWN.		1	2	3	4	5	7	9	10	11	12	13	14	15	17	18	20	21	22	23	25
		D Goods.	PASSENGER.	PASSENGER.	PASSENGER.		PASSENGER.	PASSENGER.	D Goods.	PASSENGER.	PASSENGER.	D Goods.		PASSENGER.	PASSENGER.			PASSENGER.	PASSENGER.	D Goods.	PASSENGER.
Distance from Alnmouth.	Departs from			Newcastle 6.40 a.m. p. 5			Warkworth 8.28 a.m. p. 5	Berwick 7.37 a.m. p. 14			Berwick 9.15 a.m. p. 15	Shilbottle Coll. 11.10 a.m.			Newcastle 10.27 a.m. p. 6						
																				M	WO
M. C.		a.m.	a.m.	a.m.	a.m.		a.m.	H a.m.	a.m.	a.m.	a.m.	a.m.		a.m.	p.m.			p.m.	p.m.	p.m.	p.m.
.....	Alnmouth ....dep.	6 5	6C43	7C37	8C9		8C36	8C55	9 15	9C45	10c37	—		11 35	12c11			12c49	1C10	2 10	2C20
2 79	Alnwick .. .. arr.	6 15	6 50	7 44	8 16		8 43	9 2	9 25	9 52	10 44	11 15		11 42	12 18			12 56	1 17	2 20	2 27

DOWN.	27	28	30	31	32	33	34	35	36	37	39	40	41	42	43	44	46	47	48	49	50	52
	PASSENGER.		PASSENGER.		PASSENGER.	D Cattle Empties.	Light Engine.	PASSENGER.		PASSENGER.	PASSENGER.	PASSENGER.		PASSENGER.	PASSENGER.		PASSENGER.	PASSENGER.	PASSENGER.	Empty Train.	PASSENGER.	
Departs from	Berwick 1.10 p.m. p. 16		Newcastle 1.30 p.m. p. 8		Newcastle 2.27 p.m. p. 8	Heaton J.S. 1.50 p.m. p. 8	Newcastle 3.0 p.m. p. 8				Newcastle 4.47 p.m. p. 9	Newcastle 4.15 p.m. p. 9			Berwick 5.20 p.m. p. 19		Newcastle 6.30 p.m. p. 10	Newcastle 8.15 p.m. p. 10			Newcastle 8.35 p.m. p. 10	
					SO	MO	S													SO		
	p.m.		p.m.		H p.m.	p.m.	N p.m.	E p.m.		p.m.	p.m.	p.m.		p.m.	p.m.		p.m.	p.m.	p.m.	B p.m.	p.m.	
Alnmouth ....dep.	2C47		3C13		3C58	4 6	4 45	5C0		5C35	5C43	6C18		6C45	7C13		8C13	9C4	9C30	10 5	10c15	
Alnwick .. .. arr.	2 54		3 20		4 5	4 15	4 52	5 7		5 42	5 50	6 25		6 52	7 20		8 20	9 11	9 37	10 10	10 22	

Sundays.

DOWN.	1	2	3	4	5	6	8	11	13	15	16	17	18	19	20	21	22	23	24	25	26	27
	Light Engine.		PASSENGER.	PASSENGER.	PASSENGER.		PASSENGER.		PASSENGER.		PASSENGER.		PASSENGER.		PASSENGER.							
Departs from																						
	a.m.		a.m.	a.m.	a.m.		p.m.		p.m.		p.m.		p.m.		p.m.							
Alnmouth ....dep.	6 45		7C40	9C40	11c44		2C15		5C35		7C13		8C13		10c13							
Alnwick .. .. arr.	6 52		7 47	9 47	11 51		2 22		5 42		7 20		8 20		10 20							

B—When the 7.45 p.m. train from Edinburgh is running so late as to detain the 10.15 p.m. Alnmouth to Alnwick, to make the connection this train will remain at Alnmouth and run as a passenger train to Alnwick after arrival of the North train.
E—On Saturdays starts from Newcastle at 3.51 p.m., p. 9. N—Will not run after 21st September.

Working Timetable (July-December 1914)

NOTE: *C = Collect tickets* *MO = Mondays only*

M = Not Mondays *WO = Wednesdays only*

THE ALSTON BRANCH (Opened by the Newcastle & Carlisle Railway)

In 1846 during a period of commercial depression the only railway line to be sanctioned was that from Haltwhistle to Alston and Nenthead. An application to amend the proposed route was granted in 1849 when a decision to terminate the line at Alston was confirmed. The purpose of this branch was primarily to exploit the rich deposits of lead ore and other minerals in the area.

Construction commenced from both ends in 1850. Because of the very hilly nature of the route, following the valley of the river South Tyne, heavy earthworks were necessary as the line climbed by over 500 feet in thirteen miles. It involved severe gradients, some sharp bends, cuttings and numerous stone bridges, viaducts and culverts. The most spectacular of these was at Lambley where nine semi-circular arches and six smaller ones of the viaduct strode across the valley 110 feet above the water.

The first section from Haltwhistle to Shafthill was opened for

Lambley station, 1976. The Alston branch was fully operational in 1852 once Lambley viaduct had been completed. Passenger services survived until May 1976. (J A Wells)

freight in March 1851 and for passengers on 19 July, a distance of 4½ miles. The 8¾ miles from Alston as far as Lambley opened for goods and minerals on 5 January 1852. A short stretch laid to Lambley Fell enabled traffic to travel over the Midgeholme railway to join the main line at Milton. This was no longer necessary once Lambley viaduct was completed. The branch was fully operational from 17 November 1852.

By the 1880s very little lead was being mined but the line generated good returns from coal, coke, whinstone, iron ore, some zinc, fluorspar, manure, timber, livestock and general merchandise, amply repaying the investment. Coal from collieries not served by railway sidings was conveyed to the loading points either in *tubs* running on narrow gauge tracks or by aerial ropeway.

Cartoonists and the designers of comic postcards often made fun of the railways. In this amusing sketch the 'Alston Flyer' is given a helping hand until the engine has steam up. (Courtesy of Beamish, the North of England Open Air Museum)

Bearing in mind the height of Alston at 920 feet above sea level, heavy snowfalls frequently blocked roads in the area and the railway was a lifeline. It is not surprising that a formidable snowplough was based there to keep the line open; it even had its own shed at one time.

The general pattern for passenger traffic was three or four trains in each direction though with some increases from time to time in LNER days. In the early 1950s British Railways provided seven or eight trains each way. When the colliery at Plenmeller was in production some workmen's trains were run from both ends of the branch. Special events and excursions brought additional workings. The usual locomotives in NER and LNER days were 0-4-4 tanks for passenger trains and 0-6-0s for freight, mainly J21s or J25s. 4-6-2 tanks (class A8) were used for a time and J39s appeared on both passenger and goods rosters. The branch was single line throughout with a passing loop at Coanwood (formerly called Shafthill). If necessary trains could pass at Lambley if one was shunted along the Fell branch.

The routine continued until freight facilities were withdrawn from Coanwood in September 1955 followed by Lambley and Slaggyford five years later and from Alston itself in September 1965. Passenger services survived with diesel railcars until May 1976 by which time a new 'all-weather' road linked Coanwood with Lambley.

An attempt to run the line as a preserved railway failed largely because the money demanded by BR could not be raised before the given deadline and all track was lifted. Nevertheless, the South Tynedale Railway now operates a narrow gauge passenger line from Alston station to Gilderdale on the border with Northumberland which was extended by 3/4 mile to Kirkhaugh in July 1998. The ultimate aim is to take the line to Haltwhistle.

HALTWHISTLE and ALSTON

Distance from Haltwhistle	DOWN	Weekdays 1	2	3	4	6	7	8	9	11	12	13	14	15		16	17	18	19	20	21	22	23	26	Sundays 1	2	3	4	5
								Engine and Van				PASSENGER		D Goods		PASSENGER	PASSENGER	D Goods	PASSENGER		PASSENGER	PASSENGER	PASSENGER	PASSENGER					
								Q								SX	SO	Q			SO	SX	SO	SO					
								PV						arr.	dep.														
M.C.								a.m.				a.m.		a.m	a.m.	a.m.	p.m.	p.m.	p.m.		p.m.	p.m.	p.m.	p.m.					
.....	**Haltwhistle** ....⊕							5 20				8 5		—	9 20	11 50	12 10	2 30	4 36		6 10	8 0	8 15	10 37					
0 67	Plenmeller Halt							..				..		..	..	..	..		..		..	..	..	..					
3 0	Featherstone Park Halt ..							....				8 13			.....	11 58	12 18	2x47	4 44		6 18	8 8	8 23	10 45					
4 8	Coanwood .. .. .. ✢ ⊕							..				8 17		9 37	9 52	12 2	12 22	2 50	4 48		6 22	8 12	8 27	10 49					
4 56	Lambley ....✢							....				8 20		9 56	10 46	12 5	12 25	—	4 51		6 25	8 15	8 30	10 52					
8 41	Slaggyford							..				8 28		10 56	11 6	12 13	12 33	—	4 59		6 33	8 23	8 38	11 0					
13 0	**Alston** ....✢							5 55				8 37		11 18	—	12 22	12 42	—	5 8		6 42	8 32	8 47	11 9					

Distance from Alston	UP	Weekdays 1	2	3	4	5	7	8	9	10	11	12	13		14	15	17	18	19	20	21	22	23	24	Sundays 1	2	3	4	5
							D Goods		PASSENGER			PASSENGER	D Goods			PASSENGER	D Goods	PASSENGER		PASSENGER	PASSENGER								
							Q										Q	SO			SO								
							PY						arr. M	dep.															
M.C.							a.m.		a.m.			a.m.	p.m.	p.m.		p.m.	p.m.	p.m.		p.m.	p.m.								
....	**Alston** ....✢						6 35		7 10			10 12	—	12 23		1 41	—	5 20		6 50	9 10								
4 39	Slaggyford						..		7 19			10 21	*			1 50	—	5 29		6 59	9 19								
8 24	Lambley ....✢						....		7 27			10 29	12 45	12 58		1 58	—	5 37		7 7	9 27								
8 72	Coanwood .. .. – ✢ ⊕						..		7 30			10 32	1 3	1 11		2 1	3 0	5 40		7 10	9 30								
10 0	Featherstone Park Halt ..						7b5		7 34			10 36	1 17	1b22		2 5	.....	5 44		7 14	9 34								
12 13	Plenmeller Halt						..		..			..	..	..		..	..	..		..	..								
13 0	**Haltwhistle** .... ⊕						7 16		7 41			10 43	1 36	—		2 12	3 13	5 51		7 21	9 41								

M—Barhaugh Siding *. SO departs Alston 12.43 p.m. and runs 20 minutes later.
P—Branch stations to advise station master, Alston, when they have traffic, and he will transmit the information to the Yard Master, Carlisle, specially stating when the train is required on the branch. In the latter case he will advise the station master, Haltwhistle, who will arrange staff working.
V—Carlisle dep. 4.30 a.m., p. 132.
Y—Carlisle arr. 9.19 a.m., p. 127.

b—Brakes.
x—Arr. 2.42 p.m
✢ Staff Station.
⊕ Electric Staff or Tablet Station.

SX Saturdays excepted.
SO Saturdays only.
Q Runs when required.

Extract from Working Timetable (Oct 1934-April 1935)

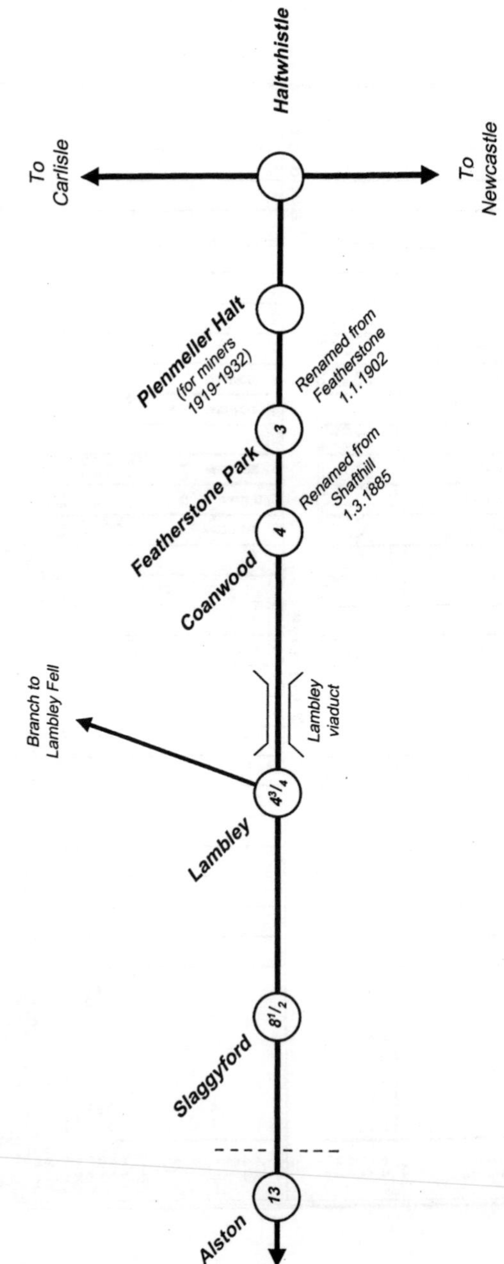
Haltwhistle
To Carlisle
To Newcastle
Plenmeller Halt
(for miners 1919-1932)
Featherstone Park
3
Renamed from Featherstone 1.1.1902
Coanwood
4
Renamed from Shafthill 1.3.1885
Lambley viaduct
Branch to Lambley Fell
Lambley
$4^3/_4$
Slaggyford
$8^1/_2$
Alston
13

The Alston Branch

THE AMBLE BRANCH (Opened by the York, Newcastle & Berwick Railway)

The Northumberland & Durham coalfield was bounded by Hartlepool, Shildon, Hexham and Amble, roughly 50 miles by 20 and covering some 700 square miles. The production of coal from Northumberland in 1910 was 13,121,691 tons, much of it conveyed by rail.

The port of Amble owed its existence to the tremendous demand for coal. Most of the output from Earl Grey's new colliery at Broomhill, together with that from other pits, was carried to Amble for shipment to London, Germany and Scandinavian countries. Coal was tipped into the holds of ships moored alongside the massive staiths by teemers and levelled by trimmers.

The railway to Amble extended for 5¾ miles from a junction with the main line near Chevington. It opened for mineral traffic on 5 September 1849. A station at Broomhill authorised in November 1877 at a cost of £263 was opened in 1878, followed by Amble station in 1879. In 1910 there were five trains each way on weekdays, eight on Saturdays with an extra train from Amble to Broomhill only at 10.45 on Saturday nights, enabling people to go to dances or 'the pictures'. Passenger services were withdrawn in July 1930.

In the early 1920s the port was handling 750,000 tons of coal a year. Other traffic was imported timber – including pit props used to support the roof in mine workings – and scrap metal. The goods yard at Amble was equipped to handle most kinds of traffic including livestock.

Having become part of the new North Eastern Railway from 1854 and the LNER in 1923, the Amble branch passed into the ownership of British Railways on 1st January 1948. Coal handling at Amble continued until the 1960s. The basic facilities for goods at Broomhill were withdrawn in May 1964 and the line closed on 14 December the same year.

THE AVENUE BRANCH

The line from Percy Main to Seghill was extended to New Hartley in 1846 to take coal from the new Hester pit* to the river Tyne. A link was also built from the colliery to a waggonway which carried coal from other outlets near Dairy House to the small harbour at Seaton

Sluice. The section between Hartley and Dairy House was upgraded and subsequently became part of the Blyth & Tyne branch to Tynemouth which was authorised by Parliament in 1854 but not opened until October 1860, for coal only. Goods and passenger traffic followed in April 1861. The line continued through the Avenue to reach Whitley station (later Monkseaton) on the way to Tynemouth, with through running from Morpeth introduced at the end of May.

A push-and-pull set with G5 0-4-4T 67261 entering Monkseaton with a train for Blyth via the Avenue branch in June 1958. (Ian S Carr)

From the village of Seaton Delaval the road to Seaton Delaval Hall was bordered by trees or small woods for a mile. The railway line crossed this belt at right angles, hence its name. A short-lived halt called The Avenue brought passengers near to the Hall and within walking distance of the coast.

When the Blyth & Tyne Railway opened its line to Newcastle in 1864 passenger trains were withdrawn from the branch, except for occasional use, and were not restored until 1904 when they became a good feeder service from Blyth and Newbiggin to the new electric service.

This line carried thousands of workers and day trippers over the next sixty years. Whitley Bay was a popular seaside holiday resort and in the 1950s the summer Saturday morning train from Tynemouth to Glasgow, composed of main line stock, travelled this way to Morpeth. About this time four signals were erected along the track from Avenue Crossing signal box towards Monkseaton for the purpose of testing drivers' eyesight.

Local passenger services in LNER and BR days were provided by push and pull trains of three or four coaches powered by G5 0-4-4 tanks but for some years Sentinel steam railcars were used on this branch. Only one of these, named *Phenomena,* was built as an articulated unit and it spent all its working life travelling mainly between Blyth, Monkseaton, Morpeth and Newbiggin. An analysis of its Saturday working is given below. The first departure from Blyth was 6.30 am and the car returned to depot at 12.14 am the following day after its duties.

Summary of Saturday Working of Articulated Steam Railcar *Phenomena* 1938		
From	*To*	*Number of Trips*
Blyth	Newsham	4
— " —	Monkseaton	6
— " —	Morpeth	2
— " —	Backworth	1
Monkseaton	Blyth	7
— " —	Hartley	1
Morpeth	Newsham	1
— " —	Newbiggin	1
Newbiggin	Blyth	1
Newsham	Blyth	3 + 1 empty stock
Hartley	Monkseaton	1
Backworth	Blyth	1

The Royal Train with HM the Queen and HRH Prince Philip on board was stabled overnight on the branch in October 1954.

Freight traffic was predominantly coal, hauled by the ubiquitous J27s.

This link between Hartley and Monkseaton was closed in 1964 and the track was lifted circa 1965.

*FOOTNOTE: On 16 January 1862 a terrible disaster at Hester pit claimed the lives of 204 men and boys.

THE BLYTH & TYNE BRANCHES

In 1874, the year the Blyth & Tyne Railway became part of the North Eastern Railway, Blyth was declining as a coal port but there followed a period of growth and expansion when new staiths were opened on both sides of the river and extra lines were laid to cope with the increasing tonnages being handled. In 1883 coal shipped from South Blyth had been little over 42,000 tons but the following year when new staiths were in use the figure rose to 252,780 tons and in 1886 429,961 tons were loaded into ships. This increased to 466,983 in 1887 despite a strike by miners lasting seventeen weeks. Another staith 1,237 feet in length and with four 'spouts' was opened to the east of the Low Quay on 1st May 1888. To connect with this at the southern end, on the south side of the river, the NER constructed a line from Newsham, 1½ miles in length, and ample siding areas thereby making an approach to the ships from two directions. When we consider that the coal was conveyed in chaldron waggons, or trucks carrying eight to ten tons, some idea can be gained of the amount of traffic even in those days.

Prior to 1886 coal from the Ashington collieries complex was taken on to the main line north of Morpeth, then if it was being transferred to Blyth for shipment it travelled either via Bedlington and Newsham to South Blyth or via Bedlington and West Sleekburn junction to North Blyth. In that year a new connection was made with the NER at Hirst station (later named Ashington) which gave a more direct route to the staiths through North Seaton and the northern side of the triangle at Marchey's House signal box.

A small section of the North Eastern Railway's staiths at North Blyth from where coal was 'teemed' into the holds of ships. In 1961 Blyth handled more coal than any other port in Europe. (J A Wells)

A Stephenson Locomotive Society tour of the Ashington collieries complex in June 1962 paused at Lynemouth. Passengers were transferred from their special train at Ashington and travelled in former NER coaches over colliery lines. (E Brack collection)

At Morpeth coal trains from the north had to reverse before proceeding along the Blyth & Tyne, a process which could take 20 minutes or more unless there was a brake van on both ends. It was not until 1980 that a new 'north curve' was laid thus giving – at last – direct access to and from the north near Hepscott. A facing crossover in the station permits a direct approach from the south. The Blyth & Tyne branch carried enormous amounts of coal throughout the ownership of the NER, LNER and BR, reaching a peak in 1961 when Blyth handled more coal than any other port in Europe, a staggering 6,889,317 tons.

From the 1960s, when many coal seams became worked out or too expensive to mine, collieries were closed until in 1995 only Ellington in Northumberland was still producing coal, under private ownership. Staiths were demolished but a new loading and storage facility was built on the jetty at the former Bates pit, Blyth. It was in use in 1991 with rail access from Newsham and the Isabella colliery line. In 1989 between 80,000 and 100,000 tons of coal were handled each week on the Blyth & Tyne, much of it from other areas. Today, apart from shipments, coal is still led to Blyth power station and Alcan.

Early in the century Blyth harbour was used to import large amounts of timber for mining, building and general purposes, a trade which had broadened considerably by 1910. The port also became recognised as a good base for fishing boats and train loads of fish were despatched. The first of these ran on 27 July 1910 but the fishing industry never fully recovered after the First World War.

A ship-building company, ship repairing and a firm of ship-breakers gave valuable traffic to rail when they were active. The largest three-deck sailing ship ever built – the *Britannia* – was one of the many vessels broken up by Hughes Bolckow of North Blyth. A sideline for this company was the manufacture of teak furniture from ships' timbers including a set of seats for the terraces of the House of Commons, and others for American universities.

The first station in Blyth, near the shipyard, was opened in 1847. This was replaced by a larger one a short distance away twenty years later which was rebuilt between 1894 and 1896. The goods yard could then hold well over a hundred wagons. It handled a variety of loads – supplies for the war time submarine base, for example, and timber, scrap metal, sand, steel, ships' engines, propellers, pipes, bricks, merchandise for local shops, even army lorries. Sadly all this has gone. Blyth Goods depot closed in September 1963 followed by all other goods facilities on the northern section of the branch between December 1963 and June 1965. Newsham and Bedlington were the last to go. The goods yards at Tynemouth and Monkseaton were closed down in March 1959.

From 1874 the North Eastern Railway continued to use the former Blyth & Tyne route to Tynemouth but a decision was taken to re-route the line between Monkseaton and Tynemouth nearer the coast. This was opened in 1882. The changes in the names and locations of stations are described in the accompanying diagrams.

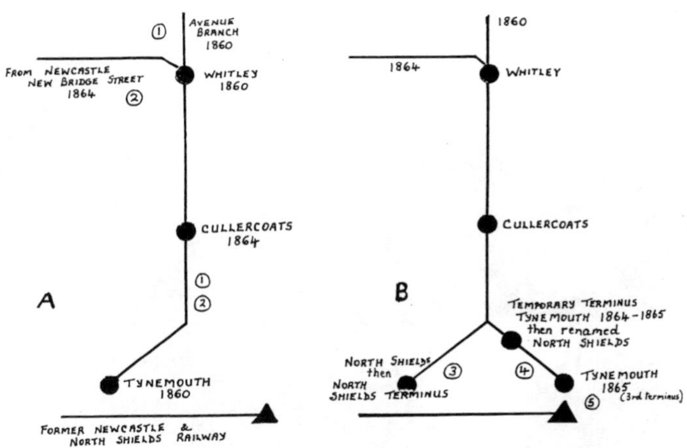

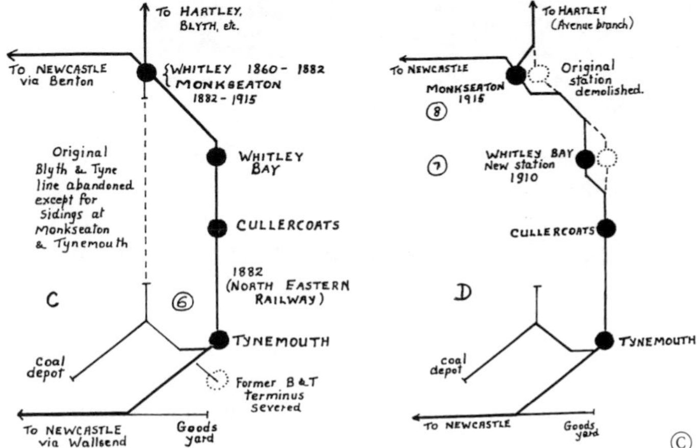

Diagram to show the Evolution of Stations at the Coast

Stations at the coast

1) Avenue branch, Hartley to Whitley, opened by Blyth & Tyne Railway for mineral traffic 1860 and for passengers and goods 1861.
2) 1864 New Bridge Street (Newcastle) to Whitley opened. These routes terminated at Tynemouth (Blyth and Tyne). Cullercoats station opened 1864.

3 & 4) 1864-65 New, temporary terminus at Tynemouth. Original terminus renamed North Shields.

5) 1865 Third Blyth & Tyne terminus at Tynemouth. Second station renamed North Shields. Original station renamed North Shields terminus.
(In 1874 the Blyth & Tyne railway became part of the NER).
6) 1882 NER laid new line nearer the coast with new stations at Whitley Bay, Cullercoats and Tynemouth. Whitley station renamed Monkseaton.
At Tynemouth connection made with former Newcastle & North Shields railway route to Newcastle via Wallsend. That terminus became a goods yard.
7) 1910 New station at Whitley Bay.
8) 1915 New station at Monkseaton.

Whitley Bay station in 1896. Opened by the NER in 1882, it was replaced by a new one alongside in 1910. (Author's collection)

Passenger traffic could be conveniently placed into three main categories, namely:-

(i) loco hauled between Newcastle Central or Manors to Newbiggin with connections to Blyth and some to Morpeth. These replaced trains from Newcastle to Morpeth with connections between Bedlington and Newbiggin.

(ii) services between Monkseaton and Blyth or Newbiggin via the Avenue branch, provided in succession by loco-hauled trains, autocars, rail-cars, push-and-pull trains of three or four coaches, and diesel multiple units.

(iii) electric trains from the city to the coast and back, introduced in 1904 which replaced steam hauled sets.

It is worth recording that favourite pastimes for the men in mining communities in the north east included racing greyhounds, whippets and pigeons. The latter were sent by rail to various destinations where they were released en masse in a whirlwind of smacking wings to fly back to their lofts. The birds were carried in large wicker baskets of uniform size and the railway provided special vans equipped with folding racks. Pigeon specials were a regular feature on some branches and were often combined into longer trains at Newcastle.

Percy Main motive power depot was originally the Blyth & Tyne Railway's engine shed and works where new engines and rolling stock were built and repaired. In NER days, up to about 1920, it was also a centre where old locomotives were broken up. It was predominantly a shed for mineral engines in LNER and BR days: in fact the 24 based there in 1950 were all J27s. South Blyth was built in 1879 to accommodate nine locos but in 1895 its size was doubled to make a six-road shed with entry at one end only. By contrast, North Blyth (1897) had a central turntable with 22 radiating stalls long enough to hold a tender engine in each one. In the early 1900s a small two-road shed was built at South Gosforth to replace a B & TR depot near New Bridge Street, but it was used for only two or three years.

The usual motive power on the branch was 0-6-0 tender and tank engines and 0-4-4, 2-4-2, 2-6-2 and 0-6-2 tanks. Larger engines including Pacifics appeared from time to time on specials, wartime troop trains and breakdown trains. By 1965 K1 2-6-0s and more Q6 0-8-0s were based at Blyth followed by ex LMS 2-6-0s before dieselisation.

Two J27 engines were involved in a serious collision at West Sleekburn on 4 November 1959. 65824 with a load of over 700 tons, running under clear signals across the junction to North Blyth, was tipped over by 65847 when it slid at walking pace past a signal at danger. Sadly the driver and fireman of 65824 were killed. At the time of this accident 40-45 coal trains or empties and sixteen passenger or parcels trains passed West Sleekburn each weekday.

Passenger services were withdrawn from the Morpeth branch on 3 April 1950 and from stations between Backworth and Newbiggin, together with Blyth, on 2 November 1964, most of which were demolished. Former Blyth & Tyne Railway stations between Newcastle and Tynemouth remain as part of the Metro system (page 189).

Percy Main shed was closed to steam on 28 February 1965 but it housed diesel shunters for a year after that, before demolition began in October 1966. South Blyth, which had seen the demise of its tough, little G5 tank engines at the end of 1958, had its remaining steam engines withdrawn on 28 May 1967 when the J27s were transferred to Sunderland. North Blyth followed on 9 September. Both sheds remained open for diesel locomotives until 29 January 1968 when they were removed to the new depot at Cambois, used until September 1994.

Diverted onto the Blyth & Tyne branch because of an accident on Morpeth curve in June 1984, an Inter-city 125 train for London is shown just after leaving the main line. (Ian S Carr)

On a Sunday in June 1966 Deltic D 9020 ***Nimbus*** *with an express from Edinburgh to King's Cross was one of the trains diverted via the Blyth & Tyne branch owing to bridge repairs on the main line. It is shown joining the electrified route from Tynemouth at Backworth. (Ian S Carr)*

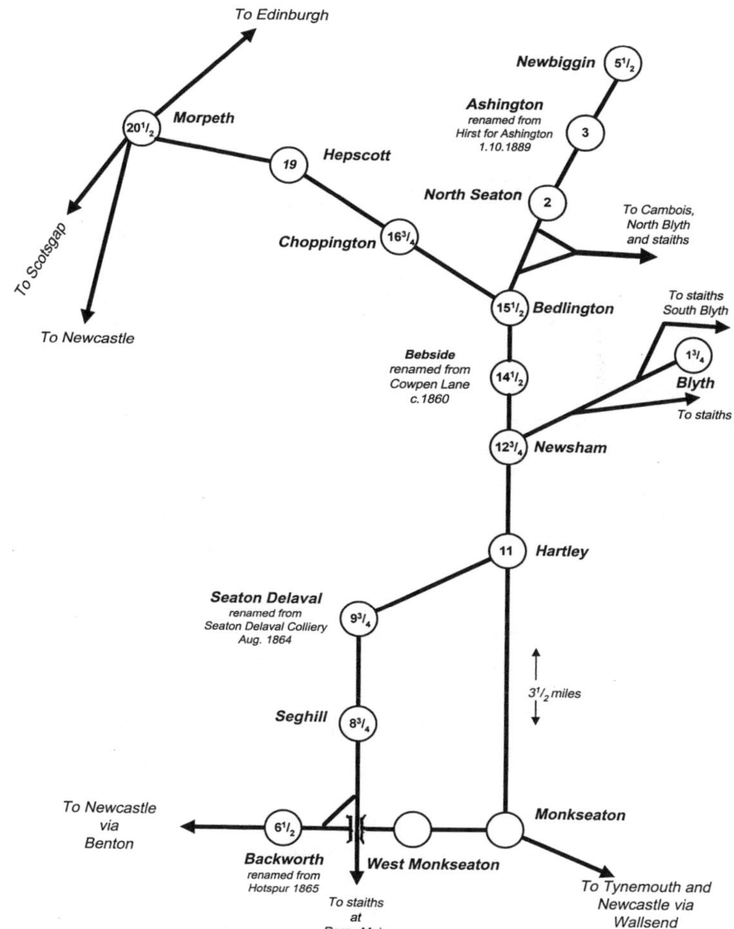

BLYTH AND TYNE BRANCH (Northern section)
Distances from Backworth to Morpeth are from Manors
(Not to scale)

THE BORDER COUNTIES BRANCH

In the North British era the single track Border Counties section provided an important route for goods and mineral traffic between Newcastle and Edinburgh which meant that running over North Eastern Railway tracks was kept to a minimum. This was no longer necessary once these two companies became part of the same organisation, the LNER; nevertheless trains conveying meat from Hawick to King's Cross continued to use the line.

After the Grouping more ex North Eastern engines were seen on this route, in fact quite a variety of motive power was used – the ubiquitous 0-6-0s and 4-4-0s, 2-6-0s and 4-6-0s of various classes. Ultimately some standard British Railways types made their appearance too.

Passenger trains in early North British Railway days usually consisted of three second-rate, four or six-wheeled coaches, a composite between two brake-thirds. The LNER replaced these with ex NE bogie coaches which were a great improvement in comfort and riding quality. Later, Gresley and Thompson corridor stock appeared. The number of passengers did not warrant a frequent service but from time to time special trains were scheduled, particularly for agricultural shows at Bellingham. These were always notable events which were well supported but the pathing of trains and the parking of empty stock between the outward and return journeys had to be carefully planned. In the 30s the Northern Belle touring train, a hotel on wheels, used the Border Counties line so that the passengers could transfer to buses to visit the Roman Wall.

Apart from coal, coke, livestock and agricultural commodities, goods traffic at various times included stone, tarred chippings for roads, pipes, cement, young trees for planting at Kielder, bricks, lime and timber. Rail transport was used more when there was a shortage of petrol during the 1939-45 war. Because of army camps, ammunition dumps, training areas for service personnel, together with gun testing in the area, there was a very considerable amount of military traffic on the line. A small station with a wartime role was Lewiefield Halt, opened in the mid-1930s to serve one of the training camps for men who had been unemployed for a long time.

The viaduct at Border Counties Junction was subjected to weight restrictions. If trains from Hexham were double-headed the leading engine was detached and sent forward 'light' to Wall before being recoupled to the train. A speed limit was in force, sometimes almost walking pace, particularly after the bridge was damaged by flash floods in 1948 and patched up. In the 1940s the naval guns which were sent for testing in the area travelled over the Border Counties route but those which were considered too heavy were sent via Morpeth.

Passenger traffic between Hexham and Riccarton Junction ended in mid October 1956, unable to compete any longer with cars and buses, though diesel multiple units were used on special trains over the route after that. Goods facilities were withdrawn on 1st September 1958 apart from those at Reedsmouth and Bellingham which survived for another five years. Closure was hastened by that troublesome bridge over the river Tyne!

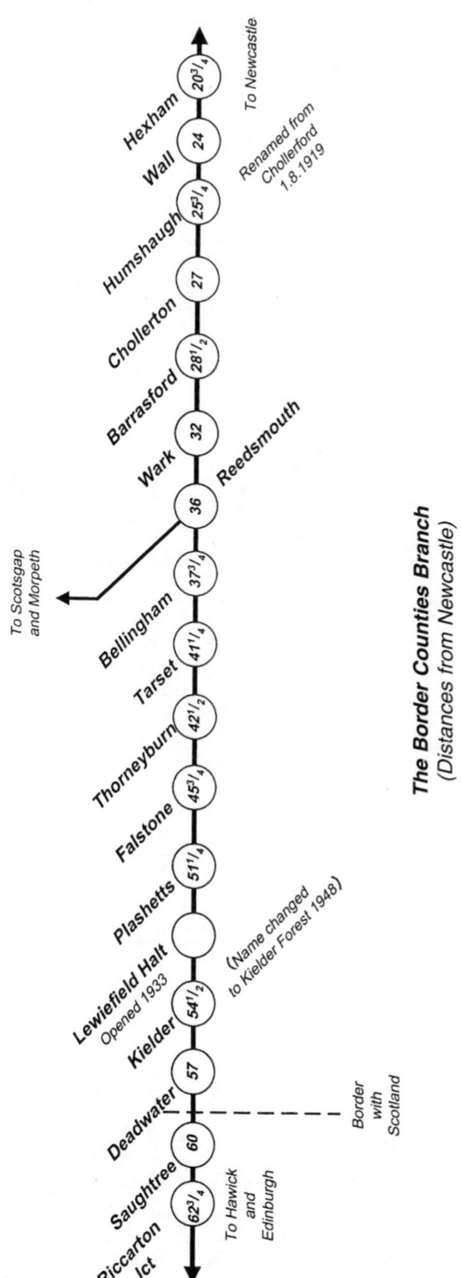

The Border Counties Branch
(Distances from Newcastle)

RICCARTON, REEDSMOUTH, and NEWCASTLE. North British.

Miles	Up	Week Days mrn.	mrn.	aft. (Saturdays only)	aft.	aft.
—	Riccarton Jcn.	6·40	10·0			6·55
2¾	Saughtree	6·46	10·6			7·1
5¾	Deadwater	6·53	10·13			7·8
8¼	Kielder	6·59	10·18			7·13
11½	Plashetts	7·8	10·26			7·22
16	Falstone	7·18	10·36			7·32
20¼	Thorneyburn	Tu.				
21½	Tarset	7·28	10·45			7·41
25	Bellingham	7·38	10·54	2·15	4·15	7·51
26¾	Reedsmouth	7·45	11·0	2·20	4·20	7·57
30¾	Wark	7·54	11·9	2·30		8·6
34¼	Barrasford	8·2	11·17	2·39		8·15
35¾	Chollerton	8·6	11·21	2·43		8·19
37	Chollerford	8·11	11·26	2·48		8·24
38¾	Wall	8·17	11·33	2·54		8·30
42	Hexham	8·26	11·45	3·4		8·40
62¾	Newcastle	9·7	12·34			9·25

Miles	Down	Week Days mrn.	mrn.	aft. (Saturdays only)	aft.	aft.	aft. (Saturdays only)
—	Newcastle dep.	6·10	10·55			4·15	(6·12)
20¾	Hexham	7·7	11·51			4·51	7·0
24	Wall	7·15	12·0			4·59	7·10
25¾	Chollerford	7·20	12·5			5·4	7·15
27	Chollerton	7·24	12·9			5·9	7·19
28½	Barrasford	7·28	12·14			5·14	7·23
32	Wark	7·36	12·22			5·22	7·31
36	Reedsmouth	7·46	12·33	2·0	3·45	5·31	7·41
37¾	Bellingham	7·51	12·38	2·5	3·50	5·36	7·45
41¼	Tarset	7·59	12·46			5·44	
42½	Thorneyburn		Tu.				
45¾	Falstone	8·9	12·56			5·53	
51¼	Plashetts	8·19	1·6			6·3	
54½	Kielder	8·27	1·14			6·11	
57	Deadwater	8·34	1·20			—	
60	Saughtree	8·42	1·28			—	
62¾	Riccarton Jcn.	8·50	1·36			6·24	

Extract from 1910 Timetable

Table 61 **HEXHAM and RICCARTON JUNCTION**

Miles		WEEKDAYS A am	SO am	B am	B pm	SO pm
	53 Newcastle ...... dep	5 52	9 45	11 10	4 27	8 20
				pm		
—	**HEXHAM** .. .. dep	6 52	10 39	12 6	5 14	9 15
3¼	Wall .... "	7 1	....	12 15	5 23	....
5	Humshaugh .. .. "	7 6	10 50	12 20	5 28	..
6¼	Chollerton .... "	7 11	10 54	12 24	5 32	9 30
7½	Barrasford .. .. "	7 15	..	12 28	5 36	9 34
11¼	Wark .... "	7 24	11 4	12 36	5 44	9 42
15¼	**Reedsmouth** .. arr	7 32	11 12	12 44	5 52	9 50
	dep	7 46	11 19	12 48	6X 1	9 55
17	Bellingham (North Tyne) "	7 51	11 24	12 53	6X 7	10 0
20½	Tarset .... "	7 58	11 31	1 0	6X13	10 6
21½	Thorneyburn .. .. "	8 2	11 35	1 4	6X17	10 10
25¼	Falstone .... "	8 10	11 43	1 13	6X25	10 18
30½	Plashetts .. .. "	8 20	11 53	1 23	6X35	10 28
32	Lewiefield Halt ...... "	8 26	11 58	1 28	6X40	10 33
33¾	Kielder Forest .. .. "	8 34	12 5	1 35	6X47	10 41
36½	Deadwater .... "	8 40	—	1 41	....	—
39½	Saughtree .. .. "	..	..	1b48	..	..
42	**RICCARTON JUNC.** arr	8 50	....	1b51	7X 2	....
55	Hawick .. .. arr	10 46	..	2C18	7X27	..
107¾	Edinburgh (Waverley) "	12p20	....	4 24	10 25	....

Miles		WEEKDAYS B am	A am	SO pm	SX B pm	SO B pm	
	Edinburgh (Waverley) dep	....	6 38	....	2 33	2 33	
	Hawick .. .. "	6 15	8 53	..	4 32	4 32	
					pm	pm	
—	**RICCARTON JUNC.** dep	6 47	10 22	....	5 3	5 5	....
2½	Saughtree .. .. "	..	..	..	5Z 8	5L10	..
5½	Deadwater .... "	6E55	10 32	....	5y13	5 17	....
8¼	Kielder Forest .. .. "	7 3	10 38	1 40	5y19	5 22	..
10	Lewiefield Halt ...... "	7 8	10 43	1 46	5y24	5 27	....
11½	Plashetts .. .. "	7 11	10 47	1 51	5y28	5 31	..
16¾	Falstone .... "	7 20	10 56	2 0	5y36	5 40	....
20½	Thorneyburn .. .. "	7 27	11 3	2 7	5y43	5 47	..
21½	Tarset .... "	7 31	11 7	2 11	5y48	5 51	....
25	Bellingham (North Tyne) "	7 38	11 14	2 18	5y55	5 58	..
26¾	**Reedsmouth** arr	7 42	11 18	2 22	5y59	6 2	....
	dep	7 48	11 21	2 26	6 4	6 4	..
30¾	Wark .... "	7 57	11 30	2 35	6 13	6 13	....
34½	Barrasford .. .. "	8 4	11 37	2 42	6 20	6 20	..
35¾	Chollerton .... "	8 8	11 41	2 46	6 24	6 24	....
37	Humshaugh .. .. "	8 13	11 45	2 50	6 28	6 28	..
38¾	Wall .... "	8 18	11 49	2 54	6 32	6 32	....
42	**HEXHAM** .. .. arr	8 27	11 58	3 3	6 41	6 41	..
62¾	53 Newcastle ...... arr	9 5	1K 8	3 48	8G 0	8G 0	....

A—Through Train between Newcastle and Riccarton Junction.
B—Through Train between Newcastle and Hawick.
C—Arrives 2.21 pm Mondays and Thursdays and 2.23 pm on Saturdays.
E—Calls when required to take up on informing the Station Master at Riccarton Junction before 5 pm the day previous to travel.
G—Passengers can arrive Newcastle 7.19 pm by changing at Hexham.
K—Passengers can arrive Newcastle 12.42 pm by changing at Hexham.
L—Calls to set down only.
SO—Saturdays only.
SX—Saturdays excepted.
X—2 mins. later on Saturdays.
Z—Calls to set down only on Mondays and Thursdays.
b—Calls to take up only on Mondays, Thursdays and Saturdays and arrives Riccarton 1.53 pm.
p—pm.
y—1 min. later on Mondays and Thursdays.

Passenger Timetable September 1954

THE COLDSTREAM BRANCH

Early in 1881 attempts were made to resurrect the idea of laying a line from Newcastle to Scotsgap then on through Rothbury, Whittingham and Wooler to Coldstream. This would have been known as the Central Northumberland Railway – not to be confused with the Northumberland Central Railway. After listening to the views of business men in Alnwick, sometimes forcefully and angrily expressed, and anxious to defend its territory in the north of the county, the board of the North Eastern Railway decided that a more practical link to Coldstream would be from Alnwick, a distance of 35½ miles. After various local meetings, both schemes were carefully considered by a Parliamentary Committee before powers to build the line were granted to the NER in May 1882, and the rival scheme backed by the North British Railway was abandoned.

The most direct route would have been north west from Alnwick but as this would have encroached on prime parkland of the Duke's estate it was not acceptable. Instead a circuitous route was necessary which took the line over the high ground of Alnwick Moor. To reach the summit at 655 feet above sea level required a four mile climb of 1 in 50, followed by a fall at the same inclination for almost three miles to Edlingham. Apart from these severe gradients, the builders at the southern end of the line were forced not only to blast their way through rocks in the foothills of the Cheviot Hills to make long, deep cuttings near the summit but also to build a five arch viaduct at Edlingham and a tunnel near Whittingham. There were dozens of bridges and culverts along the whole route but the northern section was a much simpler undertaking.

James E Wells (The author's father) was station master at Whittingham in the early 1930s. Subsequently he was SM at Seaton Delaval with Seghill, Bedlington and Benton, from where he retired. (Author's collection)

T E Harrison was given overall responsibility for the construction of the line but the ten intermediate stations were designed by the NER architect, William Bell. With one exception these were attractive stone buildings with half-hipped roofs, very distinctive if somewhat lavish for a quiet, rural branch line. The main intermediate station was Wooler which until then had had no rail connection. There were two platforms which meant that passenger trains could pass there if required. Being in the middle of a thriving agricultural area, the spacious warehouse in the goods yard was a significant stone built structure with a track through and two large access doors where carts or motor vehicles were loaded or unloaded. All stations on this single track had a passing loop but Whittingham was unique on the North Eastern system in that it consisted of an island platform with the usual station buildings surrounded by a glass canopy. It had also a signal box, coal and lime cells, cattle dock, goods shed, weigh cabin and a row of railway cottages. The two water columns were fed from an elevated tank alongside the track. The buildings were of random stone in courses. The station house (in which the writer lived as a small boy in the early 1930s when his father was station master there) stood apart. When the line opened the SM was paid 25 shillings (£1.25) a week.

Crowds turned out at Wooler to witness the first passenger train on the Coldstream branch which ran from Coldstream to Alnwick on 5 September 1887. (J Scott collection)

The first section of the branch, from Coldstream to Wooperton, was available for goods on 2 May 1887, five years after the Bill was passed. It was opened throughout for all traffic on 5 September, once the new station at Alnwick was ready for use. The first train, a set of four wheeled coaches hauled by a BTP 0-4-4 tank engine number 199 from Coldstream to Alnwick, was greeted by enthusiastic crowds. An old postcard of this train portrays the sense of excitement among the people as it stopped at Wooler.

Normally there were three passenger trains a day in each direction, none on Sundays. There were periods when an extra train was run on market days. Milk in churns, parcels, even calves with their legs tied in a lying position and with only their head and neck outside a sack, were carried in the guard's van. As this was mainly a sparsely populated area it is not surprising that passenger trains were withdrawn by the LNER on 22 September 1930 after numbers using them had fallen. They were replaced by a parcels train, sometimes with only one van but at other times taking also horse boxes or the odd covered wagon.

During the mid-1930s camping coaches were placed at most stations along the branch. At Whittingham water was collected from the station in special cans and the station master arranged with a local farmer to supply milk and eggs. The village shop was 1½ miles away. People hiring this sort of holiday accommodation had to travel by rail to their chosen site. How could they do so if there were no trains? The solution was simple – a passenger coach to carry the various families was attached to the parcels train.

As there was little industry other than farming in this very fertile belt it was livestock and a variety of agricultural traffic that formed a large proportion of the goods traffic, but there was some timber extraction and general merchandise including oil, petrol and stone. A tile works at Whittingham contributed some loads before it was closed. Sacks to carry oats, wheat or barley could be hired from the railway company. Allan Stobbs records that in the mid-30s one goods train a day ran between Alnwick and Wooler and another from Coldstream to Wooler where wagons were sorted in the sidings and some exchanged before the trains returned from whence they had come. Horses were carried in special vans which could take three animals standing in padded stalls. There was a compartment for any accompanying handlers and most horse boxes had hinged flaps at the head of each stall from where the animals could be fed, checked or reassured during the journey. At the end of the van was a small storage area for tack or food. Special cattle vans were available for transporting prize bulls and show cattle.

As with other railways in Northumberland the 1939-45 war did bring some respite from the decline because of military traffic. There was considerable movement of army personnel, equipment and stores but there was also an RAF fighter station at Milfield. The good folk of Northumberland were always grateful for the protection those crews gave. After hostilities had ceased hangars at the airfield were used for the storage of food, as rationing continued for several years, and full use was made of the railway using Akeld as the railhead.

Although the line *could* be used as a diversionary route off the main line it was not a very practical solution owing to the nature of the route and two reversals. In 1941 a bomb fell on the tracks not far from Belford, closing the main line. A north-bound express was stopped at Alnmouth then a decision was taken to send the train via Wooler and Coldstream. It proceeded to Alnwick where the locomotive, an A3, was transferred to the rear of the train then ran tender first with a 4-4-0 pilot engine to assist. A third engine had to be sent to help move the heavy load over the summit and from there progress was slow owing to speed restrictions. The train travelled along the Kelso branch to Tweedmouth where the engine again ran round its train before continuing to Edinburgh, very late but it did get through!

A good variety of motive power has been seen on the branch over the years. Normally they were based at Alnmouth or Tweedmouth but excursions and, more particularly, military specials brought engines from further afield. 1621, one of the stalwart 4-4-0s from the Railway Races, finished her service here. LNER classes have included D49s, G5s, J21s, J27s, J36s, J39s, N10s, K3s and V1s.

The Coldstream branch had its share of weather problems, one reason why hefty NER snowploughs were stationed at Alnmouth and Tweedmouth, but it was floods that hastened its closure. In August 1948, a few months after nationalisation, exceptionally heavy rain over a wide area caused severe flooding which swept away ballast, damaged bridges and left a trail of destruction. Repairs were carried out except to a bridge south of Mindrum, so the line was operable between that station and Coldstream and from Alnwick to Kirknewton. Just over a year later nature lashed out again when flash floods caused the collapse of another bridge just north of Ilderton station. As the amount of traffic could not justify costly repairs to both locations the line was reinstated at Mindrum but remained severed at Ilderton. Trains were then run between Coldstream and Wooler and from Alnwick to Ilderton. By that time there were no run-round facilities there so trains had to reverse to Hedgeley before this could be done. This part of the line closed on 2 March 1953 and the northern section on 29 March 1965.

I. 29

COLDSTREAM and ALNWICK—Weekdays.

Distance from Coldstream.	UP.	1		2	3		4	7		8	10	12		14		17		21		24	
		D Cattle.		PASSENGER.	D Goods and Cattle.		PASSENGER.	D Goods.		PASSENGER.	D Cattle Empties.	D Goods.		D Goods.		D Goods.		PASSENGER.		PASSENGER.	
	Departs from	Tweed-mouth 4.50 a.m. p. 28		Berwick 6.15 a.m. p. 28	Kelso. 7.15 a.m. p. 30		Tweedmo'th 8.0 a.m. p. 28	Kelso 9.0 a.m. p. 30			Tweedmo'th 10.40 a.m. p. 28							Berwick 2.45 p.m. p. 29			
		M O			M O		MO				M O Q	M		M O		M O					
		arr.	dep.		arr.	dep.		arr.	dep.			arr.	dep.	arr.	dep.	arr.	dep.	arr.	dop.	arr.	dep.
			B			E	EH		G		E				F		E	H			
M. C.		a.m.	a.m.	a.m.	a.m.	a.m.	a.m.	a.m.	a.m.	a.m.	a.m.	p.m.	p.m.	p.m.	p.m.	p.m.	p.m.	p.m.	p.m.	p.m.	p.m.
.....	**Coldstream**	5 41	5 51	6 53	7 35	8 0	8 30	9 20	10 5	10 40	11 20	—	—	—	—	—	—	3 22	3 23	—	6 30
3 47	Mindrum	6 5	6 8	7 2	8•14	8 48	8 39	10•19	11 0	10 49	..	—	—	—	—	—	—	..	3 32	..	6 39
5 47	*Kilham Siding*	....	....	....	8 55	9D0	....	11 7	11d12	....	....	—	—	—	—	—	—	....	....	....	....
7 76	Kirknewton	6 20	6 25	7 11	9 8	9 18	8 48	11 20	11 28	10 58	..	—	—	—	—	—	—	..	3 41	..	6 48
10 72	Akeld	6 35	6 40	7 17	9•28	9 40	8 54	11 38	11 46	11 4	....	—	—	—	—	—	—	....	3 47	....	6 54
13 42	Wooler	6 49	7 0	7 25	9 49	—	9 0	11 55	—	11 13	12 0	—	1 17	—	1 17	—	3 8	..	3 54	..	7 2
17 6	Ilderton	7 11	7 16	7 34	—	—	—	—	—	11 22	—	1 29	1 39	1 29	1 39	3 20	3 30	....	4 2	....	7 11
19 78	Wooperton	7 26	7 31	7 40	—	—	—	—	—	11 28	—	1 49	1 56	1 49	1 56	3 40	3 47	..	4 8	..	7 17
22 11	Hedgeley	7•38	7 55	7 45	—	—	—	—	—	11 34	—	2•4	2 32	2•4	2 32	3•55	4 45	....	4 13	....	7 23
24 8	Glanton	8 1	8 6	7 50	—	—	—	—	—	11 39	—	2 40	2 48	2 40	2 48	4 51	4 59	..	4 19	..	7 28
25 65	Whittingham	8 12	8 20	7 54	—	—	—	—	—	11 43	—	2 55	3 20	2•55	5 45	5•6	5 45	....	4 22	7 32	7 40
28 55	Edlingham	8•30	8 56	8 2	—	—	—	—	—	11 51	—	3 31	3 36	5 54	6 0	5 54	6 0	..	4 31	..	7 48
31 29	*Summit*	9 L6	9 9	....	—	—	—	—	—	....	—	3 L48	3 53	6 L12	6 17	6 L12	6 17	....	....	....	....
35 55	**Alnwick**	9 31	9 45	8 22	—	—	—	—	—	12 12	—	4 9	—	6 33	—	6 33	—	4 49	—	8 8	—

B—Morpeth arr. 10.34 a.m., p. 33. E—Runs on alternate Mondays, 13th and 27th July, 10th and 24th August, and 7th and 21st September. F—Runs on alternate Mondays, 6th and 20th July, 3rd, 17th and 31st August, and 14th and 28th September. G—Will not run on alternate Mondays, 13th and 27th July, 10th and 24th August, and 7th and 21st September. L—Brakes.

Extract from Working Timetable
(July-December 1914)

NOTES: *MO = Mondays only*
Q = Runs if required

Signalling arrangements on the Coldstream Branch

Edlingham Ground frame controlled by token for section.

Whittingham Box open during the passing of traffic.

Glanton Ground frame controlled by electric Staff for section.

Hedgeley Signal box.

Wooperton Ground frame controlled by key attached to electric Staff for section.

Ilderton Ground frame. Same as above.

Wooler Signal box.

Akeld Signal box.

Kirknewton Ground frame. Same as above.

Mindrum, Kilham Sidings

Points worked from ground frame controlled by key attached to electric Staff.

Mindrum station

Ground frame controlled by key.

(LNER Working Time Table, Oct. 1934-Apr. 1935)

A view of Whittingham Station modelled in 7mm scale by G. R. Mitcheson.
(Courtesy: The Railway Modeller)

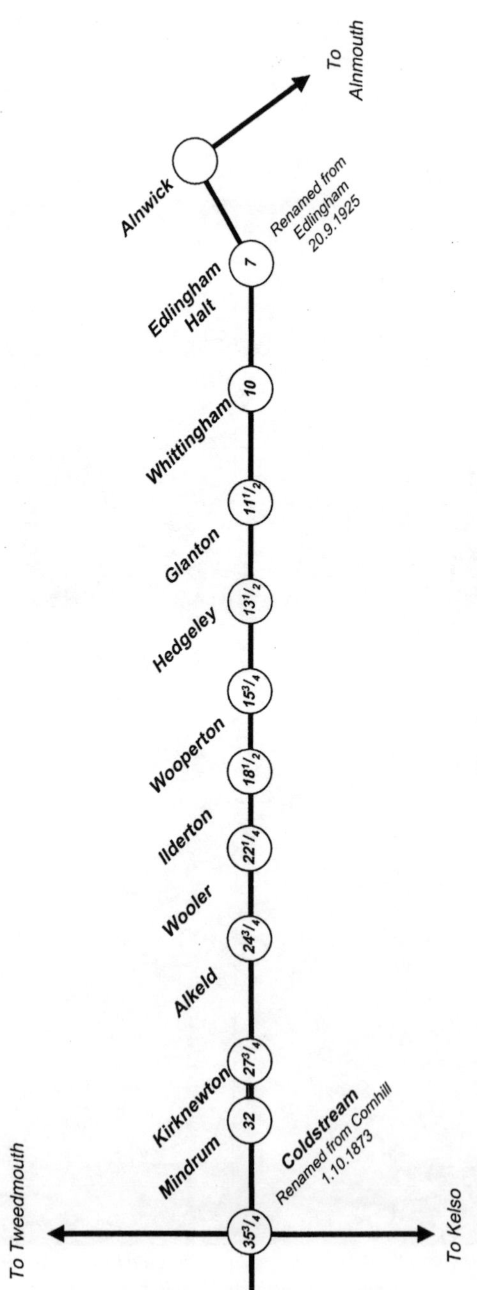

The Coldstream Branch

(Also called the Cornhill Branch and the Wooler Branch)

THE COLLYWELL BAY BRANCH

Some years after the NER introduced electric trains on Tyneside the company considered extending the system to Seaton Sluice from a junction with the Avenue Branch west of Monkseaton. This was in anticipation of the village being developed into a much larger community. The terminus station would be called Collywell Bay and an intermediate stop not far from St. Mary's Island would be Brierdene.

Platforms were built and track was laid but the outbreak of war in 1914 caused the project to be abandoned. Train services were never introduced but an armoured train with a rail mounted naval gun was deployed on the line as coastal defence. The locomotive normally used was number 545, an NER class L 0-6-0T.

The branch did not open for any traffic though there are reports that coal wagons were stored there during the miners' strike of 1921. Track was lifted in 1931.

THE ELECTRIFIED AREA

When the London & North Eastern Railway came into being in 1923 the electric trains round the coast 'circle' continued to provide a frequent and reliable service. The first part of the north Tyneside area to be electrified was just under three miles of the Riverside branch between Percy Main and Carville, in September 1903. This was used initially for testing equipment and crew training. Six months later trains were running between New Bridge Street (Newcastle) and Benton but other sections were quickly electrified so that by early July the full service was in operation, offering a train every fifteen minutes in both directions and a less frequent service via the Riverside. Live rails were also laid from Heaton along the main line to the south east curve and the south west curve at Benton thereby offering an alternative route for certain expresses and providing another way for empty trains travelling to and from the car sheds at South Gosforth which replaced those destroyed at Walkergate.

Stations on this twenty mile run are shown on the accompanying diagram. The North Eastern Railway opened a station at Benton Square, between Benton and Backworth on 1st July

1909 but it was closed in September 1915. West Monkseaton was opened on 20 March 1933 and Longbenton on 14 July 1947.

The 125hp open saloons of the 1904 stock could seat 186 passengers and there was accommodation for luggage, parcels and fish in boxes or barrels. They were built by the NER at York but all the electrical equipment was supplied and fitted by British Thomson-Houston. Power for the trains came from a generating station at Carville which fed supplies to sub-stations at Carville, Pandon Dene (near Manors), Benton, Cullercoats and Percy Main. The LNER withdrew the NER stock in 1937 and replaced them with new, articulated vehicles with bucket seats and sliding doors, hand operated by passengers. (The stringent Health & Safety rules would never allow such doors today but it was virtually unknown for anyone to fall out of a north Tyneside electric train.) These new 216 hp units, which ran in four, six or eight car formations, could complete the

A two-car electric unit leaving Carville, on the Riverside route for Tynemouth in 1967. Notice the lower quadrant semaphore signals, the water tank and 'cowhead' coupling. (Ian S Carr)

round trip from Central to Central in 53 minutes, stopping at every station, compared with 63 minutes for the older trains. Two parcel vans were also replaced. The original stock was refurbished for use between Newcastle and South Shields. A total of 341 vehicles of 33 different styles operated on the electrified area.

For many years these trains offered a twenty minute service in each direction but they were supplemented by others which just travelled part of the way. Expresses were run to and from the coastal stations at busy periods. Categories of passengers using the electric trains can be summarised as follows:-

business people and others working in Newcastle;
casual travellers to the coast and elsewhere;
staff working at the Ministry of National Insurance, Longbenton, from 1947;

To connect with ships sailing between the Tyne and Norway trains were taken to the Tyne Commission Quay. One such service was 'The Norseman' which ran to and from King's Cross. 'Peak' D170 is shown arriving at the terminal with main line stock to form a train to Newcastle and the capital in April 1969. (Ian S Carr)

workers in shipyards, ship repairing, engineering and service industries along the river Tyne;

heavy summer traffic to the coast.

Many workers travelled to Howdon, Wallsend, and stations on the Riverside branch. Apart from the normal service, workmen's trains were also provided. One of those in regular service was the *Control set* which was a rake of non-electric coaches with a powered parcels van at each end. Prior to 1929 these were a set of ten six-wheelers; afterwards six bogie coaches with individual compartments were in the formation until the mid 1950s. Electric parcels vans were modified to carry passengers with prams and were used in ordinary sets at weekends when traffic was particularly heavy. When the weather was fine and warm day trippers flocked to the coast in packed trains, but many additional sets were run as shuttles to supplement the scheduled services.

Under British Railways these coaches were painted green. All were replaced by diesel multiple units between March and June 1967. The last electric train left Newcastle Central at 6.15 pm on 17 June, the end of a remarkable era.

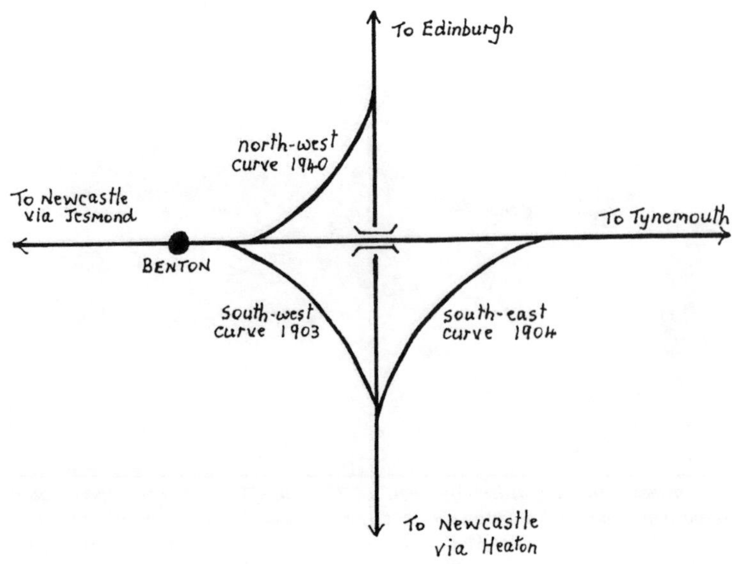

Connections with the Main line at Benton

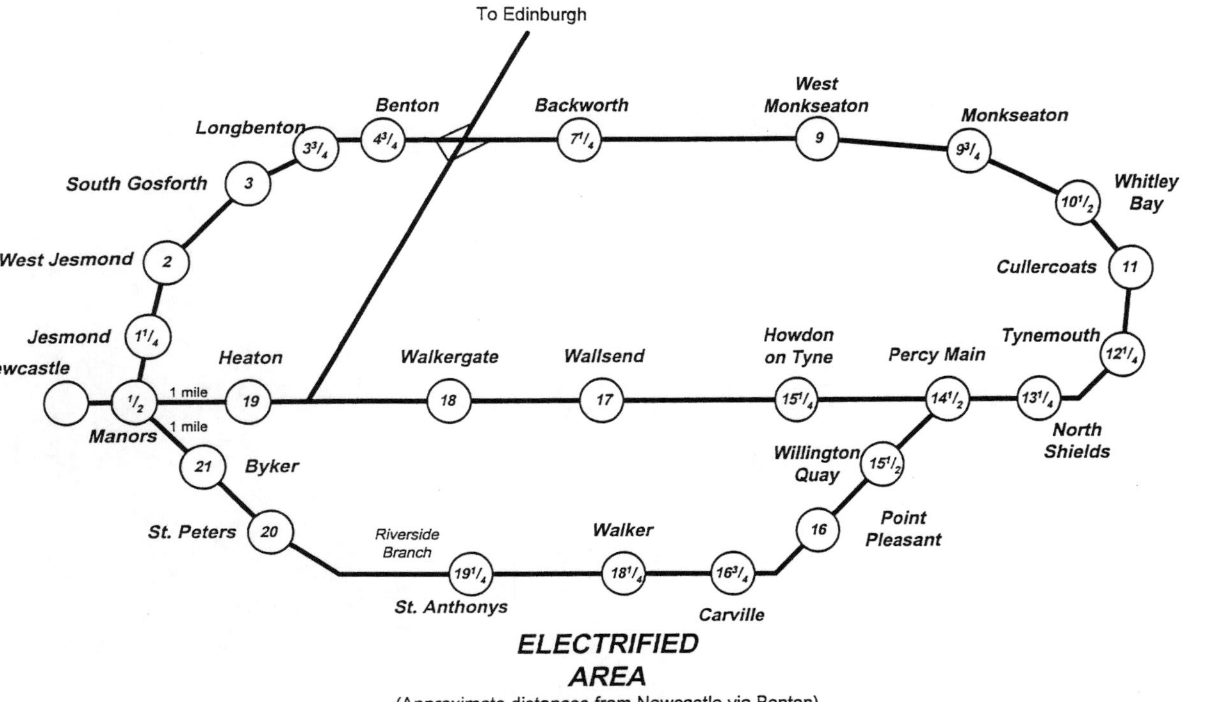
To Edinburgh
Longbenton
3 3/4
Benton
4 3/4
Backworth
7 1/4
West Monkseaton
9
Monkseaton
9 3/4
Whitley Bay
10 1/2
South Gosforth
3
West Jesmond
2
Cullercoats
11
Jesmond
1 1/4
Newcastle
Heaton
Walkergate
Wallsend
Howdon on Tyne
Percy Main
Tynemouth
12 1/4
1/2
1 mile
19
18
17
15 1/4
14 1/2
13 1/4
1 mile
Manors
North Shields
21
Byker
Willington Quay
15 1/2
St. Peters
20
Riverside Branch
Walker
16
Point Pleasant
19 1/4
18 1/4
16 3/4
St. Anthonys
Carville
ELECTRIFIED AREA
(Approximate distances from Newcastle via Benton)

THE KELSO BRANCH

Although the Stockton & Darlington Railway is recognised as the world's first public railway, an Act was passed in May 1811 authorising a public, horse-drawn railway from Spittal, near Berwick, to Kelso. It is noteworthy in that it contained the first clause in relation to the conveyance of passengers. The line was never built but a quarter of a century later, on 5 October 1836, a further effort was made to move the scheme forward – again without success as the money was not raised. Many people involved in the planning of early railways were promised financial support but, as they discovered, getting the actual cash was much more difficult!

Another thirteen years were to pass before a railway was opened between Tweedmouth and Sprouston (27 July 1849) by the York, Newcastle & Berwick Railway, a run of twenty miles. On 1st June 1851 an additional mile was brought into use between Sprouston and Mellandean Burn to form a junction with the North British Railway, thereby giving access to Kelso station after a short distance. Three years later all this became a North Eastern branch.

At Coldstream the goods yard was increased in size when the line from Alnwick through rural Northumberland reached there in 1887.

The refurbished station at Norham on the Kelso branch was converted into a private railway museum which portrays the character of a well kept country station but has other exhibits. (J A Wells)

A 50 ft. turntable built by Cowans Sheldon of Carlisle was installed behind the coal cells. In the early part of the 20th century there were facilities for handling general goods, carriages, machinery, coal and livestock. Sprouston, Norham and Velvet Hall were similar.

Norham despatched by passenger train churns of milk, cases of eggs, crates of Tweed salmon, open-topped boxes of wild rabbits hanging heads down, and some game birds. Baskets of luscious soft fruits were also sent to a London market from the Ladykirk and Milne-Graden Estates. At the appropriate time of the year loads of potatoes, sugar beet and sacks of grain were consigned to rail. Incoming traffic included household coal, lime, livestock, farm machinery and animal food. Two Clydesdale horses were kept there to haul rulleys, one for delivering coal, the other for general merchandise. According to local knowledge, the goods shed was originally an engine shed where a small tank engine was kept by the York, Newcastle & Berwick Railway for shunting the goods yards on the eastern part of the branch. The building was altered by having a large door put in the side so that carts could be loaded and unloaded. The warehouse at Norham was also used as a store for sacks which were hired to local farmers.

The Kelso branch was laid through a quiet, rural area in the valley of the river Tweed, having small populations. It was, nevertheless, an important diversionary route if the line between Edinburgh and Tweedmouth was blocked for some reason. Main line trains were then diverted via Galashiels, St. Boswells and Kelso before rejoining the main line at the south end of the Royal Border bridge, an extra fifteen miles.

In the 1920s an engine from Alnmouth shed worked a turn from Tweedmouth along the branch to Kelso but on the return trip it travelled via Alnwick. When the North British engine shed at Berwick was closed in 1924 the 21 engines based there were transferred to Tweedmouth. For some years the 4-4-0 tender engines there were those which had been displaced from fast main line duties and were ending their days at a sedate pace on country branches or on secondary expresses between Newcastle and Berwick. The most famous of these was number 1621 which had given a spirited performance in the Railway Races of 1895 when the class was the last word in east coast express engines. There was a small shed at Sprouston which was closed in 1916.

In August 1948 severe floods caused extensive damage to track, bridges and embankments north of Berwick so all main line trains had to be diverted via the Kelso branch until the line was restored.

With the exception of Tweedmouth, Norham and Coldstream which were closed to passengers in June 1964, stations on the branch were closed on 4 July 1955. Twizell lost its goods traffic in 1962, Carham two years later, and the remainder, apart from Tweedmouth, in 1965.

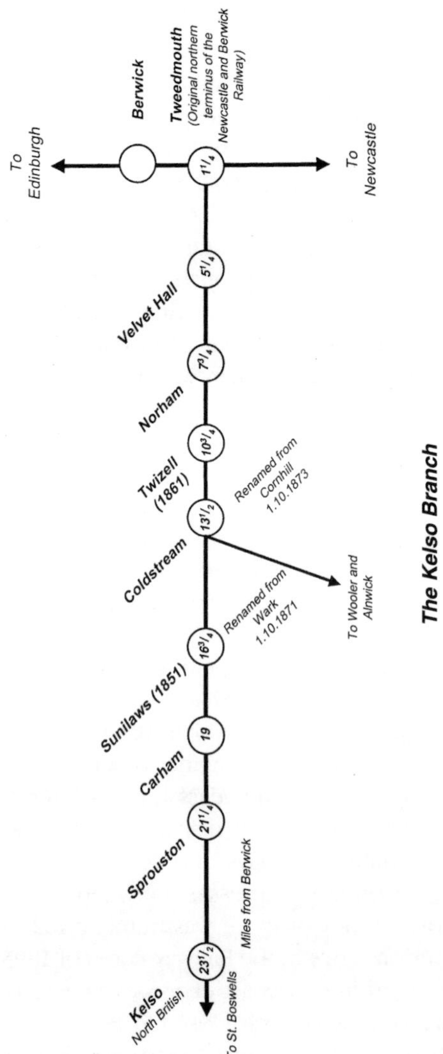

The Kelso Branch

BERWICK and KELSO.

Weekdays.

Distance from Berwick.	DOWN.	1		2		3		4	7		8		9	
		D Cattle.		D Goods.		PASSENGER.		Light Engine.	D Goods.		PASSENGER.		B Goods.	
		M O		M O							M O		MOQ	
		arr.	dep.	arr.	dep.	arr.	dep.		arr.	dep.	arr.	dep.	arr.	dep.
M.C.		a.m.	a.m.	G a.m.	E a.m.	a.m.	a.m.	a.m.	G a.m.	F a.m.	E a.m.	H a.m.	a.m.	a.m.
....	**BERWICK**	—	—	—	—	—	6 15	—	—	—	—	—	—	—
1 12	Tweedmouth	—	4 50	—	6 45	6 19	6 25	—	—	7 0	—	8 0	—	8 10
5 22	Velvet Hall	5 1	5 6	....	A	....	6 33	—	....	A	....	8 8	....	A
7 65	Norham	5 13	5 18	..	A	..	6 39	—	..	A	..	8 14	..	A
10 55	Twizell	5 26	5 31	....	A	....	6 45	—	....	A	....	8 20	....	..
13 48	Coldstream	5 41	5 51	6 15	6 35	6 52	6 53	—	7 40	8 5	8 29	8 30	8 41	—
16 53	Sunilaws	—	—	....	....	—	—	—	....	....	—	—	—	—
18 74	Carham	—	—	..	..	—	—	—	..	..	—	—	—	—
21 18	Sprouston	—	—	....	....	—	—	7 25	....	....	—	—	—	—
23 40	**Kelso**	—	—	6 55	—	—	—	7 30	8 25	—	—	—	—	—
	Arrives at destination	Morpeth 10.34 a.m. p. 29				Alnwick 8.22 a.m. p. 29					Wooler 9.0 a.m. p. 29			

DOWN.	10		11		12	13		14		15		16
	PASSENGER.		PASSENGER.			B Cattle Empties.		D Goods.		PASSENGER.		Engine and Van.
						MOQ						MO
	arr.	dep.	arr.	dep.		arr.	dep.	arr.	dep.	arr.	dep.	
	a.m.	a.m.	a.m.	a.m.		a.m.	E a.m.	p.m.	B a.m.	p.m.	p.m.	p.m.
BERWICK	—	8 35	—	9 50		—	—	—	—	—	12 10	—
Tweedmouth	8 39	8 45	9 54	10 0		—	10 40	—	11 50	12 14	12 20	12 30
Velvet Hall	....	8 53	....	10 8		....	....	12 4	12 14	....	12 28	....
Norham	..	8 59	..	10 14		..	..	12*23	12 40	..	12 34	..
Twizell	....	9 5	....	10 20		....	....	12 49	1 0	....	12 40	....
Coldstream	..	9 13	..	10 28		11 10	11 20	1 9	1 40	..	12 48	12 53
Sunilaws	....	9 20	....	10 35		—	—	1 57	2 10	....	12 54	....
Carham	..	9 25	..	10 40		—	—	2 18	2 23	..	1 0	..
Sprouston	....	9 30	.	10 45		—	—	2 30	2 37	....	1 5	....
Kelso	9 35	—	10 50	—		—	—	2 45	—	1 10	—	1 10
Arrives at destination						Wooler 12.0 noon p. 29						

DOWN.	18		19	20		21		22		23		24	Sundays. 1		Sundays. 2	
	PASSENGER.			PASSENGER.		PASSENGER.		PASSENGER.		PASSENGER.			PASSENGER.		PASSENGER.	
						S O										
	arr.	dep.		arr.	dep.	arr.	dep.	arr.	dep.	arr.	dep.		arr.	dep.	arr.	dep.
	p.m.	E p.m.		p.m.	H p.m.	p.m.	p.m.	p.m.	p.m.	p.m.	p.m.		a.m.	a.m.	p.m.	p.m.
BERWICK	—	2 10		—	2 45	—	2 55	—	5 40	—	8 30		—	8 15	—	6 0
Tweedmouth	2 14	2 20		2 49	2 53	2 59	3 5	5 44	5 52	8 34	8 38		8 19	8 33	6 4	6 8
Velvet Hall	....	2 28		....	3 1	....	3 13	....	6 0	....	8 46		....	8 41	....	6 16
Norham	..	2 34		..	3 7	..	3 19	..	6 6	..	8 52		..	8 47	..	6 22
Twizell	....	2 39		....	3 13	....	3 25	....	6 12	....	8 57		....	8 52	....	6 27
Coldstream	..	2 47		3 22	3 23	..	3 33	6 19	6 22	..	9 5		..	9 0	..	6 35
Sunilaws	....	2 52		—	—	....	3 39	....	6 28	....	9 10		....	9 5	....	6 40
Carham	..	2 58		—	—	..	3 45	..	6 34	..	9 16		..	9 11	..	6 46
Sprouston	....	3 2		—	—	....	3 50	....	6 39	....	9 20		....	9 15	....	6 50
Kelso	3 7	—		—	—	3 55	—	6 44	—	9 25	—		9 20	—	6 55	—
Arrives at destination				Alnwick 4.49 p.m. p. 29												

E—Runs on alternate Mondays, 13th and 27th July, 10th and 24th August, and 7th and 21st September. F—Will not run on alternate Mondays, 13th and 27th July, 10th and 24th August, and 7th and 21st September; leaves at Coldstream the Wooler Branch traffic for subsequent trip at 10.5 a.m. G—Runs as A Goods from Coldstream.

B—West Ord Siding 11.57—12.0. Learmouth Siding, 1.46—1.52.
E—Horse boxes and carriage trucks are not conveyed except from the South.

Extract from Working Timetable 1914

NOTES: *A, B and D refer to classifications of goods trains, particularly for braking power and speed.*

MO = Monday only *SO = Saturday only*

Q = Runs if required

THE MORPETH BRANCH (Later known as the Wansbeck Branch and locally as the Wannie Line)

The North British Railway continued to provide basic passenger and goods services along the Wansbeck section of its system. Workers at various industrial sites used the line to get to and from their jobs in mining, quarrying and at ore workings. Some people travelled to markets, to visit relatives, or to spend a few days away not far from home.

A branch approximately a mile long was laid from north of Reedsmouth along the Broomhope valley where Sir W G Armstrong had reintroduced the production of iron ore and lime in 1864. The iron was calcined at source and the major part of both commodities was sent by rail to the Armstrong works at Elswick, Newcastle. These workings closed after fifteen years and the area was then used for testing heavy guns for the army and navy. These were carried on multi-wheeled gunsets specially constructed by the NER and the LNER. Woodburn and Knowesgate continued to handle military stores and equipment until 1966.

The system of using the Blyth & Tyne station at Morpeth meant that trains from Scotsgap had to run past Barmoor junction and reverse into the station. Before the return trip the engine had to run round its train and push out beyond the junction before starting its journey. On one occasion in September 1871 the carriages for the 1.30 pm train to Scotsgap were in the bay platform coupled to three cattle trucks. The engine and another wagon of cattle were then placed on the end of the train, which from the buffer stops consisted of the locomotive, tender, two loaded and two empty cattle wagons, five coaches and a brake van. The driver reversed out of the station but when the brake was applied all the vehicles apart from the wagon next to the engine ran ahead and collided with a goods train waiting to follow along the branch. Six people were injured. An Enquiry blamed the guard for failing to couple the third and fourth wagons at the platform. Probably because of

J 25 0-6-0 65727 on the Morpeth to Rothbury goods at Scotsgap in August 1958. The string of cattle wagons awaits animals from the auction mart. (Ian S Carr)

this incident, a planned connection into the NER station was expedited. The Down side was made into an island platform with run round facilities and connections with the main line.

The Wansbeck became an LNER branch in 1923, again with limited regular services supplemented by excursion traffic. Passenger services ended on 13 September 1952, less than five years after nationalisation.

By the early 1950s a lot of goods had been transferred to road haulage though military traffic and livestock continued. Ten years later goods trains were down to one a week which conveyed coal to country merchants and stores for the army camps around Otterburn. The last such run was on 29 September 1966.

Gosforth Round Table arranged with BR to run a special diesel multiple unit train, The Bellingham Belle as far as Woodburn, from where on 19 September 1964 the 350 passengers were conveyed by buses to Bellingham Show. The train was then used to take handicapped and needy children for a day out at Morpeth pending its return journey. The venture

Angerton station, shown here in the mid-1960s, was part of the Wansbeck Railway, later the North British. Passenger services were ended in September 1952. The former coach body had been modified into a store. (J Scott)

was such a success that it was repeated the following year with a full load of 418 passengers being taken to Woodburn. A third event, again to raise funds for underprivileged children, had to be cancelled owing to foot and mouth disease in that part of the county.

As a grand finale the same group organised the Wansbeck Piper on Sunday, 2 October 1966. This was an eleven coach train steam hauled by a pair of former LMS 2-6-0 engines running back to back between Morpeth and Woodburn. As this special – the last train – left Woodburn on the return trip numerous detonators exploded under the wheels as a lament was played on bagpipes. Passengers nearly fell out of carriage windows as they, together with hundreds of spectators, recorded the scene on film; then all that lingered were memories of the Wannie line which that day had passed into Northumberland's colourful history. It also marked the final curtain of the North British Railway in Northumberland.

MORPETH BRANCH — North British

Miles	Miles	Up — Week Days		mrn.	mrn.	aft.
		Reedsmouth	dep.	7·47	11·5	4·30
3¾		Woodburn		7·56	11·14	4·39
10¼		Knowesgate		8·11	11·29	4·54
	Miles	Rothbury	dep.	7·50	11·28	4·30
	2¼	Brinkburn		7·56	11·34	4·36
	6½	Fontburn		8·7	11·45	4·47
	7¾	Ewesley		8·11	11·50	4·53
	9¾	Longwitton		8·17	11·56	4·59
	13	Scotsgap	arr.	8·24	12·1	5·6
14		Scotsgap *		8·26	12·3	5·9
16		Middleton		8·31	12·8	5·15
17½		Angerton		8·35	12·13	5·20
19¾		Meldon		8·44	12·22	5·29
25		Morpeth	arr.	8·55	12·32	5·39

Miles	Miles	Down — Week Days		mrn.	aft.	aft.
		Morpeth	dep.	9·25	2·25	6·20 c
5¼		Meldon		9·38	2·38	6·33
7½		Angerton		9·44	2·44	6·39
9		Middleton		9·49	2·49	6·44
11		Scotsgap *		9·55	2·55	6·50
	Miles	Scotsgap	dep.	9·57	2·57	6·52
	14¼	Longwitton		10·6	3·6	7·1
	16¼	Ewesley		10·12	3·12	7·7
	17½	Fontburn		10·16	3·16	7·11
	21¾	Brinkburn		10·28	3·28	7·23
	24	Rothbury	arr.	10·35	3·35	7·30
14¾		Knowesgate		10·18	3·11	7·6
21¼		Woodburn		10·32	3·25	7·20
25		Reedsmouth	arr.	10·40	3·33	7·28

NOTES. c Waits till 7 aft. for N.E. connections
* Station for Cambo.

Extract from 1910 Timetable

THE NORTH WYLAM BRANCH

The North Wylam branch was originally the Scotswood, Newburn and Wylam Railway which was bought by the North Eastern Railway in 1883. The line was laid for much of its length on the course of the historic Wylam waggonway which passed alongside the cottage where George Stephenson was born. From Newcastle it curled through Elswick, Scotswood, Lemington, Newburn, Heddon-on-the-Wall and North Wylam before rejoining the Newcastle & Carlisle route at West Wylam Junction. North Wylam, however, was used as a terminus and was only 300 yards from the other Wylam station on the opposite side of the river Tyne.

The branch was given a good passenger service which offered a wide variety of connections from Newcastle. There were twelve trains each weekday from Central in the second half of 1914 with an additional one on Saturdays and two extras which ran as far as Newburn. Only one of the twelve was shown as an autocar. The journey time was 25 minutes. The 1921 timetable offered ten trains each way, the first departure from Newcastle being at 5.27 am and the last at 9.30 pm. The LNER's Working Timetable of 1935 revealed no less than 28 trains on weekdays from North Wylam, 30 on Saturdays and ten on Sundays. Of these ten were worked by rail-motors during the week and seven on Sundays. Services on this route were first operated with the engine at the front of the train in both directions, then by autocars, and rail motors (ie steam railcars) until replaced by push-and-pull trains. The LNER bought a 95 hp diesel railbus from Messrs Armstrong-Whitworth in the 1930s which spent most of its life working in the Newcastle district including the North Wylam line.

Taking the summer of 1954 as an example, there were fewer trains in the BR era. From Newcastle there were eleven during the week but only seven on Saturdays, plus one Saturdays only to North Wylam. The last departure was 6.10 pm. In the Up direction twelve trains were timetabled on weekdays but four of those did not run on Saturdays, although two others did on Saturdays only. There was no service on Sundays.

Apart from local goods yard facilities there were various sidings along this route for sand and gravel loading, rolling mills, water works, collieries, a steel works, brick yards and for copperas. Of the five goods trains along the branch or part of it, each weekday in 1914 one which ran 'as required' (a Q train) originated at West Hartlepool.

The station at Heddon-on-the-Wall was opened in 1881, five years after the branch was commissioned. In the early 1900s there were no facilities apart from three sidings serving private customers. In 1911 the number of tickets issued at the station was just over 14,000. Passenger services at Heddon, Newburn and Lemington were withdrawn on 15 September 1958, but North Wylam remained opened until March 1968.

This branch was very useful for diversions rather than an alternative through route though goods trains from Carlisle to the Forth were sometimes sent this way if there was congestion on the west line. It was used for all trains on the Newcastle – Carlisle main line from September 1966 while repairs were carried out to Scotswood bridge, then again following subsidence at Wylam.

Heddon-on-the-Wall lost its goods traffic in September 1958; Lemington in January 1960 but it was reopened for coal traffic from June 1963 for just over a year. Goods at Newburn was withdrawn in April 1965.

The line closed on 11 March 1968.

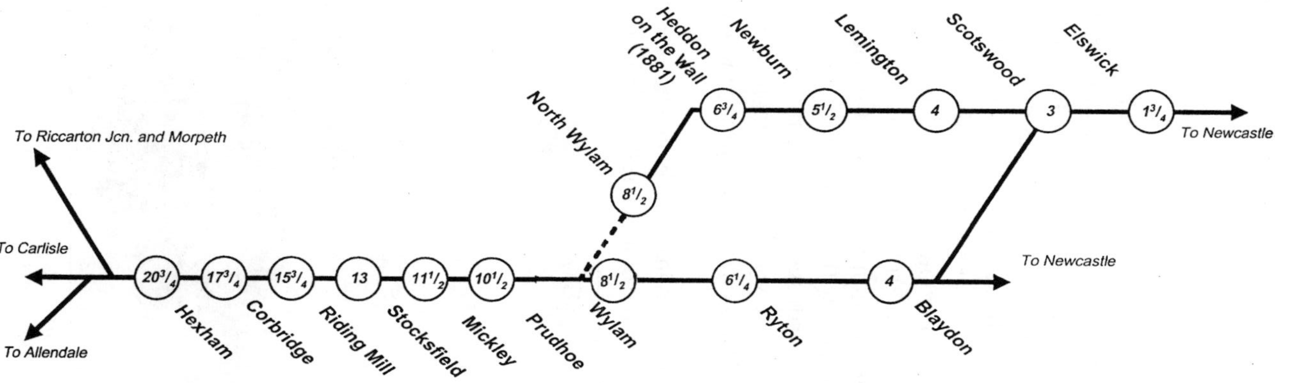

Newcastle to Hexham and North Wylam

THE PONTELAND BRANCH & DARRAS HALL

The NER was authorised to take a line from the former Blyth & Tyne station at Gosforth through West Gosforth, Coxlodge, Kenton and Callerton to Ponteland, so opening a route to more collieries and agricultural areas. Gosforth was renamed South Gosforth to avoid confusion. Part of the line was ready for goods and minerals in March 1905 and was opened throughout for all traffic on 1st June. It was intended to electrify this branch following the success of the new trains on the southern section of the Blyth & Tyne the previous year, but this was never done. A sub-station to provide electric power to the third rail was built at Fawdon though never equipped. Instead services were provided by autocars. A loop with a water column alongside was laid beyond South Gosforth station where the train could stand between each trip. The line was extended by just over a mile in September 1913 to Darras Hall, following encouraging revenues.

In 1914 there were eleven trains in each direction between South Gosforth and Ponteland, three of which reversed through to Darras

Ponteland station was opened in 1905 with autocars running to and from South Gosforth. Passenger services were withdrawn in 1929. (J Scott collection)

Hall. On Saturdays only, a traditional passenger train departed from Manors North for Ponteland at 2.10 pm and left for the return trip at 4.20 pm. There were four trains each way on a Sunday but none of these went along to Darras Hall. The service in September 1921 was very similar with nine trains Up and Down (plus one Saturdays only) and through running to and from Darras Hall for three of them.

Following the ravaging fire at Walkergate in 1918 a new depot for electric trains was opened at Gosforth in 1923. Trains from Benton and beyond had direct access via South Gosforth East junction. Those from Newcastle reversed into the spacious shed from West Gosforth. In later years servicing and maintenance was carried out on diesel multiple units and, from 1980, on Metro trains.

The competition from cars and buses caused the London & North Eastern Railway to re-assess the viability of passenger traffic with the result that the service was withdrawn in June 1929, long before the population explosion in the Ponteland area.

This branch was used for overnight stops of the Royal Train on several occasions, each one planned with military precision for several months beforehand. In October 1928 His Majesty King George V and Her Majesty Queen Mary were on board the train parked at Ponteland station. It consisted of two locomotives and eleven coaches which included sleeping cars, day saloons and the King's and Queen's private saloons. An accumulator van was attached to the rear of the train on arrival to provide power, heat came from steam from the engines, and protection of the rear of the train was given by a locomotive standing perhaps half a mile away. A rake of coaches placed alongside the Royal Special acted as a screen against inquisitive eyes. On that occasion the King and Queen were taken to Jesmond the following morning where they first opened a school before proceeding to officially open the new Tyne bridge. Another royal visit was in February 1939.

Later still, part of the Royal Train was stabled overnight on the Ponteland branch with HRH The Duke of Edinburgh on board following his journey from Aberdeen. It consisted of a power brake van, a saloon coach, the Royal saloon and a second brake van. The train departed for York on the morning of 27 September 1975 where the Duke officially opened the National Railway Museum.

After the withdrawal of passenger trains the branch continued to handle goods and minerals. The 1934-35 Working Timetable showed a goods train leaving Heaton Junction at 6 am on Saturdays only and another on weekdays at 11.25 am. There were only two *scheduled* mineral trains, between Percy Main and East Walbottle colliery. One of these did not run on Saturdays and the other only ran if required. This is not to say these were the only coal trains on the branch as supply and demand were very flexible in the coalfields with empty wagons being sent to collieries as they were needed and full train loads of coal taken wherever necessary. For this reason most coal-leading engines ran to 'Control's Orders' which varied from day to day.

The Rowntree factory at Coxlodge and the ICI explosives plant at Callerton provided some traffic for British Rail until 1987 and 1989 respectively. A special agreement with Tyne & Wear Metro permitted short freight trains to travel between Gosforth and the south west curve at Benton where they joined the main line.

Use was made of the Ponteland branch to extend the Metro to Newcastle airport.

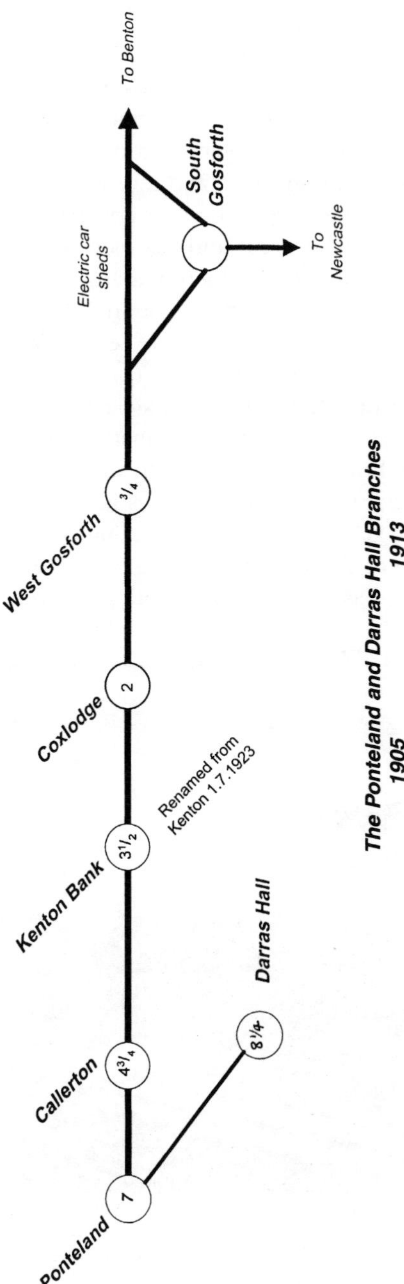

The Ponteland and Darras Hall Branches
1905 1913

THE ROTHBURY BRANCH

The North British Railway, which had acquired the Northumberland Central Railway at a knock-down price, lost no time in running trains from Morpeth to Rothbury with connections at Scotsgap for Reedsmouth, rather than the other way round. The station at Rothley was opened to the public in 1873 and renamed Longwitton.

As a general rule there were three or four passenger trains a day in each direction. In the 1920s and 30s there was a through coach from Rothbury to Newcastle which was attached to a connecting train at Morpeth and with a return working in the afternoon. This was discontinued at the outbreak of the Second World War and the service on the branch was reduced to two each way shortly afterwards. Rothbury attracted well filled special trains for people going to the races. It was also a popular destination for people wanting a few hours in the bracing countryside. In winter months excursions were run from the town to pantomimes in Newcastle. Sometimes passengers were also conveyed from Bellingham and Reedsmouth to Scotsgap where the two trains were combined. On the return journey the train was split there and both parts went their separate ways.

This was the scene at Rothbury on 13 February 1897 when an excursion train returning from Newcastle was derailed as it was about to enter the station. The cause was excessive speed through facing points but staff were criticised for "a careless, happy-go-lucky style of working". (A E Ford collection)

30 I.

MORPETH and ROTHBURY (N.B.)—Weekdays.

Distance from Morpeth.	DOWN.	1		2	3		4		5		6		7		8		9	10
		N.B. PASSENGER.			N.B. Goods.		N.B. PASSENGER.		B Cattle Empties.		N.B. Goods.		N.B. Goods.		N.B. PASSENGER.			
									MO		T		TO					
		arr.	dep.		arr.	dep.	arr.	dep.	arr.	dep.	arr.	dep.	arr.	dep.	arr.	dep.		
			B			G		E		K	J			F				
M. C.		a.m.	a.m.		p.m.	p.m.	p.m.	p.m.	p.m.	p.m.	p.m.	p.m.	p.m.	p.m.	p.m.	p.m.		
.....	**Morpeth** ....⊕	—	9 30		—	12 45	—	2 25	*2 25*	*2 40*	—	3 45	—	*5 45*	—	6 20		
5 31	Meldon .. .. .. ⊕	..	9 43		..	1 57	..	2 38	..	*3 5*	..	4 13	..	..	..	6 33		
7 53	Angerton..............	.....	9 49		.....	2 10	....	2 44	.....	*3 20*	.....	4 28	....	.....	....	6 39		
9 13	Middleton	..	9 54		..	2 20	..	2 49	..	..	..	4 38	..	..	..	6 44		
11 11	*Scotsgap Junction* ..⊕	10 0	10 2		2 30	3 14	2 55	2 57	*3 35*	—	4 48	5 15	*6 25*	*7 22*	6 50	6 52		
24 15	**Rothbury**.. .. ⊕	10 35	—		4 20	—	3 35	—	—	—	—	—	—	—	7 30	—		

B—Conveys live stock occasionally from Morpeth to Rothbury or elsewhere.

E—On Mondays conveys live stock from Morpeth to Woodburn.

F—Runs also on alternate Mondays, 13th and 27th July, 10th and 24th August, and 7th and 21st September.

G—Takes wagon for collection of spare sheets between Morpeth and Scotsgap Junction on Tuesdays and Thursdays. Calls at Middleton only to work road van goods.

J—Does not run on alternate Mondays, 13th and 27th July, 10th and 24th August, and 7th and 21st September. Calls at Middleton only to work road van goods.

K—Heaton Junction dep. 1.40 p.m., p. 8. Commences 13th July.

Distance from Rothbury.	UP.	1		2		3		4		5		6	7		8		9		10	
		N.B. PASSENGER.		N.B. PASSENGER.		N.B. PASSENGER.		N.B. Goods.		N.B. PASSENGER.			N.B. Goods.		N.B. Goods.		N.B. PASSENGER.		B Cattle.	
		MO		M		MO							T		TO				MO	
		arr.	dep.	arr.	dep.	arr.	dep.	arr.	dep.	arr.	dep.		arr.	dep.	arr.	dep.	arr.	dep.	arr.	dep.
														B		E				F
M. C.		a.m.	a.m.	a.m.	a.m.	a.m.	a.m.	a.m.	a.m.	p.m.	a.m.		p.m.	p.m.	p.m.	p.m.	p.m.	p.m.	p.m.	p.m.
.....	**Rothbury** ....⊕	—	*7 30*	—	*7 50*	—	—	—	8 10	—	11 28		—	—	—	—	—	4 30	—	—
13 4	*Scotsgap Junction* ⊕	*8 2*	*8 3*	*8 22*	*8 24*	..	*8 22*	9 15	10 0	12 1	12 3		—	1 20	—	*3 0*	5 6	5 9	—	*5 30*
15 2	Middleton	...	*8 8*	.....	*8 28*	.....	*8 27*	.....	10 15	.....	12 8		..	1 30	...	*3 10*	.....	5 15	.....	*5 45*
16 42	Angerton	..	*8 12*	..	*8 32*	..	*8 31*	..	10 35	..	12 13		..	1 40	..	*3 25*	..	5 20	..	*6 5*
18 64	Meldon ....⊕	.....	*8 20*	.....	*8 38*	.....	*8 39*	.....	11 5	.....	12 22		.....	2 6	.....	*3 45*	.....	5 29	.....	*6 35*
24 15	**Morpeth** .. .. ⊕	*8 30*	—	*8 48*	—	*8 50*	—	11 20	—	12 32	—		2 21	—	*4 0*	—	5 39	—	*6 50*	*7 20*

When required, the engine, guard, and van of the Reedsmouth passenger train will make a special goods trip from Scotsgap Junction to Morpeth after arrival at Scotsgap Junction at 11.38 a.m.

A special live stock train will leave Carlisle for Morpeth when required at any suitable hour from about 10.0 a.m., but not later than about 8.0 p.m., working general traffic on return.

B—Does not run on alternate Mondays, 13th and 27th July, 10th and 24th August, and 7th and 21st September.

E—Runs also on alternate Mondays, 13th and 27th July, 10th and 24th August, and 7th and 21st September.

F—Forth arr. 8.10 p.m., p. 19. Commences 13th July.

Rothbury Branch: Working Timetable 1914

Table 71 MORPETH, SCOTSGAP and REEDSMOUTH and ROTHBURY

Miles		WEEKDAYS				
		am	am	pm	pm	
	3 Newcastle............ dep	9 28	....	5 6	....	....
—	**MORPETH** .. .. dep	10 10	..	5 50	..	..
5¼	Meldon .... ,,	10 22	....	6 3	....	....
7¾	Angerton .. .. .. ,,	10 29	..	6 9	..	..
9¼	Middleton North........ ,,	10 34	....	6 14	....	....
11¼	**Scotsgap** (for Cambo) .. arr	10 40	..	6 20	..	..
—	**Scotsgap** (for Cambo) dep	....	10 46	....	6 27	....
14¾	Knowesgate .. .. ,,	..	10 55	..	6 38	..
21¼	Woodburn............ ,,	....	11 8	....	6 52	....
25½	**Reedsmouth** .. .. arr	..	11 15	..	7 0	..
—	**Scotsgap** (for Cambo) .. dep	10 43	....	6 22	....	....
14¼	Longwitton .. .. ,,	10 52	..	6 31	..	..
16¼	Ewesley,.............. ,,	10 57	....	6 38	....	....
17¼	Fontburn Halt .. .. ,,	11 2	..	6 43	..	..
22	Brinkburn Halt .... ,,	11 12	....	6A52	....	....
24¼	**ROTHBURY** .. .. arr	11 18	..	6 58	..	..

Miles		WEEKDAYS				
		am	am	pm	pm	
—	**ROTHBURY** .. .. dep	..	7 51	Bellingham (dep 4.5 pm)	4 30	..
2¼	Brinkburn Halt .... ,,	....	7 56		4 35	....
6¼	Fontburn Halt .. .. ,,	..	8 7		4 46	..
7¾	Ewesley................ ,,	....	8 10		4 49	....
9¾	Longwitton .. .. ,,	..	8 16		4 55	..
13	**Scotsgap** (for Cambo) .. arr	....	8 22		5 1	....
—	**Reedsmouth** .. .. dep	7 44	..	4 15	..	..
3¾	Woodburn............ ,,	7 54	....	4 24	....	....
10½	Knowesgate .. .. ,,	8 9	..	4 39	..	..
14	**Scotsgap** (for Cambo) arr	8 18	....	4 48	....	....
—	**Scotsgap** (for Cambo) .. dep	..	8 25	..	5 2	..
15	Middleton North........ ,,	....	8 29	....	5 6	....
16¼	Angerton .. .. .. ,,	..	8 34	..	5 10	..
18¾	Meldon .... ,,	....	8 40	....	5 15	....
24¼	**MORPETH** .. .. arr	..	8 51	..	5 25	..
40¾	3 Newcastle............ arr	....	9 29	....	6 12	....

A—Calls to set down only.

Passenger Timetable 1952

1877 was a year of unprecedented rainfall, said to be the worst of the century. Hay was still in the fields in September and the harvest had been poor. Nevertheless it was business as usual in the livestock marts situated adjacent to the stations at Morpeth, Scotsgap and Rothbury. At the latter sales of lambs (over 3,000 at one auction), ewes, store cattle, young horses and various breeds of sheep were widely advertised. There were special sales, too, for Cheviot and Blackface sheep only. All this demanded a constant supply of cattle trucks that had to be cleaned and disinfected after each load. Most of these were fitted with brakes which could be operated from the engine. It meant they could travel on passenger trains or by express goods. Stringent rules for the care of animals in transit indicated they had to be given water every four hours. Full train loads of cattle were a feature of this branch.

The Rothbury line served a number of small, transient industries relating mainly to quarrying and mining in earlier days. They provided some traffic in coal, lime, fireclay, stone, ganister, whinstone and timber. In 1901 work started on Fontburn reservoir for which construction materials were taken to a special siding used by the contractors. In the early 1940s soldiers sent for training in the hills and woods around Rothbury had their supplies taken in by rail.

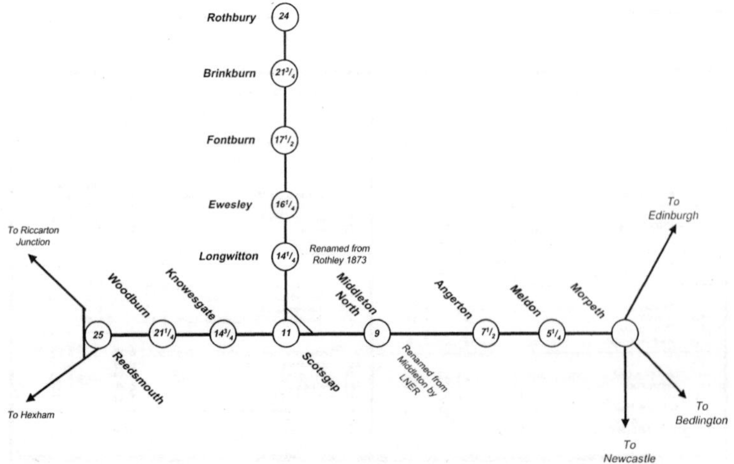

The Rothbury and Reedsmouth Branches

The North British used mainly Drummond's class R 4-4-0 tank engines for passenger working, a distinctive feature of which was the very small, spokeless wheels of the leading bogie. One was named *Morpeth* and another *Rothbury*. Goods traffic was handled by Holme's 0-6-0s. These became D51 and J36 under LNER classification but were gradually replaced by ex-NER locomotives. In the LNER and British Railways eras the usual motive power was a G5 0-4-4 tank and a J21 0-6-0 based at Rothbury.

The sheds at Rothbury and Reedsmouth were closed on 13 September 1952, the same day that passenger services were withdrawn. Goods traffic thereafter was handled by South Blyth engines culminating in J27s until they were replaced in the final days by former LMS Ivatt 2MT 2-6-0s. The last train ran on 9 November 1963 and the demolition gangs moved in shortly afterwards.

THE TYNE & WEAR METRO

Newcastle Central was one of the largest and most important stations outside London handling many thousands of passengers each day. In 1959, for example, the East-end booking office alone issued 1,973,355 ordinary tickets most of which were for electric trains. All this reflected a lively commercial centre surrounded by a progressive area of heavy industry notably mining, engineering and shipbuilding. This in itself brought problems of congestion in the city.

In the 1960s the A1 trunk road between north and south still passed right through Newcastle, Gateshead, and their suburbs, with over ten miles of continuous built-up areas. Thousands of people travelling to work by bus or car were frequently delayed by the sheer volume of crawling traffic. Clearly a bold initiative was needed to solve a growing problem. After a great deal of planning and discussion the Tyne & Wear Plan was evolved, proposing "significant investment in a public transport system with its own right of way based on the current railway with renewal and upgrading of lines and stations and improvements in central area accessibility." This was adopted by the newly-formed Tyneside Passenger Transport Authority and supported by the Tyne & Wear Council which emerged after boundary changes in 1974. Certain routes belonging to

British Rail would be taken over and those lines would be extended underground to serve new stations at more central points in the city. Interchange stations would enable passengers to transfer from buses to rail for easier access to Newcastle and motorists would be encouraged to park their cars at a convenient Metro station in the suburbs in order to travel in or out by train. In this way a great deal of congestion and pollution would be eliminated. The Tyneside Metropolitan Railway Act was passed in 1973 and major construction started the following year.

New, modern underground stations were built to serve Newcastle at the Central station, Monument, Haymarket, Manors and St. James – much more convenient for people than the original Central station and Manors which were on the fringe of the city.

On the former Blyth & Tyne route, Backworth station was closed in June 1977, followed in January by Jesmond, West Jesmond, South Gosforth, Longbenton and Benton when buses replaced the diesel trains. These stations were modified in different ways. At Jesmond a new station was built behind the existing one, just inside the tunnel where the line plunged underground. West Jesmond, which had lost its awnings some years before, was tidied up but did not need much alteration. A new, simple station with open fronted shelters was created at Ilford Road on the site of the former Blyth & Tyne station, Moor Edge. Buildings at South Gosforth were demolished to make way for a new centre which would control the whole system. Longbenton, opened in 1947 for the then Ministry of National Insurance, was provided with an extra footbridge to make it easier for people with pushchairs, or in wheelchairs, to cross the line. Four Lane Ends was one of the new interchange stations with the bus area above and a generous car park alongside. This, too, was built on the site of a former B & T station, Long Benton which was closed in 1871. At Benton the former wooden booking office on the Up platform was replaced by a covered area housing ticket machines and, in the early days, entry/exit turnstiles. The triple junction was simplified and the former north west curve was made into two sidings for trains terminating there. 'Up' and 'Down' lines were renamed *In* and *Out* under the new regime, a sensible idea when we consider that by tradition the Up line ran towards London.

As it was essential that a connection was maintained between the main line at Benton Quarry and the Blyth & Tyne route using the original south east curve, a single track was laid alongside the former BR line as far as Backworth where it curved off to pass through Seghill, Seaton Delaval, Hartley, Newsham, Bebside and Bedlington to Ashington and Morpeth. East of Benton station the old line was slewed and carried over the BR track on a flyover ready for use by the Metro.

Whereas the Tyneside electric trains had used an outside third rail, the latest development would be powered from overhead wires supplying current at 1500 volts DC. This meant that bridges had to be raised and parapets heightened for safety reasons. The whole network also had to be resignalled. Put like this it all sounds so incredibly simple but a great deal of planning, co-ordination and hard work was necessary to achieve what proved to be a very successful rapid transport system!

The station at Backworth was replaced by Shiremoor further along the line nearer to houses. West Monkseaton, Monkseaton, Whitley Bay and Cullercoats were closed in September 1979 so that work could commence on them but bay platforms at the southern end of Tynemouth remained open for BR diesel units travelling to and from Newcastle via Wallsend: closure of that section followed in August 1980, prior to the extension of the route to St. James.

At Monkseaton a standard Metro shelter was erected on the old Up platform but the covered footbridge and main station buildings were retained. The covered portions over the platforms at Whitley Bay were shortened and footbridges were renewed; similarly at Cullercoats where awnings were reduced in length. It was originally intended to demolish Tynemouth station and build a typical Metro stop instead, but public opinion forced a rethink so that the imposing 1882 station was saved.

While all this was going on a test track was introduced on the former Blyth & Tyne route to Percy Main. The prototype units were delivered to Middle Engine Lane from Metro Cammell in 1975 (numbers 4001/2) and subjected to proving trials before being used for driver training.

The splendid North Eastern Railway station at Tynemouth, with its attractive twin footbridge, was opened in 1882. It was renovated after becoming a Tyne & Wear Metro station in 1980. (J A Wells)

The initial section of Tyneside's Metro between Haymarket and Tynemouth via Benton was opened to the public on 11 August 1980, the first of its kind in the country. The coaches are lightweight sets of twin articulated cars, usually two together forming the equivalent of four vehicles. Each pair has four wide, passenger doors on each side which are opened by pressing a button but are closed

TYNE & WEAR METRO

4 weeks to 25 May 1996

Scheduled Trains Run:		
Passengers' Charter Target		98%
	Achievement	99.4%
Trains within 2 minutes of timetable:		
	Target	95%
	Achievement	97.87%

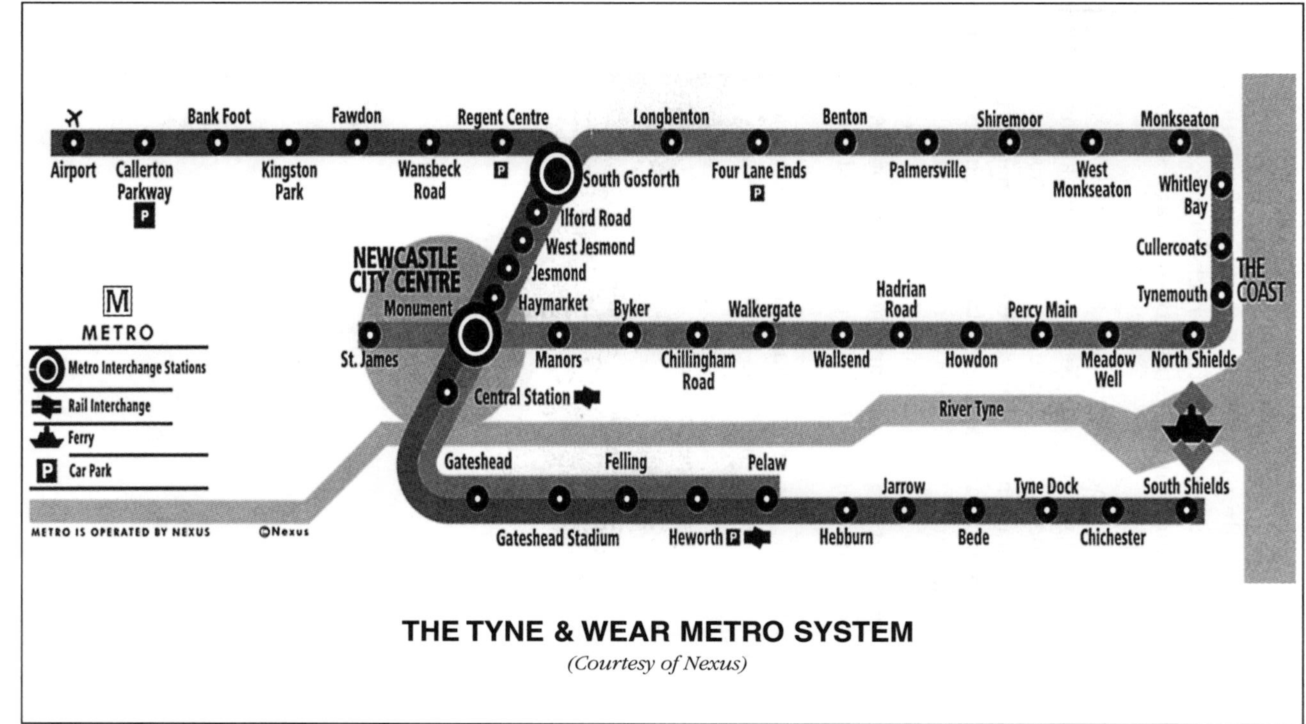

THE TYNE & WEAR METRO SYSTEM

(Courtesy of Nexus)

by the driver after a warning horn has been sounded. Each train has an identification number and when the driver activates a Ready to Start button, the information is fed into a route-setting computer which changes the points, clears signals and alters destination indicators at those stations with them.

The Metro was opened in stages and has been considerably extended. It now runs to Newcastle International airport (1991) using the former Ponteland branch. Just over a year after its inauguration the Tyne & Wear Metro made a presentation to its 10-millionth passenger. In the year ended 31 March 1996 the number of passengers carried was 35,800,000, a wonderful tribute to its success. Ironically, following the deregulation of buses, it is now just another means of transport for people going into and out of Newcastle – albeit an excellent one!

Nexus is now the professional organisation which carries out the policies of the Tyne & Wear Passenger Transport Authority.

Part 3

THE SCENE IN 1998:

The past in the present
Towards Privatisation

THE PAST IN THE PRESENT

A county so rich in railway history inevitably carries its past achievements into the present. In spite of the decimation of the railway system there is much around Northumberland to remind us of bygone days though what follows is merely a hint of what can be seen.

Of the stations still in use, Newcastle Central has been drastically altered – but how many people about to leave the building notice the stone medallions above the main exit? These celebrate the opening of the High Level bridge by Queen Victoria and Prince Albert in 1849, not the station itself. The centre one, which replaced a clock, is most probably that of King Edward VII following the opening of the second railway bridge over the Tyne, named after him, in 1906. The massive doors beside the taxi rank are perhaps the originals, bumped by generations of barrows. The former refreshment room (no longer in public use) had a very decorative ceiling, pillars and wall tiles from the Victorian era. Outside the entrance to the Royal Station Hotel the letters NER stand out in the ornate iron work of the canopy. Nearby, in a small alcove, the head of the mythical Roman god Mercury, high up on the stonework, is seldom observed; nor are the two of Jupiter? on the front of the station building east and west of the portico.

At Morpeth in 1997, apart from items previously mentioned, were six condemned goods vans used for permanent way material and storage, namely two former BR ferry vans, two covered car transporters and two 10-ton covered vans. These were advertised for sale in 1998. At the side of the curve to the south of the station, and on the A192 road at Stobhill near the top of the station bank, are the remains of two bridges which carried the Wansbeck Railway to connect with the Blyth & Tyne branch before North British trains began using the NER station in 1872.

A notice in Berwick station states:-

THIS STATION STANDS ON THE SITE OF THE GREAT HALL OF BERWICK CASTLE. HERE ON THE 17th NOVEMBER 1292 THE CLAIM OF ROBERT BRUCE TO THE CROWN OF SCOTLAND WAS DECLINED AND THE DECISION IN FAVOUR OF JOHN BALIOL WAS GIVEN BY KING EDWARD I BEFORE THE FULL PARLIAMENT OF ENGLAND AND A LARGE GATHERING OF THE NOBILITY AND POPULACE OF BOTH ENGLAND AND SCOTLAND. On the Up platform are the remains of an LNER drinking water point where passengers were urged to keep the platform dry. Outside, the damaged initials 'LNER' can be seen in the metal supports of the canopy.

Tynemouth station has been carefully restored, a particular feature being the twin footbridges across what used to be four tracks between the platforms. The roof and its supporting ironwork, together with the NER tile map, all reflect the importance of this station many years ago. This building houses a flea market each weekend, just metres away from Metro trains.

At Benton the waiting shelters from 1871 continue in use and the fancy finials on top of the one on the former Down platform still add a touch of individuality. The North Eastern footbridge at South Gosforth serves its original purpose, now for the benefit of Metro passengers.

On the west line there are for example the Newcastle & Carlisle Railway station and house at Wylam, Prosser's canopy at Hexham and the station buildings, house and water tank at Haltwhistle.

Various stations have been demolished but others have become industrial estates (Ponteland and Rothbury), or housing estates (Coldstream), whereas the station area and goods yard at Blyth were eventually covered by a supermarket and a hospital. Allendale

The former station at Ilderton on the Coldstream branch was completely refurbished and opened as a restaurant in a very nostalgic railway atmosphere. (J A Wells)

is a caravan park but the platform remains, and the circular edge of the filled-in turntable pit is still recognisable. Ashington, North Wylam and Seahouses are three which were turned into car parks. Hepscott, Scotsgap, Wall, Warkworth and Wooler are among those converted into very attractive houses. The original station at Jesmond was transformed into a restaurant with additional accommodation provided by a former Great Northern Railway coach and a mock signal box. Ilderton, too, has been professionally restored and made into a restaurant using the former waiting room. Authentic notices, photographs, timetables and an NER fireplace all add to the atmosphere. Outside is a bogie passenger brake van adapted as a camping coach, and a car carrying vehicle used as a store.

By contrast, the twin train shed at Alnwick now accommodates a huge second-hand book shop and a carpet warehouse. They have there the original iron railings, snake seats and lamps. Incidentally, Darras Hall was used for church services for a time. Langley booking office is the local Post Office and uses the ticket window as the counter. The building has changed little since it was a station. Barrasford found a new lease of life for scouting activities, and Bellingham now serves as a County Council Highways Department office.

Former station masters' houses at Akeld, Angerton, Bellingham, Hartley, Humshaugh, Lambley, Stannington, Tarset and Whittingham are a selection of those that are now privately owned.

The Newcastle & Berwick Railway goods shed at Acklington was rebuilt into "a most luxurious detached property" and linked to the original stables. The shed at Wooler offers ample space as a storage area and the one at Scotsgap is used with other buildings for agricultural purposes associated with the mart.

The signal boxes at Wylam and Hexham are good examples of the North Eastern Railway's gantry type. Most 'boxes were demolished when they were no longer needed though a few like Roseden and Reedsmouth are now holiday cottages or homes.

Bridges and viaducts built for original railway companies continue in everyday use, notably the High Level and King Edward bridges at Newcastle; also Plessey, the Royal Border bridge at Berwick and several along the Tyne Valley. Those at Bedlington and North Seaton (1929/1927) replaced earlier structures. Others, no longer needed for rail traffic, such as Lambley and North Wylam, may form part of walkways. Lambley viaduct, designed by Sir George Barclay-Bruce, was in a serious condition in the early 1990s but was fully restored by 1996 and may one day carry another railway over the gap it spans.

Forlorn reminders of the past are those bridges – some partly demolished – which stand unused but whose retaining walls may still serve a useful purpose, as at Seaton Sluice on the proposed line which led to Collywell Bay station. At Chollerton the old skew bridge still spans the A6079. An 1864 overbridge crossing the A189 road at South Gosforth East was the scene of an accident in December 1923 when the locomotive of a coal train pulled away from a signal at danger and collided with an empty electric train crossing its path. The engine and tender fell into the road below. This explains why one side of the bridge is original Blyth & Tyne but the other is not.

Former track beds, embankments and cuttings are still very much in evidence and are indicated on current Ordnance Survey maps. Some of these, together with old colliery waggonways, are now country walks for part of their length, notably those from Kielder and Scotsgap. Part of the original Plessey waggonway which was in use in 1723 can be seen from the A192 overlooking Bog Houses (reference NZ276791) and not far away, near the Three Horse Shoes inn, the familiar double line of hawthorn – only a short length now – indicates the general direction taken to the river Blyth (ref. NZ279792). Between Halton Lea Gate and Lambley on the

In 1852 a short branch was laid from Lambley to join the Midgeholme Railway. The track bed is still in evidence, together with a sheep bridge, in 1997. (J A Wells)

A689 three roads lead to Haltwhistle. A short distance along the middle one the old trackbed of the connecting line between Lambley and the Midgeholme Railway is still clearly visible together with a sheep bridge.

Coal drops still exist at Norham but those at Glanton were removed to Beamish Museum some years ago and rebuilt as part of their railway scene. At Staward two of the original coal cells have been roofed over and wooden fronts fitted to make substantial sheds. Remains of others can be found at Belford and Chathill.

Two of the cottages in which George Stephenson lived draw visitors from a wide area though opening times may be restricted. The famous sundial above the door at West Moor, near Killingworth, is yet another reminder of the great man's versatility. The cramped room at Wylam in which he was born and where the family lived is administered by the National Trust. A short distance away a small but fascinating museum showing the importance of Wylam as a centre of railway development is housed in the local library. It has an interesting collection of railwayana in addition to providing information on those railway pioneers, all of which is well displayed.

At Norham the present owners have carefully maintained the character of a well kept country station which is presented as a private railway museum. The booking office, waiting room, warehouse, signal box and goods shed have been retained together with items of railway interest.

The Stephenson Railway Museum in Middle Engine Lane near Shiremoor has larger exhibits two of which are a restored NER electric parcels van from 1904 and the cab from what was once a Blyth & Tyne 0-6-0 engine. The LNER A4 *Bittern,* masquerading as *Silver Link* stayed there for a period then was replaced by Deltic number 55002 *The King's Own Yorkshire Light Infantry* which remained for two years. From this museum a standard gauge single line runs along the old B & T trackbed to Percy Main and is used from time to time to carry passengers in steam hauled trains.

Woodhorn Colliery Museum, near Ashington, opened a short narrow-gauge, passenger carrying line in the spring of 1996 running from the museum to the Lakeside hotel. The locomotive, stock and track had been donated by British Coal and other sponsors.

Further afield from the county Beamish Museum and the Tanfield Railway are fascinating centres as is the Monkwearmouth Station Museum at Sunderland. Also well worth a visit are the Darlington Railway Museum and the National Railway Museum at York.

Members of the North Eastern Locomotive Preservation Group (NELPG) have made an excellent job of restoring and maintaining in working order a K1, J27, Q6, J72 0-6-0 tank engine and the A2 class 60532 *Blue Peter.* Their home base is the North Yorkshire Moors Railway.

Finally, although steam was officially withdrawn in 1968 what better reminder of our heritage than the road signs still in use which warn drivers of unprotected level crossings by depicting a 4-6-0 locomotive with a good head of steam!

PRIVATISATION: THE WAY AHEAD

In April 1994, following a total restructuring of British Rail and as a prelude to privatisation, ownership of some 2,500 railway stations together with control centres, signal boxes and 90 or so light maintenance depots came under the auspices of RAILTRACK. Infrastructure Services became responsible for the maintenance and renewal of the infrastructure and track. Passenger services were provided by 25 Train Operating Companies one of which was Intercity East Coast, the jewel in the crown. 'TOCs' leased locomotives and rolling stock from three Rolling Stock Leasing Companies, ROSCOs for short. Railtrack required track access charges for every train and for the use of stations. They retained and operated fourteen major centres but all other stations including Newcastle were leased to train operators.

Southbound 'Capitals Mail' passing Morpeth. These class 325 electric four-van units, finished in striking red and yellow livery, commenced service in the autumn of 1996, replacing Royal Mail trains hauled by class 86 electric locomotives. (J A Wells)

Rail Express Systems, known as RES, was introduced to carry Royal Mail and parcels, also to provide motive power for charter services and excursions from the Special Trains Unit. The names of those locomotives which carried them started with the letters RES (until they ran out of possibilities) and resulted in such oddities as *Restored* and *Restitution*.

From 1987 freight services had been sectorised into trainload coal, metals, petroleum products, and construction materials, each with its own distinctive markings. In addition there were Railfreight for mixed general merchandise and Freightliner trains for containerised traffic of various kinds, but from April 1994 completely new freight divisions were created. *Load Haul* was the trading title of Train Freight North East; *Transrail* was the name chosen by Train Freight West, and *Mainline* was adopted for TF South East. Each could provide services countrywide away from their operating areas if they had competed successfully for traffic. Load Haul locomotives were painted black with the mandatory yellow ends and with orange below the cabs. The logo was displayed very prominently on the sides. They became quite a common sight in the north east working alongside those plain, grey 56s which had not been repainted.

A shortage of class 91 electric locomotives sometimes meant it was necessary to hire a class 90 from another operator. Here a Railfreight Distribution engine, 90021, waits at Newcastle at the rear of an express to King's Cross in October 1997. (J A Wells)

Freightliners Limited – its new name following a management buy-out in 1996 – carries containers on long, flat, bogie wagons between major ports and rail terminals or customers' centres. Railfreight Distribution became responsible for operating freight services to and from various concentrations and private sidings and, later, through the Channel Tunnel.

This was the chosen way forward towards the complex privatisation of the railway network yet many people thought it would have been preferable to have a system based on the four companies that operated the railways between 1923 and 1947, if that had been possible. So, how was all this implemented?

Carefully controlled franchises were awarded to the private sector to operate passenger trains over specified routes, usually for seven years initially. The first two, both in the London area, were granted in February 1996. The following month Sea Containers Ltd. were the preferred bidders for Intercity East Coast. With a historical perspective, it was proposed to trade under the name of Great Northern Railways but as there was already another company which had the words 'Great Northern' included in its title a change was made to the Great North Eastern Railway (G**NE**R) in August. The new livery for east coast expresses, dark blue with a broad crimson stripe, was launched in October. Sea Containers Ltd. also operates the British section of the Orient Express.

The Rolling Stock Leasing Companies were sold in November 1995. One of these, Porterbrook leasings, painted its stock-moving locomotives and barrier vehicles in a splash of purple and white. It was the object of a successful buy-out by Stagecoach Holdings in July of the following year, a large bus company which had been granted railway franchises.

The whole of the Special Trains Unit was bought by Mr. Pete Waterman, the pop-music entrepreneur. The assets included more than 200 passenger coaches – some of them luxury stock – and six class 47 locomotives. The first of these to be repainted in Waterman Railways livery appeared in lined black and was named *Lady Godiva.* An agreement with RES allowed for an interchange of locomotives when required. Mr Waterman, however, withdrew from involvement of leasing trains and control passed to Rail Charter Services. More than 150 mark I and mark

II coaches were put up for sale shortly afterwards, being surplus to requirements.

It was thought that the three freight companies would be sold off individually but they were bought collectively by an American consortium led by Wisconsin Central Transportation in January 1996. The company already owned the railway system in New Zealand and some in Canada, both of which have produced spectacular results. It is committed to providing an excellent standard of service to its customers and is winning more and more traffic to rail. Goods yards and sidings which had been closed by BR are being reopened where there is traffic potential; furthermore, wagon loads (where customers send less than train load numbers of wagons) which had previously been withdrawn in 1991 as being uneconomic, have been reintroduced as the Enterprise service and are proving very popular. 250 new, powerful locomotives of proven design and reliability were ordered almost immediately from North America. The first of these class 66s was delivered in May 1998. In December 1995 Wisconsin had been the successful bidder for Rail Express Systems which owned 1,250 locomotives though

High above the River Tyne at Wylam, English Welsh & Scottish Railways 60022 heads west with a train of empty limestone hoppers from Teesside to Hardendale Quarry, Shap, in August 1998. (J A Wells)

many of them were not in good condition. The company is also responsible for running the Royal train. The choice of name was originally to be North & South Railways but this was changed to the more embracing English, Welsh and Scottish Railways. Their locomotives are gradually being repainted maroon with a broad, gold band prominently displaying the initials E W & S originally or EWS and the engine's number in matching red, a welcome contrast to dirty grey. Their crest features the heads of a lion, a dragon and a stag. The company, which is breathing new life into the movement of freight, further strengthened its position in 1997 by taking over Railfreight Distribution. Goods traffic is now thriving as a result of enterprise, initiative and positive attitudes. Yards, sidings and depots are leased long term from Railtrack.

Contracts have been agreed to provide infrastructure maintenance and renewal on an area basis. All lines in Northumberland apart from the Metro are now the responsibility of Messrs. Balfour Beatty. All aspects of track work are conducted by Fastline Track Renewals but this company is now part of the Jarvis group even though its name has been retained for the present. In the interests of safety, planning and co-ordination close liaison is necessary between contractors and Railtrack.

Railtrack, owned by Her Majesty's Government, was floated on the stock market in May 1996.

The following November it was announced that Cross Country Trains – whose operations include Dundee to Penzance via York, Newcastle to Plymouth, and Edinburgh to Bournemouth – would be operated by Richard Branson's Virgin group as Virgin CrossCountry for fifteen years. The day after the franchise began their first refurbished 125 train was launched in an eye-catching livery of bright red with three horizontal white stripes and with executive grey at the end of power cars and coaches. Virgin is committed to introduce completely new stock for its entire network operation within eight years and expects to double the number of passengers it carries nationally. The company is interested in running Eurostar trains between Glasgow and the continent from January 1999.

High speed train in Virgin CrossCountry livery, with power car 43153 on the rear. This locomotive was named ***The English Riviera Torquay Paignton Brixham*** *to advertise a special service. (J A Wells)*

One of the last to go, Regional Railways North East was franchised to Merseyside Transport Limited (MTL) in February 1997 but by the end of the year there had been no change of title and the stock remained in a variety of liveries which were inherited from BR. From May of the following year RRNE became Northern Spirit and began repainting local trains in blue and green livery and the trans-Pennine 158 units in purple and gold.

Considering the lack of real investment in the national system, many changes and challenges lie ahead but even after a few months the benefits of privatisation were becoming apparent and, given a chance, the railways of this country should have a bright future.

When a canal was opened in March 1823 for shipping between the Solway Firth and Carlisle hopes were expressed that it could be extended to join with the river Tyne in Northumberland. In September 1996 serious proposals to resurrect the idea were being discussed. Initial estimates put the cost at *six billion pounds.* Think what could be done for the county which gave railways to the world with money like that!

BIBLIOGRAPHY

ANTHONY C R & RODGERS B Rail Freight Today
Oxford Publishing Co. 1989

CLINKER C R Clinker's Register of Closed Passenger Stations & Goods Depots in England, Wales & Scotland 1830-1977
Avon-Anglia Publications & Services 1978 ed.

COOK R A & HOOLE K North Eastern Railway Historical Maps
Railway & Canal Historical Society 1975

HARESNAPE Brian Design for Steam 1830-1960
Book Club Associates by arrangement with Ian Allan Ltd. 1981

HOOLE K The North Eastern Electrics: The History of the Tyneside Passenger Services 1904-1967
Oakwood Press 1987

HOOLE K Railway Stations of the North East
David & Charles 1985

IRVINE R J The North Eastern Railway 1870-1914: an Economic History
Leicester University Press 1976

JENKINS S C (i) The Alston Branch
(ii) The Rothbury Branch
Oakwood Press 1991

MARSHALL John Guinness Book of Rail Facts and Feats
Guinness Superlatives Ltd.
Second edition 1975

SEWELL G W M The North British Railway in Northumberland
Merlin Books Ltd. 1992

STOBBS Allan W (i) Memories of the LNER: Rural Northumberland
(ii) Memories of the LNER: Tyneside
Published by the author at Penrith

TOMLINSON W W The North Eastern Railway: Its Rise and Development
Andrew Reid, Newcastle 1915

TUFNELL R M Gresley Pacifics Super Profile
Winchmore Publishing Services Ltd. 1985

WEBB B & GORDON D A Lord Carlisle's Railways
Railway Correspondence and Travel Society 1978

WELLS J A (i) The Blyth & Tyne Railway (Blyth & Tyne Part I) 1989

(ii) The Blyth & Tyne Branch,1874-1989 (Blyth & Tyne Part II) 1990

(iii) Blyth & Tyne – A Pictorial Record, 1840-1990 (Blyth & Tyne Part III) 1991

(iv) Signals to Danger: Railway Accidents at Newcastle upon Tyne and in Northumberland 1992

All published by Northumberland County Library.

WHISHAW Francis Whishaw's Railways of Great Britain & Ireland 1842

David & Charles Reprints 1969

WRIGHT A The North Sunderland Railway Oakwood Press.

ABBREVIATIONS OF RAILWAY COMPANIES IN NORTHUMBERLAND

B & T R	Blyth & Tyne Railway
B C R	Border Counties Railway
B R	British Railways / British Rail
E W S	English, Welsh & Scottish Railway
G N E R	Great North Eastern Railway
H & A R	Hexham & Allendale Railway
L N E R	London & North Eastern Railway
M (or T & W M)	Metro (or Tyne & Wear Metro)
N & B R	Newcastle & Berwick Railway
N & C R	Newcastle & Carlisle Railway
N & N S R	Newcastle & North Shields Railway
N B R	North British Railway
N C R	Northumberland Central Railway
N E R	North Eastern Railway
N S R	North Sunderland Railway
S N & W R	Scotswood, Newburn & Wylam Railway
W R	Wansbeck Railway
Y N & B R	York, Newcastle & Berwick Railway

INDEX

NOTES

NOTES

NOTES

NOTES